Fateful Years
1938–1945

Fateful Years 1938–1945

Vilmos Nagybaczoni Nagy

with a Foreword by
George Schöpflin

© 2017 Béla Nagybaczoni
All rights reserved

KKL Publications LLC, Helena History Press
Reno, Nevada USA

Publishing scholarship about and from Central and East Europe

H P
www.helenahistorypress.com

Distributed by IngramSpark and available through all major e-retail sites
info@helenahistorypress.com

Originally published as
"Végzetes Esztendők: 1938–1945" (Budapest, Körmendy, 1947)
Translated from the Hungarian second edition (1964) by Thomas Cooper
Maps created by Károly Kocsis and Norbert Agárdi: MTA RCAES Geographical Institute: Budapest

The translation of this work was underwritten in part by Edina Gaspar Jennison in memory of her father Dr. Edmund Gaspar
Graphic Design: Sebastian Stachowski
Archival Photography: Péter Szikits

Table of Contents

Foreword – *George Schöpflin* vii

Introduction 1

Chapter I At the Head of the First Army Corps
· The March into Upper Hungary · In Szolnok
· At the Head of the First Army 3

Chapter II The Minister of Defense's Negotiations in Early 1941
· The Collapse of Yugoslavia 39

Chapter III War with Russia 49

Chapter IV In Retirement 55

Chapter V At the Head of the Ministry of Defense 63

Chapter VI Again in Retirement 137

Chapter VII Another Attempt to Occupy Serbia
by Hungarian Soldiers 145

Chapter VIII 19 March – 15 October 1944 169

Chapter IX What Happened After 15 October 1944 213

Chapter X The role of the Army in the Events of October 1944 237

Name Index 263

Photo Gallery 267

Map Depicting First and Second Vienna Awards 286

Foreword

György Schöpflin

History, as is so often repeated, is generally written by the victors. Sometimes, though, the victors are defeated and the suppressed voices of those the victors had intended to cast on the scrapheap of history are heard again. This does not mean the rewriting of the past, an exercise in falsification, but accepting the diversity of how the past is understood and how different eras see their pasts differently.

Secondly, memoir literature must be understood on its own terms. Crucially, it is written within the moral assumptions of its own time, not ours. To repeat L.P. Hartley's oft quoted sentence, "the past is a foreign country: they do things differently there". What the author of a memoir regarded as self-evident modes of feeling and perception are not ours and, given the inevitable psychological remoteness involved, we have to make an effort of interpretation that can go counter to our own assumptions, to our own baggage. If we fail to read the view of the past as seen by contemporaries on their terms, we readily fall into the trap of projecting our moral values onto that past and thereby misjudge it. The temptation to do so is very strong, especially if there is a political or cultural agenda lurking in our assessments.

The communist rulers of Hungary did this consciously and deliberately, for they were seeking actively to rewrite the past for their own needs. The residues of these rewritings have not disappeared. There are far too many who paint the past in the darkest hues possible in order to secure their own values in the present. The Hungarian past, not least the interwar period, is widely seen in overwhelmingly negative terms and the actors of that time are written off as fools or knaves, the latter mostly.

Fateful Years

This is the significance of the memoirs of Vilmos Nagybaczoni Nagy. It casts a light different from the one insisted on by the communist historians of Hungary on Hungary's role in the Second World War. And because the memoirs were written immediately after the events – first published in 1947 and then republished in 1986 – they have an authenticity and immediacy that the best of memoir literature provides.

What is clear from this account is that Nagybaczoni was well aware of the dilemmas besetting Hungary before and during the War. This demands an analysis and will establish a context in which to place the memoir. Basically the dilemma is that of the small state at risk from the machinations of more powerful international actors and the limits to agency. In the case of Hungary, the dilemma was made more acute by "the loss of empire" syndrome, the Treaty of Trianon, by which pre-1914 Hungary lost two-thirds of its territory and around a third of its indubitably Hungarian population, to which can be added the c.6-7 million non-Hungarians. This was an acute trauma, a defeat for the pre-1914 ruling elite, and a perpetual reminder of the radical reduction in the country's room for manoeuvre.

Furthermore, the end of the First World War was followed by around a year of political chaos (1918-1919) during which incompetent leftwing governments sought to find a way out of the mess and ended up creating an ever larger one. The 133 day Hungarian Soviet Republic was finally put down by the military intervention of the Romanian armed forces, intervention being justified as the defeat of communism and, equally, by the spirit of revanche for the defeat of Romania during the War itself. The occupation of the country by the Romanian army (from August 1919 to March 1920) and the depredations that accompanied it only added to the sense of trauma and humiliation.

Then, before 1914 Hungary was broadly confident of its modernity – still visible in Budapest's architecture – and its particular sense of the future. That future was wholly destroyed by the War and its consequences. During the War, Hungarian casualties were around 800,000 and after Trianon, a substantial number of Hungarians (over 300,000 according to estimates) opted to go to Hungary rather than live in one or other of the successor states; some were expelled. The integration of these returnees, not least members of the state administration dismissed by the successor states, took a long time and added to the trauma. In all, the chaos added up to a collapse – political, economic, social, cultural.

Not surprisingly in the circumstances, the year of chaos effectively destroyed the chances of a social transformation, such as was introduced in neighbouring Austria, and ensured that the pre-1914 elite would return power as the only elite with the necessary political skills and experience. This meant that the pre-1914 social order changed only marginally and remained hierarchical.

Much has been written – mostly negatively – about the backward-looking, "reactionary" character of this elite. This view (favoured by the left) seriously distorts the situation and misstates the problem of consolidation after the year of chaos and the trauma of Trianon. Hungary's political system after Trianon placed stability and security at its centre. The confidence of the pre-1914 period was gone, but it was the only elite with the political skills to re-establish a viable system. This system preserved some of the elements of the pre-1914 order under the aegis of Admiral Horthy as regent. The monarchy remained in being, but there was no agreement as to who the monarch should be; gradually the issue slipped off the agenda. In practice, the system was put together above all by István Bethlen, the prime minister from 1921 to 1931; it was semi-consensual and semi-authoritarian. And there was striking contrast between the modernity of Budapest and the pre- or semi-modernity of the countryside.

The Horthy order allowed a good deal of latitude to the expression of various opinions, as long as the system itself was not threatened. Elections were indeed held to ensure the hegemony of the ruling party and these were neither fully free or fair, but there was competition and parliamentary debates were real enough. By the criteria of the 1920s, the system worked adequately to secure the power of the elite and, equally, to offer some space for alternatives. But it had an Achilles heel, the peasantry, which the country's economy could not really integrate fully. The problem of rural poverty, of the landless peasantry, smallholders and dwarfholders could not be resolved without industrialisation and the country lacked the capital resources to achieve this. Besides, with consolidation as the primary aim, the elites preferred a rather static model of rule – unsurprisingly in the circumstances. It should be added that the competence of the technical intelligentsia and the professional classes was good.

Under the terms of Trianon, Hungary was permitted only a very small army of 35,000, no armour, no heavy weaponry, no air force. This added to the sense of insecurity, given that the system of client states constructed by France – the little Entente – had their own anti-Hungarian perspectives, their own rather more sizeable armies. To this can be added the presence of sizeable Hungarian minorities in the successor states whose attitude to their new citizenship was mixed and whose loyalty was generally questioned by the new rulers. In effect, the country was all but surrounded by ill-disposed, hostile neighbours, which meant that it would need a patron from beyond the region. All the successor states had gained territory from Hungary and had thereby acquired ethnic Hungarian minorities. This created a security problem for the successor states and meant that they necessarily saw Hungary itself as hostile, bent on reacquiring what it had lost. The Western powers, France above all, which had created this vicious circle, never cared about the security issues that would ensue. Everyone was the loser.

This dilemma was well understood by much of the post-1918 elite. It was a severe constraint on action, but it left some room for manoeuvre. Over time, Italy came to play the role of patron with the 1927 accord with Rome. After the 1929 economic crisis and the rise of Hitler, Germany took over. This posed a problem for the elite. Most of them had little time for the radical solutions adopted by Nazism, but there was also a strong pro-German faction. This tension endured and was one of the markers of inter-war Hungarian politics. Clearly, small states had a much more restricted freedom of action and had to align themselves with one or other more powerful state and that affected domestic politics too. The difficulty for the Hungarian elite was that none of the potential patrons was particularly interested in the central Hungarian issue – the injustice of Trianon and the insecurity that came with it. If anything, France and to a lesser extent Britain were content to see Hungary on a leash; any attachment to the Soviet Union was obviously out of question given the country's experience with the communist experiment in 1919; Weimar Germany was not interested, which left Italy as the only player, albeit the newly launched Fascist system under Mussolini was unattractive to the conservatism of the dominant elites.

The 1930s economic crisis hit the country very hard. The massive shrinkage of the international market left the economy in a poor state. In any case, Hungary was far too heavily dependent on agriculture – up to two-fifths of the GDP and over half the population – and remained capital poor. The structure of the agricultural sector was dominated by underfunded large estates, the latifundia, and it lost much of its export markets with the crash. There was some small sector production, but this too suffered from capital shortage and technological backwardness. The outcome was an insoluble peasant problem. The country was described, with only some exaggeration, as the land of "three million beggars".

By 1932 the conservative elite associated with Horthy and Bethlen effectively found itself incapable of dealing with the crisis of growing social discontent, the short-lived government of Gyula Károlyi resigned and in 1932, Gyula Gömbös, a contested figure if ever there was one, took over as prime minister. Gömbös was a right-radical figure with a military background, but he recognised that the strategy of stability followed in the post-Trianon years was exhausted. Broadly, he sought to revitalise the country by launching his National Work Programme which aimed at the modernisation and rationalisation of the public sphere. This included social reforms and attention to the peasantry. He was also successful in rejuvenating the army with the retirement of 22 senior officers in 1935. In foreign policy, Gömbös launched various openings, the net effect of which was to move the country closer to Germany; he was not alone at the time in admiring the dynamism of Nazism, whether in Hungary or elsewhere. All the same, the alignment was not total and there remained some choices. Not least, the conservative elite around Bethlen, together with the Smallholders and Social Democrats, were less than delighted with this course and opposed it.

Gömbös died in 1936, but his mobilising, reform policies were not altogether successful. Above all, both he and the conservatives were increasingly challenged by various right radical movements. The opening of the franchise made the Hungarian variant of Nazism, the Arrow Cross, a serious problem for the adherents of stability and equally for the moderate right. In any case, as Gömbös's successors were to discover, Germany's growing political and economic dominance meant a growing constraint on what the country could do.

For the elites, whether conservative or right-radical and to some extent even the relatively weak Social Democrats, the question of Trianon and frontier revision was central. There was agreement on this revision being peaceful, but there was division on whether Hungary should aim for total revision – everything back – or only the indubitably Hungarian inhabited areas. Revision necessarily brought the country closer to Germany and Italy, given that neither was satisfied with the Paris Peace Settlement.

The year 1938 was a turning point. With Anschluß, Germany had become a direct neighbour and the Munich agreement created an opportunity to satisfy the revisionist claim against the disintegrating Czechoslovakia by reattaching the overwhelmingly Hungarian-inhabited strip of southern Slovakia. Germany and Italy were the midwives of this agreement, the first Vienna Arbitration, but Hitler regarded Hungary as a troublesome, not altogether reliable semi-satellite. Much the same applied to the second Vienna Arbitration, when around of two-fifths of Transylvania was returned to Hungary from Romania. In the interim, Hungary reoccupied Sub-Carpathian Ruthenia and, following Germany's attack on Yugoslavia in 1941, the Bácska (Bačka) region of the Vojvodina.

Hungary was able to remain neutral during this period, though closely attached to the Axis, but that ended when the town and airport of Kassa (Košice) were bombed (26 June 1941). Horthy decided that the Soviet Union was responsible and entered the war. (Who was actually responsible remains a mystery. The least implausible theory is that Soviet planes bombed Kassa in error, intending to attack the nearby Eperjes (Prešov) in Slovakia instead.) Hungary's participation in the war lasted until 1945, but with the destruction of the Second Hungarian Army at Voronezh in January 1943, it was hardly an active role. The story ended with the Red Army invading Hungary in 1944, the siege of Budapest, far-reaching devastation and a collapse as deep-seated as that after 1918. It is against this background that Nagybaczoni's career and memoirs are to be understood.

Nagybaczoni was born in 1884 in Transylvania, his family was of rather poor lesser nobility and Calvinist. He received his education at the Ludovika and Vienna military academies, fought on the Serbian and Russian fronts in the First World War and remained in military service after Trianon, reaching the rank of colonel in 1925. He wrote regularly on military strategy and tactics and was promoted to major-general (vezérőrnagy) in 1934, to lieutenant-general (altábornagy) in 1937, was commander of the Budapest army corps in 1938.

It was in this function that he took part in the military occupation of southern Slovakia and, as commander-in-chief of the First Hungarian Army, of northern Transylvania. This was evidently a distinguished career, but Nagybaczoni had his opponents, chief among Henrik Werth, chief of staff, who succeeded in having Nagybaczoni sent into retirement in 1941. Werth was strongly pro-German, was of the view that Germany could not lose the war and objected to those, Nagybaczoni among them, who harboured doubts on this score.

Indeed, as he makes evident in the memoir, Nagybaczoni was of the view that war would be a disaster for Hungary. There was a clear rivalry between the two senior soldiers. Werth, however, lost the contest and with the coming to office of the Kállay government in 1942, Nagybaczoni was appointed minister of defence. Kállay recognised that the German war was doomed and he pursued a semi-neutral policy, in the hope that after the war, this would gain recognition and Hungary would not be as badly treated as after 1918. This was illusory, of course, given the determination of the Allies to wage a war of unconditional surrender. And Kállay's policies brought Hungary increasingly into Hitler's bad books, which culminated in the German occupation of the country in March 1944.

As defence minister (1942-1943) Nagybaczoni was responsible for various moves to improve the condition of the Hungarian armed forces, above all, his determination to end the inhuman treatment of Jews. One of the anti-Jewish measures introduced in 1939-1941 was that Jews could not serve in the regular armed forces, but were required to do labour service (munkaszolgálat). This service was coercive, those serving were unarmed, and the guards regularly treated Jews with marked inhumanity. It should be added that those obliged to do coercive labour service included non-Jews, so-called "unreliable elements", communists, Roma, members of ethnic minorities, but the majority, several hundred thousand, were Jewish.

Fateful Years

Nagybaczoni tried, and to some extent succeeded, in diminishing this brutality, but the extent of anti-Semitism in military and civilian circles was deeply rooted. His measures generated growing opposition among the right-radicals of the pro-German elements and they succeeded in forcing Nagy into retirement in 1943. On the 15 October 1944, with the collapse of the Horthy system, the Arrow Cross seized power and a day later, they arrested Nagybaczoni, imprisoned him, moved him to Germany as the front was disintegrating in 1945 and he was only able to return to Hungary well after the end of the war. It was then that he wrote this memoir.

His tribulations were not over. The communist regime regarded him as a class enemy, stripped him of his pension and his work as a gardener. But chance intervened. Petru Groza, the then Romanian head of state, had been a class mate of Nagybaczoni's at the Szászváros (Orăştie) Secondary School, they graduated together, and Groza invited him to the 50th anniversary of the graduating class. Nagybaczoni replied that he had neither the money nor the passport and Groza then intervened with Rákosi, the communist leader, who allowed Nagybaczoni to take part and the authorities gradually lifted the restrictions that they had imposed on him. In 1965, his actions to improve the treatment of Jewish forced labourers during the war were recognised by Israel and he was awarded the title of "righteous among nations". Nagybaczoni died in 1976 at the age of 92.

Two thoughts can be added to these memoirs. One of these is that Nagybaczoni's life was characterised by professionalism and a fundamental decency. As a serving soldier, he accepted that his duties were military and not political, whether he accepted the views of the political leadership or not, but only up to a given point. While he recognised that Hungary's situation left it and him with few choices, within those constraints he acted as thoughtfully as was possible to mitigate human suffering and to minimise damage.

The second thought that comes to mind is that while the interwar elites of Hungary were far from flawless, they were not the consummate villains depicted by the communist period. Some certainly were, notably the hardline, pro-German anti-Semites, but the majority of the elite sought to sustain a degree of moderation and propriety. That elite was swept away by the Second World War and their successors did what they could to blacken their predecessors. But history is not carved in stone and today we can or, at any rate have the capacity to, adopt a different, more nuanced understanding of the past. After all, the current elites will also be judged by their successors. So when making judgements of the past, it is always worth doing so with care and moderation. I am certain that Nagybaczoni would have endorsed this and would have done so firmly and rigorously. That was his character.

Introduction

It would be best to erase from my memory the dark days which are now behind me, but I must remember them, for those who will come after me may read my recollections, and I believe they may learn something from them.

I think of you, my dear son Béla, as I commit these lines to paper. I realize that I must leave something for you of the experiences that I have gathered over the course of the past years. I must explain the considerations that guided me in my assessment of certain questions. I must explain them at the very least so that you will be able to judge the last chapter of your father's life properly and draw important lessons from my recollections, lessons which will be useful as you shape your future and your frame of mind.

I do not like to recall those times, for the years in question were the saddest period of my life, both as an individual and more generally. It was then that I reached the highest rank in my military career: I had become a minister. And it was then that I had my greatest fall, for I was held for six months in the prison in Sopronkőhida as a political prisoner, and I then spent another four months in an internment camp after the Arrow Cross[1] had me deported to Germany.

I never wanted to cause anyone any harm. I embraced the notion that one must help everyone. And yet, what was the reward for this conduct? The prison in Sopronkőhida, and the fact that the people in whose interests I had done so much, some of the members of the officer corps, turned against me, people in whose eyes my name meant "the great traitor." The Arrow Cross

---

1 The Arrow Cross Party – Hungarist Movement (or Nyilaskereszt Párt – Hungarista Mozgalom) was a national socialist party founded by Ferenc Szálasi in 1935 as the Party of National Will and then, after having been banned by the Hungarian government in 1937, reestablished as the Arrow Cross Party in 1939. The party was based on an ideology of extreme nationalism, referred to by its leader and members as Hungarism, and it conceived of Hungarian identity in unambiguously racial terms. It was anti-communist and anti-Semitic, and it championed agrarianism and anti-capitalism.

general staff called me this when I was a minister, because in their assessment I had betrayed them, I had betrayed the Hungarian army, because I was not a faithful follower of the Germans, I was not a friend of the Axis powers, and, finally, because I had espoused the cause of the persecuted Jews.

But I must remember those times, those fateful years. I cannot allow the events in which I took part and of which I was at times the helmsman to be forgotten.

People who were active in public life and who played roles in the events of recent years should speak out. They should record their standpoints, for those who come in our wake will only be able to avoid making the kinds of mistakes that were made if they have a thorough knowledge of the events of the past.

So I too will not permit myself respite, for I wish to finish this task. I will attempt to gather my memories.

Read attentively everything that I recount in the following pages. I wish to affirm in you the conviction that I sought only to improve the lots of my fellow men, both today and always.

Chapter I

At the Head of the First Army Corps
The March into Upper Hungary
In Szolnok
At the Head of the First Army

In 1938, I was commanding officer of the first army corps of Budapest. I oversaw the autumn army maneuvers near Nógrádbercel. We resided in the Dégenfeld manor house, from where we would go to observe the individual groups practicing their maneuvers. Later, we moved our quarters to Nógrádbercel. The momentous events that would soon be at hand were already casting shadows. I am compelled to reflect on the mobilization of the Hungarian army in the autumn of 1938 and the partial liberation of the territories of Upper Hungary.[2] One must consider whether everything had been properly prepared. Had we, as soldiers, done everything to ensure that, with regards to the military, the political leadership of the country rested on certain and solid foundations? Had our government leaders done everything to win friends who would support Hungary's just aspirations as devotedly as we Hungarians felt necessary? Finally, one could raise the question of responsibility as well. We must discern the path to be taken in the future in order to ensure that no blunders are made similar to those that have been made now.

These thoughts flow inexorably from my pen, for the military and political leadership merit harsh criticism. Our officers, who followed the events closely as they unfolded and who were themselves part of the events, often made condemnatory statements about these problems, and as their commanding officer I could do nothing more than listen to their outbursts. I could not even seek counter-arguments, for I myself was convinced that our officers were correct.

---

2   This is a relatively literal translation of the term "Felvidék" in Hungarian, which could also be translated as "the highlands." The term refers to what today is the territory of Slovakia.

Fateful Years

In the autumn of 1938, the orders concerning the re-annexation of Upper Hungary changed three times. The last-minute rejection of measures that would have had grave consequences gave rise to the conviction that the military leadership was not on the same path as the civilian leadership. The military leadership was not properly informed of the government's intentions, and at their own initiative they implemented measures of grave import and potentially involving foreign policy complications, measures for which the government did not dare accept responsibility. It was also conceivable that the military leadership did not have the patience to take the necessary steps to prepare a given operation thoroughly and prudently from the perspectives of domestic and foreign policy. Thus, a situation arose in which the measures adopted by the military could well be ahead of the events. They did not fit the political circumstances, and in the last minute the high command was compelled to change or—as happened in this case—withdraw the steps it had taken.

There may be lacunae in my account, for without complete knowledge of the actual background, I did not see everything clearly.

First, I will recount the difficulties I experienced involving the mobilization of the Hungarian army. According to the original thinking and the plans that had been drawn up, measures were taken to ensure preparedness and proper footing for war, referred to as an increase in our "effective force of arms." Peacetime preparations, if they are done attentively and well, make it possible to increase the number of units in peacetime to wartime strength with conscripts called up for military service. Accurate records are the foundation of a good system of conscription. Whether or not the soldiery will reach the footing desired and specified depends on the precise delivery of calls to arms addressed to conscripts by name. The plans contained preparations for the conscription of four classes.[3]

Following the visit of the regent[4] and his wife[5] to Germany in September, news came according to which Germany was going to take steps to resolve the

---

[3] In this context, the term "class" refers to all of the students in given year of schooling, or what in American English is referred to as a grade.
[4] Miklós Horthy (1868–1957) served as Regent of the Kingdom of Hungary from March 1920 until October 1944.
[5] Magdolna Purgly (1881–1957).

Chapter I

question of the Sudetenland once and for all, and in accordance with German designs. I was of the belief that the German-Czech conflict could easily lead to armed clashes, in which Hungary should not intervene. If, however, this was unavoidable, Hungary must only take military steps if it were absolutely clear that the German-Czech affair would remain an isolated incident which would not grow into a European conflict. If Hungary were to meddle in an armed clash that were to spread to the rest of Europe, this rash step could lead to the complete dismembering of our homeland in the event of defeat in war. I did consider it necessary, however, that the Hungarian army be at the ready. In the course of a discussion with the leader of the first division of the general staff directorate, I said that the most effective solution would be to keep the troops who had been sent to practice maneuvers where they were and to issue orders calling for an increase in the standing army. Thus, by mobilizing the army gradually and without attracting notice, we would be prepared for any eventuality.

Major Zákó, who had been brought in to serve as chief of the general staff of the first division and thus was my commander, later implemented measures for the forces in Szirák according to which the soldiers who were conducting military exercises were to remain in their current area of engagement and, in addition, two more classes would be conscripted for service.

The soldiers remained at the sites where they had been conducting their exercises. My corps, the first army corps, had been given the task, in the event of an order for aggressive border defense, to cross at the line of the Ipoly River and take control of the high ground on the far bank, securing territory for the advancement of the forces drawing up behind it. I would note, we entrusted the commanding officer of the southern unit with a similar task during the winter campaigns. Now, when the actual execution of this plan seemed nigh, I was compelled to acknowledge that reality is very different from theory. To assign such a task and to think that a corps consisting of three brigades can perform this task was a mistake. The relatively large extent of the territory in question, the enemy's system of fortifications, and the enemy's freedom of movement made the success of this kind of isolated advance doubtful. Indeed, there was no real need of this maneuver, since the advance of the army behind the line of the Ipoly River, which could have been secured in a moment of peace, could have been accomplished without any difficulty in a time of peace. As we shall see, this idea of an isolated advance occurred to later commanders as well. To this day, I cannot understand why they stuck to this design, which was neither strategically nor tactically sound.

A few days after my general staff commander's consultation in Budapest, I was ordered to report to the chief of the general staff on 7 September. At this meeting, I was informed of the tasks of the first army corps in border defense and possibly attack.

In the meantime, I myself went to the border several times. On the basis of the available photographs and my examinations on site, we determined that it would be possible to launch an attack to the east of Balassagyarmat, in the area around Őrhalom, and to the west of Balassagyarmat, by Ipolyszög and Ipolyvecze.

These observations and plans, however, were in vain, because in the assessment of Lieutenant General Lajos Keresztes-Fischer, the first army corps needed to advance to the northwest by Ipolyság,[6] take control of the high ground on the far bank of the river, and thereby create the foundation for the further use of the larger area. This was the second modification to the command within three days, and it was still based on the incomprehensible idea of having the first army corps, with three brigades, attack completely on its own, before the main body of the army.

On 12 September, the chief of the general staff came from Budapest to observe the exercises being held by Colonel Paduschitzky.[7] I waited for a long time with the commander of the exercises in the mountain pass to the north of the village of Becske. Later, Paduschitzky sent word that he was consulting with the commander of the southern unit. He instructed us to go to the observation point that had been prepared in advance in the hills. He would soon come himself. I waited for him there for a good half hour, and when he did not come, I decided that this waiting was senseless. I had not come to wait, but rather in order, after having observed the soldiers and the commanders in action, to instruct them in proper tactical conduct and procedure. I ordered the commander of the infantry to inform Lieutenant General Keresztes-Fischer

---

6   Today Šahy, Slovakia.
7   Alfréd Paduschitzky (1887–1940).

Chapter I

that I had gone on horseback into Cserhát Mountains, since the decisive attack had been launched from there. If Keresztes-Fischer wanted to speak with me, we could talk at the meeting in the school in Becske.

At roughly noon, Keresztes-Fischer finally arrived in Becske. He offered excuses for his tardiness and expressed his regret that we had not yet been able to meet. He had immediately hurried after me, so he said, but I had already left the observation point. I used the occasion to clarify with him the army corps' direction of attack. I explained the Czechoslovak system of fortifications. I informed him that, according to our reconnaissance, the Czech defense system was strongest precisely where he wished to attack. I noted that in my opinion the attack should be launched where it was tactically the easiest and the least dangerous. In other words, to the east of Ipolyság. From there, one could always curve around in the direction of Léva,[8] which was considered tactically important.

Keresztes-Fischer, however, insisted on his original decision to have the first army corps break through the Czech system of fortifications at Ipolyság and to the west of the city and to create a bridgehead on the high ground on the far side of the river. I requested that at the very least a gravel road suitable for any kind of vehicle be accessible behind the army corps in order to make it possible to provide supplies, since the road that ran beside the Ipolyság train station and essentially overlapped with the border could not be used. He promised that this would be done, and he also informed me that in order to increase the standing army, he would order the conscription of an additional five classes.

Soon, construction of the road, which ran some 16 kilometers, began. 4,000 men were working on it. Three days after the work had begun, I traveled by car from Diósjenő to Kemence. Four weeks later, the road was finished, but we did not actually need it, since events had taken a peaceful turn.

The commander-in-chief of the Hungarian army [Hugó Sónyi] ordered the military forces to remain where they were. He chose Vác as the new seat of the army headquarters. The Minister of Defense, however, decided in favor of Budapest instead, since in his view there was need of me in Budapest.

---

8   Today Levice, Slovakia.

Fateful Years

The concluding exercises began in the area around Bercel, Romhány, and Diósjenő on 13 September. Minister of Defense Jenő Rátz[9] was there on the first day of the exercises. We watched the exercises from the hills to the north of Becske. The German and Italian military delegations were also there, along with a great number of journalists. I sought a chance to learn directly from Minister of Defense Jenő Rátz, who had only recently returned from the celebration of the launch of the Prince Eugen cruiser in Germany, of his experiences there. He informed me that the Germans had been extremely accommodating in every respect, and they had striven in their own way to rein in their "traditional tactlessness." He also said that Hitler had proclaimed that he absolutely wanted to solve the question of the Germans of the Sudetenland. His generals had endeavored to dissuade him, since in their assessment an attack on Czechoslovakia would mean world war. England and France would support Czechoslovakia and would attack Germany. Hitler, however, was convinced that there would never be a better moment to attack Czechoslovakia. Neither France nor England was prepared for war, and thus their threatening gestures would not be followed by armed intervention. Russia would not interfere. This was the situation at the moment, but if he were to wait any longer, England and France would grow stronger militarily and thus armed intervention on behalf of Czechoslovakia would be much more likely.

The German Reich had no need of Hungary's direct assistance, Hitler had said. He had suggested, however, that we use the opportunity to take back Upper Hungary. He had no claims on territories this side of the Carpathian Mountains. We could even take Pozsony.[10] If this important city were for some reason not to become part of Hungary, then Germany would occupy it, but under no circumstances would he leave this important juncture on the Danube River in Czechoslovak hands.

Rátz said that in the course of the conversation, Hitler had told him that it would be easier for him if the Hungarians were to come forward with their demands and the Czechs were to refuse to meet these demands and perhaps

---

9   Jenő Rátz (1882–1949) served as Hungarian Minister of Defense in 1938. After the war, he was put on trial by the People's Court of Hungary for having served as Deputy Prime Minister in the government of Döme Sztójay. Initially, he was sentenced to death, but the sentence was then changed to life imprisonment. He died after having spent four years in prison.
10 Today Bratislava, Slovakia.

Chapter I

even attack Hungary. Germany would mobilize immediately and attack Czechoslovakia. Germany would appear to the world in a very different light if it were not to play the part of aggressor or the initiator of armed conflict.

In Rátz's view, we could not embark on such a plan, since we were not militarily prepared.

I summarize my opinion of this historical meeting between Hitler and Minister of Foreign Affairs Rátz here. Small states should not venture in where great powers do battle. If Germany were to start a war, it would be a world war. The consequences of this kind of conflagration would be incalculable. Hungary could not permit itself to take part. Defeat in war could mean its complete annihilation! The Little Entente still existed. Yugoslavia and Romania would unquestionably move into action against us if we were to launch military operations against Czechoslovakia.

Rátz mentioned that Mussolini had shown complete support for Hungary's claims, but he had cautioned us to wait patiently. We should not begin an attack too soon, for in time, Upper Hungary would fall into our lap more easily and more safely. Mussolini had also declared that, were Yugoslavia to attack Hungary, Italy would turn against Yugoslavia.

Disregarding the promises made by Hitler and Mussolini, I believe—and this belief has only become stronger over the years—that our leadership bears grave responsibility, for even in the case of the most peaceful political and military stance, it should have done everything to ensure that the army stood at the ready, properly equipped and organized. Our preparatory measures were sluggish, and thus, when events, which had taken a rapid and unexpected turn, made immediate action necessary, the Hungarian army was not prepared, and we were unable to keep pace militarily with the diplomatic efforts.

The orders intended to sound the alarm were given so slowly that they could not possibly have been effective. Everything was protracted and confused, and hampered by innumerable complications. There were almost no units that were actually ready to march. For the moment, the military exercises had been extended for the army corps along the border with Czechoslovakia. We had been commanded to call up only five new classes for conscription, and we had had to do this using conscription cards, which put an inhuman burden on the shoulders of the people who kept the registers. The fact that the registers themselves were not precise made the process particularly difficult, and thus we had to work with a very large margin of error. If the conscriptions had been issued through public announcements, the individual classes would have shown up to join the fighting force much more quickly and with a more complete participation rate. The use of conscription cards was seen as necessary in order to maintain secrecy. According to our specialists, conscription through public announcement would have made it immediately clear to the rest of the world that Hungary was preparing to take military measures. Clearly, this contention was incorrect: conscription could not be kept secret. For this reason, in my view, we should have chosen the system that would have been the most rapid and precise. The conscriptions had to be completed by 27 September. Thus, the standing army had grown enough to make it possible to assemble twin infantry formations. The officers who were needed in order to assemble the army commands, however, were only summoned much later. The first orders that were given for the assembly of the supply formations were withdrawn before we had even had the chance to hand them down, and as a consequence, the soldiers, whose numbers had been increased, did not have a train (i.e. a supply unit).

The concluding exercises came to an end on the afternoon of 15 September.

When negotiations began between Germany and the western great powers, we were not prepared. Not only were the army divisions not in a state of readiness for war, even the Budapest army corps did not have the necessary supply formations. After the autumn military exercises, the army headquarters had been moved to Budapest. By 23 September, the soldiers had come to the sectors to which they had been assigned and had begun training the new conscripts and honing their skills.

On 1 October 1938, a reorganization of the Hungarian army was scheduled to have begun. In light of the uncertain situation, the Ministry of Defense suspended the reorganization of the army, or rather postponed its implementation until 1 November. I responded to this measure with the remark that it would be better to abandon the idea of reorganization for a long time. If war were to break out, the plan would hardly be timely anyway. If we were to get something of Upper Hungary back, the structure of the Hungarian army

Chapter I

would have to be placed on entirely different foundations. In my view, it would have been better to have dropped all organizational plans until 1 May 1939.

We were relocated to Budapest. I observed the troops training on several occasions. In the meantime, the international situation had become increasingly complex. The reports indicated ever more seriously and ever more emphatically the dangers that could be triggered by the increasingly forceful German demands. The pronouncements that were being made by English statesmen and the failure (which became clearer with every passing day) of the peacemaking delegation of Lord Runciman to yield any results made clear that we would soon face grave and fateful events. Although I was entirely aware of the tremendous accomplishments of German military development, and I knew that additional efforts would be made that would only add to these achievements, I nonetheless believed that the German military could be outmatched by united French and Anglo-Saxon attacks and the western reserves that could be brought into the struggle in the future. The English declarations always emphasized that if the security of France were to be threatened, England could not sit idly by, and it would support its ally under any circumstances. The French Prime Minister and Foreign Minister, Daladier[11] and Bonnet,[12] again proclaimed: if Germany were to attack Czechoslovakia, France would meet its obligations as an ally and would attack Germany. Under the circumstances, it seemed certain that if Germany were to issue an ultimatum to Czechoslovakia and Czechoslovakia were to fail to meet it, there would be war, a war into which Hungary could not allow itself to be swept.

On 15 October, English Prime Minister Chamberlain[13] met with Hitler in Obersalzberg. Hitler informed Chamberlain of his claims against the

---

11 Édouard Daladier (1884–1970), a leading figure in France's so-called Radical Party, served as Prime Minister of France for two short periods in the 1930s and then again from 1938 until 1940. He was prime minister during the negotiations which preceded the Munich Agreement, when France failed to meet its obligations to protect Czechoslovakia from Germany.
12 George Bonnet (1889–1973) served as French Foreign Minister in 1938–1939. Bonnet was consistent throughout the upheavals of his two years in office in his insistence that France take almost any measures necessary to avoid war with Germany, for instance even after Germany invaded the rump state of Czechoslovakia and proclaimed the Reich Protectorate of Bohemia-Moravia. He was demoted from his position as foreign minister in September 1939, after the German invasion of Poland.
13 Neville Chamberlain (1869–1940) served as Prime Minister of the United Kingdom from 1937 until 1940. He is best known for his failed foreign policy of appeasement, of which the Munich Agreement, according to which Nazi Germany could annex Czechoslovak territories inhabited primarily by German speakers, is the best example.

Czechs. He said he was prepared to make one concession: he would agree that for the duration of the talks he would not attack Czechoslovakia. At the same time, reports in the Italian press suggested that, in addition to the question of the Germans of the Sudetenland, the question of the Polish and Hungarian minorities in Czechoslovakia also had to be addressed.

On 19 September, Mussolini demanded that a plebiscite be held for all of the nationalities living in Czechoslovakia. The plebiscite should determine whether or not the minorities wished to belong to Czechoslovakia or not.

The English prime minister fought for peace. He did everything he could to avert the looming catastrophe. He by no means wanted to allow the question of the Sudetenland Germans to upset peace in Europe. For this reason, on 20 September, together with the French government, he sent an aide-memoire to the Czechoslovak government drawing attention to the necessity of a territorial arrangement. They demanded that the Czechoslovak government solve the problem peacefully.

On 22 September, Chamberlain again negotiated with Hitler, this time in Godesberg. Hitler presented Chamberlain with a detailed plan for the cession of the Sudeten territories, and he also emphasized the fulfilment of the Hungarian and Polish demands.

In the speech held in Nuremberg on 24 September, Hitler left no doubt that Germany was prepared to take military action. If Czechoslovakia would not cede the Sudeten German territories within a fixed period of time, Hitler would send in his army. Göring's statements, according to which Germany had an air force larger than any other power in Europe and Germany's western borders were impenetrable, did not fail to make an impression on the great powers, and these statements also left no doubt that Hitler had complete faith in Germany's success if aggressive measures were to be taken.

The Hungarian government also began to take action. On 3 October, it delivered a sharply worded aide-memoire to the Czechoslovak government in which it called attention to the solution of the Hungarian question. It suggested beginning bilateral negotiations in Komárom on 6 October. Krofta,[14]

---

14 Professor of history at Charles University in Prague and member of the Czechoslovak Academy of Sciences, Kamil Krofta (1876–1945) served as Czechoslovak Minister of Foreign Affairs from 1936 until 1938. He was an active member of the resistance against German occupation of Czechoslovakia during the war.

Chapter I

the Czechoslovak foreign minister, replied evasively. Every sign suggested that the Czechs still had faith in the possibility of preserving the status quo. After Hitler insisted on his demand that the Czechs cede the Sudeten German territories on 1 October, the situation became so tense that the English prime minister proclaimed that a German attack against Czechoslovakia would lead to a European war.

Mussolini's intervention created a transitional state of calm. He suggested that representatives from England, Germany, France, and Italy meet to discuss the matter. Thus, on 29 September, the Munich conference of the four great powers was called. Here, an agreement was reached concerning the Germans of the Sudetenland. According to the agreement, by 10 October, the Sudeten German territories had to be ceded to Germany, and within three days the Czechoslovak government also had to reach agreements with the Polish and Hungarian governments. If no agreement were reached, the Polish and Hungarian issues also had to be submitted to the four great powers for a decision.

On 30 September, the Czechoslovak government accepted the Munich Agreement, and with this resolution it also expressed its willingness to begin discussions concerning the Hungarian demands.

In accordance with the Munich Agreement, on 10 October, German troops crossed the Czechoslovak border and began their occupation of the territory which, according to the Munich decision, had ended up in Germany's possession...

At this point, Poland took action: it submitted an ultimatum to the Czechoslovak government demanding the immediate cession of the disputed territories. Facing the threat of military force, the Czechoslovak government agreed to allow the Polish troops to enter Teschen[15] and the disputed territories. With this step, the Polish and German issues were approaching resolution, or at least so it appeared. Only the Hungarian demands remained unaddressed. It seemed as if, while the Czechoslovak government had agreed to fulfill the demands of the German Reich and Poland, it was preparing to use military resistance to prevent the assertion of the Hungarian demands.

---

15   Today Cieszyn, Poland.

Fateful Years

On 3 October, the Hungarian government submitted a new aide-memoire demanding the immediate discussion of the Hungarian issue. On 5 October, Beneš,[16] President of the Czech Republic, resigned. In the meantime, the Slovaks had begun their "independence" movement. This caused a certain delay in the Hungarian-Czech negotiations, and the talks only began on 9 October in Komárom. During the negotiations, the Hungarian delegates used ethnic borders drawn on the basis of data from the 1910 census as their point of departure. The Czechs did not recognize either the accuracy or the legitimacy of the Hungarian standpoint. In order to demonstrate their intention to arrive at a compromise, however, they agreed to cede the city of Ipolyság and the small railway station of Sátoraljaújhely to Hungary immediately.

The Hungarian committee was headed by Minister of Foreign Affairs Kálmán Kánya.[17] Tiso,[18] the newly named [Slovak] prime minister, was at the head of the Czechoslovak delegation.

The Hungarian committee soon realized that the Czechoslovak approach to the negotiations was only intended to allow the Czechoslovak army, regrouped in the meantime along the Hungarian border, to exert armed pressure on the talks. The Czechs offered the Hungarians of Czechoslovakia autonomy. When the Hungarian committee rejected this offer, on 12 October the Czechs offered to cede Csallóköz,[19] excluding the city of Komárom, which would have meant the return to Hungary of a territory of some 1,840 square kilometers and 105,000 inhabitants, in contrast with the Hungarian demands, which sought the return of 14,150 square kilometers of territory with 1,090,000 inhabitants.

The Hungarian committee considered the offer unacceptable. Going one step further, the Czechs were willing to return a bit more of the territories inhabited by Hungarian-speakers, but this meant little more than a few border

---

16 Edvard Beneš (1884–1948) served as President of Czechoslovakia twice (1935–1938 and 1945–1948), as well as Minister of Foreign Affairs (1918–1935) and President of Czechoslovakia in exile (1939–1945).
17 Kálmán Kánya (1869–1945) served as Foreign Minister of Hungary from 1933 until 1938.
18 Jozef Tiso (1887–1947) was a Roman Catholic priest and a leading member of the Slovak People's Party. In 1939, following the German invasion of Czechoslovakia, Tiso became the head of the First Slovak Republic, which functioned essentially as a satellite state of Nazi Germany. After the end of the war, Tiso was convicted of treason, war crimes, and crimes against humanity by the National Court in Bratislava. He was hanged on 18 April 1947.
19 Today Žitný ostrov, Slovakia. Žitný ostrov is a river island between the Danube, one of its tributaries, and the Váh River, or Vág River in Hungarian.

Chapter I

adjustments. Thus, it was clear that the Czechs were guided not by the ethnic principle, but rather by tactical, economic, and transportation policy considerations, and they were completely unwilling to approach the Hungarian demands in the same manner as they had approached the German and Polish demands.

In the meantime, Lieutenant General Lajos Keresztes-Fischer had submitted his resignation. He had not been able to withstand the nerve-racking work and anxieties that went with the position of chief of the general staff. Henrik Werth,[20] his successor, became lieutenant general. The regent appointed Keresztes-Fischer adjutant-general and head of the military office. The position of adjutant-general allowed the former chief of staff to avoid being demoted to a position that would have meant a loss of prestige.

On one occasion, Minister of Defense Jenő Rátz summoned me to meet with him. I knew that he wanted me to be given the position of chief of the general staff. I assumed that he wished to speak with me about this. Rátz received me at 7:00 in the evening. We discussed matters not worth any mention, of which I no longer have any recollection. What I do remember, however, is that he recounted the story of the appointment of the new chief of staff, Werth. He had learned of this appointment when the regent had called him on the phone and informed him that Henrik Werth, the new chief of staff, would soon seek him out. Minister of Defense Rátz was very disgruntled over the manner in which the appointment had been made. No one had sought his opinion, and indeed he had even been avoided. He would have expected the regent to have sought his opinion of the person to be named chief of the general staff before the appointment had actually been made. The issue bothered him all the more because he was not on good terms with Werth. When Lieutenant General Hugó Sónyi had been named to serve as commander-in-chief of the Hungarian army, Lieutenant General Werth, who as the commander of the fourth army corps felt that he had been overlooked, had asked to be allowed to retire, and now the regent had called him out of retirement.

---

20 Henrik Werth (1881–1952) served as Hungarian Chief of the General Staff from 1938 until 1941. He vigorously supported Hungary's declaration of war against the Soviet Union in 1941. He was arrested by Soviet forces in 1945 and in 1948 he was put on trial by the Hungarian People's Court for war crimes. He was found guilty and sentenced to death. He died in Soviet captivity in 1952.

Fateful Years

As I have mentioned, the negotiations in Komárom began with the Czechs announcing their willingness to cede Ipolyság and the small railway station of Sátoraljaújhely. We soldiers followed the Komárom negotiations closely, and we were overjoyed when the order came for the troops in the first Budapest army corps to enter Ipolyság on 11 October.

The first infantry regiment of the Hungarian army was stationed across from Ipolyság, under the command of Alfréd Paduschitzky, in the area around Diósjenő and Nagyoroszi. The order did not specify that I was to lead the troops to Ipolyság, but I still decided to oversee the entry into the city. We departed from Budapest by car, and as we didn't want to bother the troops marching in columns, we traveled by way of the new road through Diósjenő and Kemence. We were late nonetheless. I went out onto the balcony of the county hall to listen to the welcoming speeches. When I appeared on the balcony, I was told that the people of the city wanted me to speak too. I greeted the people of Ipolyság as the commander of the Hungarian soldiers who had arrived in their city. I assured everyone that we had come to Ipolyság as representatives of peace and reconciliation and that we would be just defenders of all those who proved faithful children of the Hungarian homeland.

Following the arrival of the soldiers in Ipolyság, events became complicated. The Komárom negotiations were broken off on 13 October. The Czechoslovaks were not willing to recognize the ethnic borders. Initially, they had wanted to return Csallóköz, not including the city of Komárom, and they had then shown themselves willing to cede other territories, but not the cities of Kassa,[21] Rozsnyó,[22] Léva,[23] Losonc,[24] Ungvár,[25] or Munkács.[26] On 26 October, the Czech government suggested allowing Germany and Italy to decide the fates of the disputed territories.

A rumor was spreading according to which Hungary might have to give the Czechs back the territories that it had already ceded, and so we were given orders to take all the necessary preparations to defend the territory around

---

21 Today Košice, Slovakia.
22 Today Rožňava, Slovakia.
23 Today Levice, Slovakia.
24 Today Lučenec, Slovakia.
25 Today Uzhhorod, Ukraine.
26 Today Mukachevo, Ukraine.

Chapter I

Ipolyság. We began digging entrenchments, and we set up artillery batteries on the southern bank of the Ipoly River so that we would be able to support the defense positions of the infantry on the right bank effectively.

In the meantime, however, the tension eased. The two parties to the negotiations had agreed to let German and Italian representatives decide on the questions of the territories under dispute. On 2 November, the first Vienna arbitration decision was issued.[27] According to the decision, a territory of 12,400 square kilometers and 1,100,000 inhabitants, a majority of whom were Hungarian, was ceded to Hungary.

The gradual occupation of the Hungarian-inhabited territories began. Since a long line of the northern strip of the territory to which my army corps (the first army corps) had been assigned bordered the territory left to the Czechoslovaks, my soldiers had to march through several cities. On 5 November 1938, I crossed [the Danube] at Esztergom and entered Párkány[28] at the head of the first army corps.

I took part in the entry of the corps into Losonc and, on 13 November, Léva as well. According to higher orders, while the military administration was functioning in the territory, I had to set up my headquarters in Ipolyság. This lasted until 20 December. I was then ordered to return immediately to Budapest with my command.

During the time I spent in Ipolyság, Jenő Rátz left his position at the head of the Ministry of Foreign Affairs. He was succeeded by Colonel General Károly Bartha. I later heard that Prime Minister Count Pál Teleki[29] wanted

---

27 This decision, which is referred to in secondary literature as the First Vienna Award, constituted the first modification of the borders of Hungary as dictated in the Treaty of Trianon. The Award was the result of arbitration in Vienna led by German Foreign Minister Joachim von Ribbentrop and Italian Foreign Minister Galeazzo Ciano. Both Germany and Italy were eager to see a peaceful resolution to the territorial conflict between Hungary and Czechoslovakia. According to the Award, Hungary was given permission to annex territories in southern Czechoslovakia and Sub-Carpathian Ruthenia (which today is part of Ukraine). The Treaty of Paris signed after the Second World War declared the Award null and void.

28 Today Štúrovo, Slovakia.

29 Pál Teleki (1879–1941) served as Prime Minister of Hungary from 1920 until 1921 and from 1939 until 1941. During his time in office in 1939–1941, Teleki strove to maintain Hungary's status as a non-belligerent in the conflicts that were enveloping Central Europe. When Germany invaded Poland in September 1939, Teleki refused to allow the German forces to use Hungary's railway system and allowed more than 100,000 Polish soldiers and hundreds of thousands of civilians to take refuge in Hungary. Teleki took no steps, however, to modify or annul Hungary's anti-Semitic laws. In December 1940, Teleki, eager to build an alliance with another power in the region, signed a Treaty

to get me to serve in his cabinet, and he had tried to find me. The newspapers referred to me as the minister designate of the Ministry of Defense. Since I was not in Budapest and the crisis in the Ministry of Defense had to be resolved quickly, the regent had asked Colonel General Bartha to accept the portfolio. Until then, Bartha had served as the head of the main department in the Ministry of Defense, and he was thus well-versed in managing affairs, so this solution seemed the most obvious. Whether or not it was the most auspicious was debatable. During the time in which I served as minister, István Bárczy, state secretary in the prime minister's office, told me that when the question of entering the war against the Soviet Union had been raised in the course of a cabinet meeting, Bartha had threatened to resign if we did not declare war against the Soviet Union. Henrik Werth also supported the declaration of war.

I served as the commander of the first army corps of Budapest until May 1939. The regent then appointed me to serve as infantry observer. My successor was General Zoltán Decleva. My new position did not give me a broad scope of authority. According to my title, the entire infantry was under my oversight. Since as infantry observer I was an expert who worked directly under the commander-in-chief, I needed the preliminary permission of the commander-in-chief of the Hungarian army to make an inspection. I was able to exert influence through the training exercises, and I also had some say when it came to the appointment of commanders. I served in this position until 1 March 1940.

When war broke out between Germany and Poland on 1 September 1939, the Soviet Union mobilized its army and occupied the territories of the old czar's empire that had been acquired by Poland. After this, in the summer of 1940, the Soviet Union also moved against Romania, demanding that Bessarabia, which had been unlawfully occupied by Romania in 1917, be returned, along with the part of Bukovina that had been occupied by the Ro-

---

of Eternal Friendship with Yugoslavia. In 1941, when Germany decided to invade Yugoslavia, Hitler demanded that Hungary allow German troops to pass through its territory. At first, Horthy resisted the German demands, in early April he gave in, and Chief of the General Staff Werth gave the German army permission to pass through Hungary. On the eve of 3 April, Teleki, having failed in his attempts to honor the Treaty of Friendship with Yugoslavia and believing that Hungary had inescapably become an ally of Nazi Germany, committed suicide by shooting himself.

Chapter I

manians. At the time, the Soviet radio addressed Hungary in a very congenial tone, calling on the Hungarian government to assert its claims against Romania. Romania reacted with lightning speed. Realizing that it could not hope for help from Poland, it accepted the Russian demands, regrouping the Romanian troops stationed on the border with Russia and moving them to Transylvania, lest the Hungarians be able march into Transylvania unopposed.

Among our leaders there was then resolve, or, rather, the resolve awoke to begin the work against Romania. The preparatory work for a possible mobilization began. I was in Rozsnyó at the time on an inspection. While the exercises were being done, I received a telephone call informing me that the regent had entrusted me with the position of commander of the second army, because infantry general Sónyi,[30] who was serving as the commander-in-chief of the Hungarian army and had been selected for the post, was taking over command of the units in the hinterland. I immediately went from Rozsnyó to Budapest and reported to the head of the general staff to discuss the next steps. Werth informed me that since things had taken the turn they had taken, it was easily imaginable that military measures would be taken against Romania in order to assert Hungary's claims. I was being entrusted with command of this army. My chief of staff would be Colonel Károly Beregfy (Berger), commander of the Military Academy. I noted that in my view, we should work together with the Russians and take advantage of the circumstances to act against Romania. The Soviet Union's simultaneous move guaranteed success, and we would acquire its support in the ensuing events. To this, Werth replied that we could not work together with the Soviets. I could already sense that the regent and those surrounding him did not relish the idea of entering a joint campaign with the Russians, even if this held out the promise of serious political and tactical success. In my view, it would have been the best moment to have improved our relationship with the Soviet Union and thus put an end to the hostilities that had been artificially inflamed and maintained for decades.

The order was given to assemble the command of the first army. Beregfy began his efforts to organize the headquarters at the Ludovika Academy. I had

---

30 Hugó Sónyi (1883–1958), commander-in-chief of the Royal Hungarian Army from 1936 until 1940.

not yet taken over the leadership, since at the time we were only dealing with the internal makeup of the command. In the end, the command headquarters was never actually active, because before the organizational work had been completed and the staff assembled, the Germans cautioned us to desist and made it known that they did not support Hungary over the Romanians. They needed Romanian oil, and they were already counting on war with the Soviet Union. They regarded Romania as a more valuable ally than us.

On 1 January 1940, I was informed that I would soon be given a different position. Essentially, I was going to be named deputy chief of staff. General István Náday, section head in the Ministry of Foreign Affairs, informed me of this as if it were a fait accompli. I was amazed that Werth had not summoned me to speak about this. True, we had never been on the friendliest of terms. In the course of our collaborative work, I had become convinced that I could not count on any goodwill from him. On only one occasion had he spoken to me person to person with a show of respect. At the time, he had been serving as the commander of the fourth army corps of Pécs. I had been the aide-de-camp of Infantry General and Commander-in-Chief Kamilló Kárpáthy. He had once congratulated me on the publication of the second volume of my book *Szerbiai hadjárat* [The Serbian Military Campaign], which examined the political events leading up to the world war and the roles and work of diplomats.

I was never actually made deputy chief of staff, because the chief of the general staff chose the commander of the Miskolc army, Lieutenant General András Littay, instead, suggesting that I be made part of the command of the newly formed first army.

Szolnok was chosen as the garrison for the command headquarters of the first army. The headquarters of the newly formed rapid deployment force was also stationed there. At the time, it was under the command of General Béla Miklós.[31] Here I found myself reunited with Béla Miklós. When I had been

---

31 Béla Miklós (1890–1948) was a military officer who became General of the Hungarian First Army in the tumultuous month of August 1944. He supported leaving the Axis and entering an alliance with the Soviet army. On 16 October, fearing arrest by the Germans, he fled and joined the Soviet forces. On 17 October, at the request of the Soviets, he made a plea over the radio to the commanders of the Hungarian army, asking them to turn on the Germans and fight alongside the Soviets. In late 1944, he became the head of the Hungarian Interim Assembly in Debrecen, a position which he held until he was replaced by Zoltán Tildy after elections in November 1945. His name in Hungarian is Dálno-

Chapter I

the chief of staff of the first mixed brigade, as lieutenant colonel he had served as my deputy for two years.

In the meantime, the foreign policy situation had become increasingly complex. The relationship with Romania had become increasingly tense. The Hungarian government thought that the time had come to solve the Transylvanian question. It began negotiations with delegates of the Romanian government on 16 August 1940 in Turnu Severin.

On 1 July, the soldiers of the army, whose numbers had been increased, began to move to the eastern borders. The army command, on almost a full footing for war, was stationed in Sóstó, near Nyíregyháza. This meant that if the negotiations did not lead anywhere, we would solve the Transylvanian problem with force of arms, and my army, which consisted of some 208,000 people, had been given a decisive role in this. In Sóstó, we took all the preparatory measures for military operations against Romania. I examined the border and considered the options for attack. With my officers of the general staff, we sought out every spot along the border that offered a good vantage point. We discussed the possibilities for attack. In the meantime, I was ordered to have the first army ready to begin attack on 28 August if the Romanians were to reject the conditions set by the Hungarian government and prove unwilling to return and evacuate from the territories we were demanding.

I convened a meeting with my army corps commanders in Sóstó: General István Schweitzer, commander of the second army corps, General Zoltán Decleva, commander of the first, Lieutenant General László Horváth, commander of the fourth, and Lieutenant General József Bajnóczy, commander of the sixth.

I laid down the guiding principles according to which we would proceed in the course of the military operations and the launch of an attack. I established the goals to be reached and the tasks to be carried out by the individual army corps.

No military action was taken, however, because the Romanians asked the German and the Italian governments to settle the issues under debate

---

ki Béla Miklós, which in English would be something like Béla Miklós of Dálnok. The title "of Dálnok" was used by his father, Gergely Miklós. Dálnok (or Dalnic in Romanian) is a commune in the Székely Land in eastern Transylvania, which today is part of Romania.

through a court of arbitration. This was the second meeting of the court of arbitration, held in Vienna on 2 August 1940.[32] The Romanian government accepted its decision. On the basis of this decision, Hungary got back northern Transylvania and the Székely Land.[33] Thus, instead of an armed resolution, Hungarian forces entered the territory peacefully.

During the time in which the army headquarters was stationed in Sóstó, an interesting event took place that had serious consequences for me for the rest of my life. I received a letter from Jenő Rátz, the former Minister of Defense. In this letter, he called my attention to the fact that Béla Imrédy,[34] the former prime minister, had been assigned to my army as a so-called "train commander." According to Rátz, it was not fitting that the former prime minister be in a subordinate position. He asked me to make Imrédy part of the army command and use him as a commanding officer or in some other position that better suited his standing and dignity. Naturally, I agreed. Imrédy had been made a train commander not because he was needed as a train officer, but rather simply as a way of striking a blow to someone who had fallen out of government. Everyone knew that Imrédy had left the prime minister's seat in part because it had been learned that his grandparents had not all been of Aryan descent.

I immediately ordered that Imrédy be given a position in the army command. What was unusual was that it was precisely the right-wing politicians who did not attribute much significance to Imrédy's lineage. They claimed that the whole attack against Imrédy was the work of the members of circles who saw in him a representative of the radical tendency and feared that

---

32 This arbitration resulted in the so-called Second Vienna Award, according to which Hungary was granted northern Transylvania, all of Máramaros (or Maramureş in Romanian), and part of Körösvidék (or Crişana in Romania). It total, Hungary re-annexed a territory of 43,104 square kilometers.
33 The Székely Land is an ethnographic region is eastern Transylvania (roughly the middle of Romania today) inhabited primarily by Hungarian speakers known as the Székelys. The origins of the Székely people remain a subject of debate among historians.
34 Béla Imrédy (1891–1946) served as Prime Minister of Hungary from 1938 until 1939. He resigned from his position as prime minister in February 1939, after having been confronted by his opponents, who observed that his great-grandfather had been Jewish, a fact which seemed difficult to reconcile with Imrédy's support for Nazi Germany and the right wing in Hungary. In 1940, Imrédy founded the anti-Semitic Party of Hungarian Renewal. In 1944, he served in Döme Sztójay's government as Minister of Economic Coordination. After the war, he was arrested and put on trial by the People's Court for war crimes and collaboration with Nazi Germany. He was found guilty and sentenced to death. He was executed by firing squad in 1946.

he would deprive them of their influence, and also those who feared that by kicking aside the constitution, Imrédy sought to create a dictatorship.

As someone who did not engage in politics, I did not attribute any significance to this political game, and I thought that it was not my place to pass judgement as to who was correct in this matter. I had no interest in Imrédy's lineage. I could not leave him, as the former prime minister and head of the foreign policy committee, in the insignificant position of train commander.

At the same time, Antal Kunder, the former Minister of Industrial Affairs, was also part of the army command. Imrédy worked as a hussar captain in the general staff division. I brought him with me many times when I made inspections because I felt I was doing the Hungarian army a service by giving a leading politician a chance to glean a glimpse into the life of the soldiery. I wanted there to be more people in parliament who were informed friends of the army. I was of the opinion that politicians often failed to grasp military questions because they had never had a chance to get to know the army from up close.

The politicians who took note of my conduct did not approve of this, because, as I later learned, they reported to the prime minister and the regent that Imrédy and I were as thick as thieves. They even took photographs of us in secret with which they sought to prove to the regent that I was an adherent of Imrédy's. They claimed that when lunch was served, I did not sit down until Imrédy had arrived. Imrédy always sat at the head of the table. This, of course, was not true. I never waited for Imrédy when lunch was served, and I sat at the head of the table. I could not prevent these rumors, indeed I did not even know of them at the time.

On one occasion, I received an order from the military office of the regent to go immediately to Gödöllő with Ferenc Jékely, the lord lieutenant of Nyíregyháza, to see the regent, because he wanted to speak with us on an important issue. I could not imagine what this important issue was that required us to report to the regent. When we arrived, the regent immediately received us. He said that he had reason to believe that Imrédy was using his position in the army command to engage in political agitation among the officer corps. If this were indeed the case, it must be prevented. I was to report my observations to him directly. This order surprised me, because I had not seen any sign whatsoever suggesting that Imrédy was engaged in political agitation in the circles of the officer corps. I assured the regent that I would do everything to make it impossible for Imrédy to engage in political agitation.

I was convinced that this accusation was merely the consequence of a rumor that had been spread by Imrédy's enemies. I did not know that, together with Kunder, Imrédy had used other official channels, including in civilian circles, to acquire followers and begin the organization of the political party that would later emerge as the Party of Hungarian Renewal, the party of which Jenő Rátz, the former Minister of Defense who had approached me on the question of Imrédy's position, was to become a stalwart pillar.

I later learned that Imrédy's machinations were one of the reasons I was discharged with a pension, because according to what the regent was told, I had helped further Imrédy's political maneuvering, and as army commander, I had not put any obstacles in his way.

With regards to the imminent entry of Hungarian forces into Transylvania, I was given no part. I can only attribute this to the antipathy between me and the chief of the general staff, which had become palpably sharper. The bulk of the military force that had been mobilized against the Romanians—four army corps—had been put under my command. As already mentioned, we would have used armed force to open the road towards Kolozsvár[35] if the Romanians had clung to their rigid standpoint. This attack never took place. However, since the regent and the entire government wanted to take part in the march into Kolozsvár, the chief of the general staff gave orders for the soldiers under Lieutenant General Jány,[36] the regent's former adjutant-general

---

35 Today Cluj, Romania.
36 Gusztáv Jány (1883–1947) served as commander of the Hungarian Second Army during the Battle of Stalingrad. In Autumn 1942, Jány asked the regent to relieve him from his position, since he felt that the German demands that have been placed on the Hungarian army were unrealistic and put the Hungarian forces in grave danger. His request was denied. In December 1942 and January 1943, Jány ordered the Hungarian forces along the Don River to hold their ground, as a consequence of which the Hungarian Second Army was virtually annihilated by the numerically superior and better equipped Soviet forces. As the Red Army occupied Hungary, Jány fled with his family to Germany, but in 1946, following his wife's death, he returned voluntarily to Hungary and turned himself over to the authorities. He was put on trial by the People's Court and sentenced to death. Although the judge in his case argued in support of a reprieve, the request was rejected by President of the Republic Zoltán Tildy, and Jány was executed in November 1947. He was exonerated posthumously in October 1933.

Chapter I

(the second army), to march into Kolozsvár. According to the old plans, Lieutenant General Jány would have joined my right-wing and led the southeastern frontline, which fell on the side towards Arad. Now that the lion's share of the entry of our forces had fallen to me, I had to press northwards, leaving space for the second army (for Jány), and thus even Nagyvárad[37] was no longer in the territory into which I was to advance, though in the event of an attack it would have been.

On 26 August, the difficult situation was finally resolved. The Romanians realized that we were not going to withdraw, and if they continued to prolong and postpone the issue, we would resolve the question by force of arms. It is possible that the allies also exerted pressure on them. As a consequence of this, the Romanians accepted the decision of the Vienna court of arbitration, according to which a territory of 43,000 square kilometers with approximately 2.5 million inhabitants was returned to Hungary. Thus, the second Vienna Award did not fulfill all of the hopes of the Hungarian government or the Hungarian public. The fact that the new border ran roughly 4 kilometers to the south of Kolozsvár was met with great disappointment, as was the fact that Marosvásárhely[38] had also become a border city. The public in Hungary was also disappointed that the train line connecting Kolozsvár, Nagyenyed,[39] and Tövis[40] was severed by the new border, and the city of Brassó[41] remained in Romania, along with the gas fields of Nagysármás.[42] Allegedly, Göring's brother had business interests there. He was also the leading shareholder in the industrial enterprises in Resica.[43] It seems that, in the process of making the decisions concerning the border, they had not wanted to disrupt Göring's interests. Instead, they shaved a bit off of the Hungarian claims. Thus, the Székely Land was not connected by rail to the western territories of Transylvania, because the stretch of railroad between Apahida and Marosludas[44] was not in the territory returned to Hungary.

---

37   Today Oradea, Romania.
38   Today Târgu Mureș, Romania.
39   Today Aiud, Romania.
40   Today Teiuș, Romania.
41   Today Brașov, Romania.
42   Today Sărmașu, Romania.
43   Today Reșița, Romania.
44   Today Luduș, Romania.

Fateful Years

According to the order received on 26 August, we were to begin our march into the territories which the Romanians had evacuated on 5 September. The first major city which the soldiers of the first army corps entered was Szatmárnémeti.[45] I was informed that the regent would take part in the ceremonies held on the occasion of our entry into the city.

There was very little time for the preparations for the march into the city, so the date on which we were to begin was postponed a bit. The regent had to wait for a little while outside the city of Szatmárnémeti while we removed the roadblocks and antitank traps that had been built by the Romanians so that the soldiers could set out towards the city. Prime Minister Pál Teleki was with the regent, as was Minister of Defense Károly Barth and Chief of the General Staff Henrik Werth.

Werth did not let this opportunity to confront me slip either. While the procession was underway and the motor units were proceeding in front of us, ignoring the momentous nature of the situation, he suddenly turned toward me and heatedly asked why motorized vehicles were part of the procession when, allegedly according to his orders, only the columns of soldiers were to march before the regent, without any supply formations.

Because, I answered, the army corps commanders had arranged the procession in this way with my approval. The troops were only accompanied by the combat train—ammunition and food. Up to the last minute, the Romanians had said that they were not going to accept the decision, and they would attack the arriving Hungarian formations in the Avas Mountains.[46] As responsible leaders, the commanders of the army corps had taken measures to ensure that the soldiers take ammunition and food with them, since if they were now to be separated from their supply units, they would not be able find each other, and thus they would not be guaranteed to have supplies.

When the regent heard this—though I had not said it in order for him to hear it—he interrupted: "Your Honor is right." With that, the debate came to an end. The regent and his entourage were taken to the city hall for brunch before the procession of soldiers had even come to an end. I felt that I should not leave the soldiers who were still marching, so I did not join the regent, but

---

45 Today Satu Mare, Romania.
46 Today the Oaș Mountains in Romania.

waited instead until the procession had ended. As the highest ranking military officer present, the chief of the general staff should have paid attention to this, and he should have kept the regent there, at the procession. And I would note, the command that had been given by the chief of the general staff made no mention of the trains not following the columns of troops or of having only the troops march in front of the regent.

The army headquarters remained in Szatmárnémeti for a few more days, because according to the orders of the chief of the general staff it was not important that the army command remain in constant and close contact with the soldiers, but rather that communications with Budapest remain intact. Thus, the soldiers and their commands advanced in front of us by a stretch of several days, making it difficult for us to receive reports from them or give them orders. When I gave orders—without Werth's permission—that we reduce the distance between us and the soldiers and proceed to Dés,[47] he wanted to order us to return to Szatmárnémeti, as if he were dealing not with an army command, but rather a simple squadron. When I spoke out against returning, he agreed under protest to allow the army command headquarters to remain in Dés. He insisted that we could proceed onward only with his permission. If he had led the army in this manner in a combat situation and not in a peaceful advance, I do not know how the campaign would have fared. Would I have been able to withstand this impossible leadership, and, most importantly, would our troops and commanders have withstood it?

Since according to the plans for our advance we were to arrive in Marosvásárhely on the 10th, and the regent, together with his family, wished to take part in a procession planned in his honor in Szászrégen[48] and in the review of troops in Marosvásárhely, I decided that on the 10th, I would march into Marosvásárhely. From here, following the celebration to mark the arrival of the Hungarian forces, I would return to Dés. Then, if the chief of the general staff gave his consent, I would return in plenty of time to Marosvásárhely to make the necessary preparations for the regent's arrival here and in Szászrégen.

The Hungarians of Transylvania welcomed the Hungarian soldiers with enthusiasm. We felt a great sense of joy when we set foot on the soil of the

---

47   Today Dej, Romania.
48   Today Reghin, Romania.

Fateful Years

Székely Land. The high point of the march into Transylvania came on 10 September 1940, when we arrived in Marosvásárhely. Since the procession would have been too long for the infantry units, I gave orders for the cavalry and rapid deployment units of the fourth army corps to enter and take control of the city, from which the Romanians had evacuated. The march into the city was planned for 4 o'clock in the afternoon. The body of the army command went from Dés by car. Before arriving in Marosvásárhely, we were going to switch to horseback. In all of the previous such marches, I had ridden on the back of a bay horse, because it had calmly born the people's cheers and the rain of flowers they had thrown. At the border of the city, a few minutes after we arrived, the animal suffered an unfortunate accident. When Géza Szabó, a lieutenant colonel in the artillery, arrived with the horses at the spot where we were to switch to horseback, iron protruding from a truck driving past us ripped open the horse's hindquarters. Blood gushed from the poor animal's wound. We did not think it would survive. It was immediately given care in the yard of a nearby house. Another horse had to be found for me. There was a fine-looking gray. I had not selected this gray for the march into the city because I had known that the regent usually rode a gray horse on these occasions. Now, however, I had to set aside this consideration and mount the gray. We barely had time, because of the accident, to saddle the horse with a general's harness. We set out, as it was almost 4 o'clock.

At the edge of the city, the municipal leaders were waiting for us, the arriving troops, in front of a triumphal arch. I had to reply to the moving speeches of welcome from horseback. I endeavored to express gratitude for the enthusiastic welcome in a short speech. From the triumphal arch, I went at the head of the troops through a rain of flowers to the main square, where a crowd had gathered that filled the entire square. People had even climbed nearby trees and gone up onto the roofs of nearby buildings to see and hear everything. On one end of the square stood the Greek Orthodox church, and on the other stood the Uniate church, both of which had been built by the Romanians as a sign that they now regarded this territory as theirs, permanently. If the Romanians had only been guided by the desire to serve God in their decision to build these churches, one could hardly have spoken a word of protest, for the freedom of religion is an important and inalienable right for everyone.

Chapter I

The series of celebratory speeches was opened by the local Roman Catholic parish priest, Béla Jaross, who spoke of earlier times with tact and eloquence and expressed his conviction that here, in Transylvania, everyone must pursue a policy of understanding and reconciliation. Of the many speeches, I recall one very clearly. It was held by the Romanian Greek Orthodox priest. He spoke Hungarian very well. One could hardly tell that it was not his native tongue. Among other things, he said that one should not be surprised that the Romanians were not pleased by the arrival of the Hungarians, because for them, this meant the loss of their homeland. This was met with almost continuous protests from the crowd. I could understand this Romanian priest. Indeed, it hurt for him to see that the Romanian dreams were fraying, and again they would have to recognize Hungarian rule. I understood this pain, but I faulted him too, much as the people protesting faulted him, for having spoken about the wounded Romanian national dreams precisely at a place and time when Hungarian crowds were enthusiastically celebrating their liberation from Romanian captivity.

Then I too spoke. I was moved, and I spoke in fervent words about the twenty-two years that had passed, and I stated my conviction that we must rebuild the Hungarian Transylvanian country of the people. And I noted that the land had been Hungarian for one thousand years!

When I think back now on those days and on the feelings that surged in me and, in my opinion, in every true Hungarian heart, the question inevitably arises within me: is it possible that we Székelys must prepare ourselves again to recognize Romanian rule over us? True, in a speech he held in Kolozsvár, Romanian Prime Minister Petru Groza[49] guaranteed on his life and on his honor that in Transylvania no one would suffer any harm simply because he was Hungarian. These are beautiful words that arouse hope, and Petru Groza takes them seriously, but who can guarantee that his successors will not begin from the beginning, perhaps with other tools, the oppressive

---

49 Petru Groza (1884–1958) was a Romanian politician who served as prime minister of several governments in Romania dominated by the Communist Party from 1945 until 1952. As a communist ideologue, he strove at least in his rhetoric to downplay the importance of national differences among the citizens of Romania. On 10 March 1945, four days after Groza had become prime minister, the Soviet Union agreed to annul the Second Vienna Award and return northern Transylvania to Romania. Groza held a speech in which he promised that the rights of all of the ethnic groups in Transylvania would be respected by the new government.

and violent policies of Romanianization that in the past thrust the staff of a wayfarer into the hands of thousands and thousands of Hungarians.

The decision of the great powers again has made all of Transylvania part of Romania. Again, Romania has been rewarded, a country which served German interests more actively and more effectively than Hungary. The Romanians were rewarded for having left the alliance with Germany and having turned against their former allies in time.

Our political leadership, alas, was to the end unable or unwilling to grasp that the Germans could only emerge from this war as losers, and that we must not remain by their side to the bitter end, for the Germans had never been true friends of ours. They also did not see that a possible—though very unlikely—German victory might very well have had fateful consequences for Hungary.

To our misfortune, after the Second World War, we were regarded as the most faithful followers of the Germans and the people who had served them without thinking. We are not seen as deserving a fate any better fate than that of the Germans, or if so, then only slightly better. If, in the inebriation of the lightning German victories, they had been unable to prevent the Hitler fanatics from sweeping our country into war, at least they should have discerned the right moment at which to unhitch ourselves from the German cart, which, under Hitler's leadership, had been racing towards the precipice. We should not have missed the many chances to unfasten our nation's little boat from the sinking ship of Germany.

But I will return now to Marosvásárhely, because I wish to address the thoughts I raise above later. The celebration in Marosvásárhely lasted late into the evening. It was beginning to grow dark when the celebration ended.

There was a group dinner in one of the restaurants. During the meal, Count Mihály Toldalaghy and the parish priest János Jaross sat next to me. With the exception of Toldalaghy, the aristocrats of the area around Marosvásárhely did not take part in the dinner. At the beginning of the meal, Count Toldalaghy asked me to go with him to the home of physician Dr. Czakó after dinner, where the magnates had gathered because they wanted to meet me. I found it strange that even on this unforgettable day of celebration the local wealthy lords preferred to remain separate. The magnates explained this with the contention that it was not a sign of any desire to remain separate, but rather an expression of particular respect for me and for the army. I nonetheless did not approve of it.

Since Werth, the chief of the general staff, had not given permission for the first army command to move its headquarters to Marosvásárhely, we returned the next day to Dés, where I waited for the chief of staff's next command. In the end, I had to compel him to give his consent. I explained that careful preparations had to be made on site for the regent's inspection.

The celebrations in Szászrégen and Marosvásárhely had been splendid. The crowds had remained in spite of the drizzling rain. The arrangements for the lunch, however, were not to my liking. The delegate from the military bureau had forcefully insisted at all costs that the lunch be held in the hunting lodge of the Romanian king in Laposnya.[50] I disapproved of the idea of having the Hungarian regent use the manor house, which was the property of the Romanian king. It was entirely unnecessary. The representative of the military bureau, however, was so insistent that in the end I had to give in.

After the lunch, the regent and his entourage prepared to leave and travel back to Budapest by special train. Werth then informed me that the permanent headquarters of the army command would be Kolozsvár.

Following the regent's inspection, the preparatory work for the move began. I made a round and inspected the troops, and I then hurried to pay a visit to the village in which my wife had been born, her family's ancient nest, Nagybacon.[51] I had not been able to come into the village with the soldiers when they had arrived, because I had had to make the preparations for the regent's inspection and so had been unable to leave Dés. So I set out on the 17 as a private citizen to see my relatives in Nagybacon.

My path took me through Parajd,[52] the village of my birth. I went to the village cemetery to find my mother's grave, which I had last seen in 1905. In 1905, the gravestone had still been standing. I remember, as a young second lieutenant I had come with my friend Hugó Hirsch, a medical student. I was lost in reveries for a long time, thinking about the past, and it occurred to me

---

50   Today Lăpușna, Romania.
51   Today Băṭanii Mari, Romania.
52   Today Praid, Romania.

how strange it is that one does not even remember one's father, and one can only make pilgrimages to his burial mound. Strange, one is not tied by a single memory to the person whose blood and life one carries onward or continues, so to say. As much as I would like to, I do not remember my father, for I lost him when I was only two years of age, and the image of the loving father cannot remain firm and fixed among the memories of a two year-old child.

Several decades had passed since my last visit to the cemetery. And now I had come in vain. I searched in vain for the places where I thought the grave might be. In the thirty years that had passed, the cemetery had become completely wild. It was overgrown with underbrush, and I could find neither the gravestone nor the rose bush that had been on top of it. On the way back to the village, I asked the commander of the gendarmerie to have someone try to find the grave, and if they did find it, to inform me so that I could have someone tend to it.

The moon was already high in the heavens when I arrived in Nagybacon. I can hardly find words to express the joy with which Elek Nagy, my brother-in-law, and his family welcomed me in the vicarage. We embraced, and I am not at all ashamed to confess that I shed tears. We had not seen each other for twenty-two years, since August 1918. At the time, I had been a staff captain. A young man. Now I was a gray-haired old soldier. A great deal of time had passed, and we had gone through a great deal in the twenty-two years that had passed. We were sitting, talking by the intimate light of a petroleum lamp, when suddenly a Székely woman came in and said, "the men are waiting for you, general! They even set up a triumphal arch by the parish hall!" We had to go, we could not leave our Székely kinsmen waiting. All the people of the village, young and old, had come, everyone who had learned of my arrival. The first person to speak was my brother-in-law, Elek Nagy, a Calvinist deacon. He was followed by Ferenc Pataky, the village clerk. Then many others also spoke. Again, my eyes filled with tears when I shook hands with the people, one after the other, who were thronging towards me and asking questions, one after the other: "captain, do you still remember me?... You know, captain, we lived in Felszeg." Their openness and warmth was moving. Over the course of the past twenty-two years, many people have departed from this world and joined their forebears in the better home of the next world. Those

Chapter I

who had been children before had grown up. The youths, the young men, had become heads of families, and I had grown old. It was nice to see them again. It was nice to think back on the happy days I had spent here, on youth!

The next day we awoke to a Sunday. It was moving and heart-rending to hear the hum of the organ. I stood to the left of the door, in the first "upholstered chair," just as I had in times past, and sang with the same fervor as I once had: "Lord, thou hast been our dwelling place in all generations." All around me, Székely farmers and their wives, people of faith, sang the psalm, and I felt as if the beautiful, timeless melody had taken me on its wing to lift me into the infinite.

The next morning, I went to Sepsiszentgyörgy[53] and Kézdivásárhely[54] to muster the soldiers for inspection. We returned to Nagybacon in the afternoon. When we were approaching the village, coming from Hatod, I could see a large crowd waiting at the edge of the city. There was a triumphal arch. The youths of the village welcomed me with great jubilation. From here, we went to the vicarage, together with the crowd. Proud joy shone on every face: the blood of our blood, a Székely man, is the leader of the Transylvanian Hungarian army!

The next day, I bid farewell to the people of Nagybacon and went to Csíkszereda.[55] Lieutenant General Béldy, the commander of the cavalry division stationed in Csíkszereda, immediately presented himself and asked where I wanted to take up quarters. He recommended the hotel, but I decided to stay with my old friend, head physician Dr. Hugó Hirsch. I had to show that I considered the old friendship, which we had had some forty years earlier, sacred. Hugó and I had attended all eight years of secondary school at the Kun Boarding School in Szászváros.[56] We had always lived together in friendship and shared affection. I always thought of him with these feelings in my heart. What would he have thought of me if I had not heeded the call of this old bond, but rather had given in to the fashionable, stylish catchphrases just because short-sighted soldiers might speak ill of me?

---

53 Today Sfântu Gheorghe, Romania.
54 Today Târgu Secuiesc, Romania.
55 Today Miercurea Ciuc, Romania.
56 Today Orăștie, Romania.

Hugó and his family welcomed me with indescribable affection. I spent an unforgettable evening at their home.

I returned from Csíkszereda to Marosvásárhely, passing through Gyergyószentmiklós.[57] On the way, I crossed paths with the units of the cavalry division, which had already been given the order to return home. I saw that the saddles had galled the horses, and the cavalrymen had to lead the animals on foot by their reins, since they could not be ridden. This episode had an interesting sequel. After my arrival in Marosvásárhely, I received a report from General Béla Miklós, the commander of the rapid deployment force, who suggested that the division not return to its peacetime station on foot, but rather that the chief of the general staff permit transport by train. As I considered the commander's suggestion a good one, I requested permission from the chief of the general staff to use a train transport. I added to this request a note indicating that until the chief of staff's decision came, I had given the division permission to rest, since this was necessary given the condition of the horses.

The chief of the general staff sent a brusque rejection of my request, which made it quite plain that, with no regard for the importance of sparing the men, he wanted to strike a blow against the army command, or against me. In his reply, Werth contended, among other things, that the army command was fostering laxity. He objected to the fact that such a request had even been presented to him.

To this, I gave a brusque and measured reply. I referred to the Military Service Regulations, which obliged me to spare the men, the animals, and the supplies. I never received any reply to this.

Werth, however, did even more unusual things than this. He summoned me with a vindictive report because at the ceremonies marking the arrival of the Hungarian forces in Szatmárnémeti the officers of the army command had worn white collars instead of green. He must have known perfectly well that when the decree had been issued concerning the green collars we were no longer in our peacetime stations. In Nyíregyháza, it would have been preposterous to have bothered with obtaining green collars. I confess, I had not

---

57 Today Gheorgheni, Romania.

even thought about this nonsense until then, for I had never imagined that, when one must consider whether or not the sound of gunfire will soon be heard, the chief of the general staff has nothing better to do than worry about whether the officers of the army command are wearing green collars or white collars. As if the debate between Lázár Mészáros and Sándor Petőfi concerning collars were taking place all over again![58] A statement that Henrik Werth once made in my presence in the minister's antechamber in Budapest is similarly characteristic of his thinking: "Hungarians are only capable of doing great things when they are under foreign leadership."

He was right in the sense that it was indeed foreigners who had led Hungary into the unfortunate situation in which it found itself: the Beregfy-Bergers, the Szálasi-Szalajosáns, the Jurcseks, the Reményi-Schnellers, and the Werths.

We remained in Marosvásárhely until 1 November, at which point we moved to Kolozsvár, which was to become the permanent headquarters of the army command as of 1 November 1941. I stayed for a time in the New York Hotel and then moved into the home of Dr. Vitályos, relatives of whom had always given me lodging on previous occasions when I had not been able to rent a suitable apartment and had had to come from Szolnok to deal with the matters of the move. I must recount one thing that in my opinion was important. I mention it because it makes quite clear that, as military leaders, we were not hostile to the Romanians. We regarded them as citizens with equal rights.

A few days after the army command headquarters had been relocated to Kolozsvár, I informed the chief of the general staff of my wish to meet the local civilian and church leaders and share with them a few words concerning the policies and principles I sought to assert as long as the administration was under military leadership. I invited the Romanian Greek Orthodox and Greek Catholic bishops to join me for this conversation, as well as the lead-

---

58 Nagy is referring to a disagreement between Hungarian poet Sándor Petőfi and Lázár Mészáros, who served as the Minister of Defense in the government of Lajos Batthyány at time of the 1848 Revolution against the Habsburgs. In early 1849, Petőfi, who as a poet and public figure had been an impassioned supporter of Hungarian independence from Vienna, was put at his request among the fighting forces in Transylvania. He was rebuked by Mészáros, however, for not wearing a proper collar. On 17 February 1849, in response to Mészáros' reproaches, he submitted his resignation from his post as an officer.

ers of the civilian administration who had not left Kolozsvár when we arrived in the city. In the course of the conversation, I emphasized that the fact that the northern part of Transylvania had been returned to Hungary did not mean that anyone would come to any harm or suffer any persecution. We were bringing peace and understanding, and I did not want anyone to feel persecuted or restricted in his or her rights. In my eyes, Romanian, Saxon, German, Jew, and Hungarian were equal. I would not allow anyone to suffer disadvantage because of his or her ancestry. Everyone should boldly live a free life. I asked only one thing of everyone, that they respect the laws of the state.

I traveled from Kolozsvár to Budapest to attend a sitting of the Upper House. This trip coincided with a request of the seat of the Order of the Valiant[59] in Budapest to hold a speech at the Saint Nicholas' Day celebration of the Order on 6 December.

After Saint Nicholas' Day, I sought out Minister of Defense Bartha, because I wanted to know when I could expect to retire, since in October 1941 I would have completed my 36th year of service, and according to the statutes in effect at the time, someone who had been in the service for that long had to retire unless the Council of Ministers wished to retain him. At the time, from my class at the Ludovika Military Academy (1905) Lieutenant Generals Gusztáv Jány, András Littay, Elemér Novák, Sándor Bengyel, and Lajos Keresztes-Fischer were in the service, in addition to me. I was the oldest among them in rank. I asked Bartha about his plans for the future. He openly said that as far as he knew, the chief of the general staff was going to suggest beginning to put the members of the Armed Forces from our class into retirement. Since I had already become an infantry general (full colonel) and I was the highest in rank, they would begin with me. It bothered me that I would be the first to leave, and a half year before having complet-

---

59   The Vitézi Rend, or Order of the Valiant, was a Hungarian order of merit founded in 1920. The term "vitéz," which means "valiant" or "knight," constituted an officially recognized title. During the Second World War, many of the most prominent members of the order were virulent anti-Semites and actively collaborated with the Nazis. The organization is therefore sometimes thought of as having been unanimously supportive of Nazi Germany. However, many of its members, including Vilmos Nagy, opposed the Germans. For instance, in 1944, Vitéz Ferenc Koszorús, who was an officer in the Hungarian army, deployed his troops to prevent a putsch by the Hungarian gendarmerie, which sought to implement the deportation of the Jews of Budapest. Today, there is a plaque in his memory by the synagogue in Dohány Street in Budapest.

Chapter I

ed my 36th year of service. This alone made it clear that, in addition to the reasons that Bartha had given, other factors were coming into play. Later, I discovered that the principal reason for my rapid dismissal was that the regent had been told I was a supporter of Imrédy. They said that I had helped Imrédy organize his political party in Transylvania. The rumors that were spread about me and my alleged ties to Imrédy were nothing but fictions and baseless calumny. I wrote as much to Bartha, but he never replied to my letter. On one occasion, I met with him in the Upper House, and I asked him whether he had gotten my letter. He said that he had received the letter and that he would reply. He never did.

My stay in Kolozsvár did not last long. I asked to be given leave for Christmas. I was still on leave when I received an official summons from Werth to find him in his office. On 9 January 1941, I reported to the chief of the general staff. Werth informed me that the Crown Council had decided gradually to put the 1905 class from Ludovika into retirement, and the pensioning off of the members of the class who were in the service would begin with me. The chief of the general staff did not even bother with the customary gesture of politeness, saying not a word about the extensive work I had done in the service of the Hungarian army.

It is amazing that they cannot arrange the process of putting us, soldiers, into retirement so that the person who is being pensioned off leaves the armed services in a manner that will allow him always to think back fondly on the years he spent in his army unit. Because of the manner in which we are dismissed, we do not leave the service with a pleasant sense of satisfaction. Old soldiers always depart with a feeling of pain in their hearts. I too suffered this fate. True, I had never expected warm words of recognition from Werth. He had never had any feelings of friendship for me, but nonetheless, he could have offered at least one or two words of recognition.

My most immediate task was to see to it that we be able to move to Budapest as quickly as possible, since now all of my ties were with the capital. I completed my service in Kolozsvár on 31 January 1941. Lieutenant General István Schweitzer, commander of the second army corps, was my successor. I bid farewell to the Kolozsvár army command headquarters and the officer corps and officials of the garrison on 9 February 1941. I gave thanks to all of the people who had served under me and who had stood by me faithfully and trustfully over the course of my long career as a soldier.

On the morning of 10 February, when we drove to the train station, we found many members of the officer corps waiting for us there. They presented my wife with a beautiful bouquet of flowers.

This farewell was touching, and it made clear that I had many followers among the subordinates, who did not feel that from now on they could not expect anything from me simply because, as an infantry general and former army commander who had gone into retirement, I no longer belonged to the active circles of the army. The troops had been lined up on either side of the railway tracks for some ten kilometers in order to allow my soldiers to bid farewell to me. In Nagyvárad, a delegate of the officer corps boarded the train under the instructions of General Gothay, and here too my wife was presented with a bouquet of roses. It was a gratifying show of attentiveness.

Chapter II

The Minister of Defense's Negotiations in Early 1941 The Collapse of Yugoslavia

In Budapest, I was preoccupied first and foremost with the tasks of setting up house. In the meantime, I endeavored to renew all my friendly ties to people in civilian circles, which had broken when I had been transferred from Budapest.

This did not mean, however, that I did not take an interest in political events. I was continuously preoccupied by thoughts of the war that was underway and, in particular, the fate of Hungary, and I followed the developments closely. Though I did not receive continuous reports or notifications, I nonetheless could see that our ties to Germany and Italy were increasingly close. The principal reason for this, in my assessment, was that the Western powers had failed to appreciate the grave situation and economic difficulties that Hungary had suffered because of the Treaty of Trianon,[60] and they had failed to support our endeavors to assert our legitimate claims. In contrast, Germany and Italy had striven to bind Hungary ever more tightly to them. In particular, the leaders in Germany had nurtured the conviction among the Hungarian leaders that we could only expect support for our rightful claims from them. The Hungarian government had sought to come to an agreement with Yugoslavia (under Pál Teleki). The Yugoslav-Hungarian negotiations had begun in 1940. The negotiations had taken place with the tacit agreement that Hungary would not have to abandon the prospect of

---

60 The Treaty of Trianon was the peace treaty with which the First World War came to an end between the Kingdom of Hungary and most of the Allies (notably, though the United States signed the treaty, it was never ratified by the U.S. Senate, and the United States concluded a separate treaty with Hungary in 1921). According to the Treaty of Trianon, the Kingdom of Hungary, which had been part of the Austro-Hungarian Monarchy, lost roughly two-thirds of its territory and population to Czechoslovakia, Romania, and the Kingdom of Serbs, Croats, and Slovenes (which later became Yugoslavia). Although in principle the treaty was based on the idea of national self-determination, the Treaty of Trianon left large Hungarian minorities in the neighboring states, including in areas directly contiguous with Hungary. Border revision was the principal foreign policy of every Hungarian government in the interwar period.

a possible settlement of its territorial claims against Yugoslavia. The negotiations led to the signing of a treaty of friendship between Hungary and Yugoslavia in early December 1940.

Neither Rome nor Berlin was enthusiastic about the signing of this treaty.

The Yugoslav government had been hesitant to join the Axis powers. In January 1941, Minister of Defense Károly Bartha had traveled to Berlin to introduce himself to Hitler. In his notes concerning the trip, Bartha wrote down his impressions of the welcome he was shown.

In the course of their discussion, Hitler had proclaimed that German victory was beyond any doubt. The only thing he did not know was when this victory would come and when the English would realize that they had no chance of triumphing. He was waiting for the English to attack. He was so certain of German victory that he would have been perfectly happy to evacuate Holland in order to allow the English to land there, and then he would have defeated them decisively.

"Germany is invincible. There is ample proof of his analysis. They have sufficient raw materials, and the German army is the most powerful in the world." Hitler would now continue to expand the German army and strengthen it with new equipment and supplies. He was not able at the moment to grant the Hungarians' wish that Germany support the provision of supplies and arms for the Hungarian army, because the materials and equipment were all necessary for the development of the German fighting force. Only after a few months had passed would he be in a situation to provide greater support for the Hungarians. Germany had to secure itself towards the east. Yes, it had signed a treaty of friendship, not attack, with Russia, but "Russian expansion and the communist peril threaten from the east, and a Russian attack is likely."

Germany definitely needed the oil wells in Romania, and they had already secured control of them. Thus, it was in Germany's interests that there be peace in the Balkans.

The presence of the English in Thessaloniki did not yet constitute a serious danger in the Balkans. But nonetheless, Germany could not simply watch this idly. (And here one sees the seeds of the idea that, if necessary, Germany would move into the peninsula, even if it meant having to occupy Yugoslavia,

Chapter II

in order, by capturing Greece, to prevent the English from gaining ground and prevent them from building airports there.) Italy continued to fail to make advances against Greece. This failure was unpleasant, but it had no decisive effect on the course of the war. The Italians had not asked for help from the Germans only because they sought to protect their prestige. He knew the mood in Yugoslavia. Yugoslavia did not want war.

He emphasized: *"Hungary should strengthen its armed forces. At the inevitable general reordering that would come with the end of the war, possible gains were imaginable for a friendly Hungary."*

"The Hungarians had a mission at the crest of the Carpathian Mountains, for if Russian Bolshevism were to break through that barrier, they might advance as far as Vienna or perhaps even farther."

"A strong Hungarian army will also have an appropriate and calming effect on Yugoslavia."

Hitler's contentions were interesting indeed, in particular his contentions concerning Hungary. Hitler was kindling and attempting to lure us with the hope that if Hungary were to remain at Germany's side, it could count on enjoying "possible advantages," probably territorial gains. Herein lies the explanation for why Minister of Defense Bartha and, after Teleki's death, Prime Minister László Bárdossy[61] insisted so resolutely on attacking Russia, even though there was no conflict of interest between Russia and Hungary. Bartha had always been pro-German, and in my view the conversation he had with Hitler had a decisive influence on the rest of his career and bound him forever to the German line.

---

61 László Bárdossy (1890–1946) served as Prime Minister of Hungary from 1941 until 1942. He became prime minister after Pal Teleki's suicide. On 26 June 1944, the city of Kassa was bombed by three unidentified planes. The Hungarian military concluded that the attack had been launched by the Soviet Union, and Horthy ordered reprisals. Bárdossy held a meeting of the Council of Ministers, and the next day he announced to the Hungarian parliament that Hungary was in a state of war with the Soviet Union. Thus, he was one of the people most immediately responsible for Hungary's declaration of war against the Soviet Union. Bárdossy was also responsible for the enactment of the Third Jewish Law in 1941, which limited Jewish employment opportunities and prohibited intermarriage between Jews and gentiles. In 1942, Horthy forced him to leave office. He was replaced by Miklós Kállay. After the German occupation of Hungary in March 1944, Bárdossy collaborated with the puppet government of Döme Sztójay and, later, the Arrow Cross government led by Ferenc Szálasi. As Soviet troops advanced into Hungary, Bárdossy fled the country, but he was eventually extradited back to Hungary and put on trial by the People's Court. He was found guilty of war crimes and collaboration with the Nazis and was executed by firing squad in 1946.

The government had gotten little more than vague promises, but on the basis of these promises, the Hungarian leaders saw Germany as Hungary's only source of support.

Ribbentrop[62] had also spoken with Bartha, but he had not made any promises. It was common knowledge that he did not like the Hungarians, and so he had not made any mention of possible Hungarian gains. He had only mentioned the Russian question, which in his view, however, was not pressing for the moment.

Germany was adopting an increasingly threatening stance with regards to Yugoslavia, and Germany had demanded that Yugoslavia join the so-called Tripartite Pact. In the end, the Yugoslav government, under the leadership of Cvetković,[63] gave in to the German demands, and on 25 March 1941 Yugoslavia signed the Tripartite Pact. The officer corps, which was unhappy with the pro-German policies, overthrew the government with the approval of the king and formed a new government under the leadership of General Simović. In response to this, on 6 April Hitler sent German soldiers to occupy Yugoslavia and, by taking control of the entire Balkan Peninsula, to prevent the English from landing and secure the right wing and hinterland of the attack he was planning to launch against the Soviet Union. Thus, the measures taken against Yugoslavia were closely intertwined with the attack that had been planned against Russia.

The Soviet Union had also recently signed a treaty of friendship with Yugoslavia, so the two states were in the same relationship with each other as they had been in 1914. Much as the Austro-Hungarian Monarchy's attack against Serbia had set the Russian war machine in motion back then, the attack against Yugoslavia in April 1941 provoked the Soviet Union to stand up to German aggression.

The introduction of further steps began with announcements in the German press which shifted the focus of German public opinion to the Ukraine

---

62 Joachim von Ribbentrop (1893–1946) served as Foreign Minister of Nazi Germany from 1938 until 1945. He was one of the most prominent among the accused at the Nuremberg Trials. He was convicted of war crimes and crimes against humanity and was hanged on 16 October 1946. He was the first person sentenced to death at Nuremberg to be executed (Hermann Göring, who had been scheduled for execution before Ribbentrop, killed himself the night before he was to be hanged).

63 Dragiša Cvetković (1893–1969) served as Prime Minister of the Kingdom of Yugoslavia from 1939 until 1941.

Chapter II

in an effort to demonstrate that German interests were tied to the Ukraine. All signs suggested that Germany first was striving to create an independent Ukraine and then planned to annex this valuable territory.

The armed resolution of the Serbian question and the rekindling of the Ukrainian question caused relations between Germany and the Soviet Union to cool. The non-aggression pact that Germany had signed with Russia created an advantage for Germany that would have been worth putting to use, even at the price of some sacrifices. If Germany had not attacked Yugoslavia, without the support of the Soviet Union, the Anglo-Saxons would have had great difficulty defeating a Germany that was not tied down in the east by an enormous Soviet fighting force.

Germany's attack against Yugoslavia was met with great excitement in Hungary. On 27 March, Hitler summoned Döme Sztójay,[64] the Hungarian ambassador to Berlin. He called Sztójay's attention to the fact that if Germany were to take armed action against Yugoslavia, Hungary would be given the ideal moment to address the dictates of the Treaty of Trianon, which were disadvantageous and unjust to Hungary. Sztójay flew to Budapest that day to give Hitler's letter to Horthy. Hitler asked that Hungary take part with its army in the war against Yugoslavia and that it allow German troops to pass through Hungarian territory. Prime Minister Pál Teleki, who had crafted the recently signed treaty of friendship, was torn. The launch of a German attack against Yugoslavia, which seemed imminent, raised the question: what should Hungary do? Should it follow Germany, or should it adhere to the treaty of friendship it had so recently signed? This crisis drove Teleki to his death. On the morning of 3 April 1941, the prime minister was found in his bed, dead. Teleki had committed suicide. Thusly he had escaped from the grave conflict he faced. He had not wanted to break

---

64 Döme Sztójay (1883–1946) was a Hungarian diplomat who served as Hungary's ambassador to Germany from 1935 until 1944. Following the German occupation of Hungary in March 1944, Sztójay was appointed prime minister by Horthy. As prime minister, Sztójay took a number of drastic steps, including increasing the Hungarian troop presence on the eastern front (in response to German demands) and having political opponents arrested. As prime minister, Sztójay oversaw the deportation and murder of the vast majority of Hungarian Jews in the summer of 1944. In October 1944, when Horthy was removed from power by the Germans, Sztójay was not kept as prime minister because he was in poor health. He fled the country, but was captured by American soldiers and extradited back to Hungary. He was put on trial by the People's Court and found guilty of war crimes. He was sentenced to death and executed by firing squad in 1946.

his word, and he had not wanted to consent to the attack against Yugoslavia, with which Hungary had recently signed a treaty of friendship. The struggle that Teleki fought with himself explains his suicide. He had not wanted to follow Germany in an attack against Yugoslavia. Before committing suicide, he had sent a letter to the Regent. However, Horthy had already sent a letter to Hitler.

On 28 March 1941, Horthy had given the following response to Hitler's message:

"I express my warmest thanks for your message, brought to me by the Honorable Ambassador Sztójay. I feel I am completely indebted to Germany. In the past, the Hungarian nation has always stood on the side of the German Empire, and today too, it is the firm resolution of the Hungarian nation, in full awareness of our common fate, to adhere to this political line and, as its strength permits, to remain with unwavering faithfulness at the side of the German empire.

The territorial claims to which Your Excellency was kind enough to refer in your message still stand and await fulfillment.

In the course of its rapprochement with Yugoslavia, which was suggested by Your Excellency, my government never made any secret of these claims and even insisted on them as a possibility in the second paragraph of the treaty of friendship.

Your Excellency was kind enough to suggest to Ambassador Sztójay that the command headquarters of the army would be in touch with the Hungarian military leadership. I look forward to this with sincere hope.

The events that have taken place in Yugoslavia over the course of the past few days indicate that, had it not been for Soviet-Russian influence, Yugoslavia hardly would have taken this misstep. The situation which has thereby been created reveals the outlines of Russian strivings, which are in the service of common fundamental Slavic interests. Furthermore, one must take into consideration the continuous hostile sentiments of the Russian state leadership.

Please accept, Your Excellency, this expression of my highest esteem.
Miklós Horthy"

Chapter II

On 28 March, the Council of Ministers discussed the question of our participation in the campaign against Serbia. At a sitting of the Supreme Council of National Defense on 1 April, the final decision was made to take part in the attack, in spite of the treaty of eternal friendship.

In his letter, Teleki wrote the following:

"Your Highness!
We broke our word, out of cowardice, with respect to the Treaty of Permanent Peace outlined in your Mohács speech. The nation feels it, and we have thrown away its honor.
We have allied ourselves to scoundrels, since not a single word is true about the alleged atrocities. Not against Hungarians, not even against Germans.
We will become grave-robbers! The vilest of nations.
I did not hold you back.
I am guilty.
Pál Teleki"

He also wrote his letter of resignation as prime minister at the same time.

"Your Honor!
If I should not succeed entirely in my act and I am still alive, I hereby resign.
With deep respect,
Pál Teleki"

On 2 April 1941, Minister of Defense Barth ordered the mobilization of the fourth and fifth army corps, the rapid deployment force, the river forces, the air force, and the high command. On the evening of 3 April, Bartha received an order from the regent to give his letter to Hitler. He was also entrusted by László Bárdossy, the new prime minister, to clarify how the Germans intended to use the Hungarian fighting forces.

Hitler received Bartha on 3 April at 13:30. After having read the regent's letter, Hitler expressed his condolences on the tragic death of Prime Minister Pál Teleki.

Fateful Years

In the course of the discussion, Bartha proclaimed that Teleki's death would not in any way hinder German-Hungarian cooperation. He had already given orders for three army corps and the high command to mobilize. On behalf of the Hungarian government, Bartha asked Hitler to have the German troops create a situation, before the Hungarian troops were actually sent into action to intervene, that would make it possible for Hungary to intervene in spite of the treaty of friendship. From the perspective of the Hungarian government, the most fitting thing would be if it could be claimed that Serbia had attacked Hungary.

The Yugoslav state ceased to exist de facto. A Croatian government had been formed under the leadership of Ante Pavelić,[65] and an independent Croatia had been created.

In Hitler's assessment, Hungary had no obligation to keep a promise given to a Yugoslavia that for no reason had terminated a treaty that had been accepted and signed. He also asserted that Germany had no territorial claims on Yugoslavia. He wanted to see Bácska[66] and Bánát[67] made part of Hungary. Because, together with Croatia, we were advancing at Germany's side down the path of a victorious war, the road to a favorable resolution of territorial claims would also open for Hungary.

The Hungarian soldiers were under the leadership of Regent Horthy. The cooperation would consist of Hitler merely making suggestions and giving advice concerning the military operations.

On this occasion too, the Hungarian government took Hitler's promises seriously. Soon the government leaders were compelled to confront the fact

---

65 Ante Pavelić (1889–1959) was a Croatian politician who as early as the 1920s called for Croats to revolt against Yugoslavia. He was the head of the Ustaša, a Croatian revolutionary movement, which was racist in its ideology and terrorist in its means (for instance, the Ustaša planned and carried out the assassination of King Alexander of Yugoslavia in 1934). After the invasion of Yugoslavia by Germany and Italy in April 1941, an independent Croatian state was created. Pavelić, who had been in exile in Italy, returned to Zagreb, where he formed a puppet government. His regime was infamous for its brutality, and under his rule, hundreds of thousands of Serbs and tens of thousands of Jews and Roma were murdered. After the war, Pavelić fled to Austria and eventually Argentina. He was wounded in 1957 in an assassination attempt and died two years later in hiding in Spain from his wounds.
66 Bácska or Bačka in Serbian is a region bordered by the Danube River to the west and south and the Tisza River to the east. Most of the region lies in Serbia today.
67 Bánát or Banat in Serbian and Romanian is a region bordered by the Danube River to the south, the Tisza River to the west, and the Mureș River to the north, and the Carpathian Mountains to the east. Most of Bánát lies in Romania today, though a substantial share of the territory to the west is in Serbia and a small corner in the northwest is in Hungary.

that, although Hitler had claimed not to have any territorial claims with regards to Yugoslavia, Bánát nonetheless remained in Germany's hands. The Hungarian population there suffered a fate of which they never would have dreamed under Serbian rule. Not only did the Germans seize the produce of Bácska, they began to pursue policies the goal of which was to create a German "Südgau." The Baranya and Bácska regions and Torontál and Temes Counties would have been part of this Südgau, along with the southern part of Transylvania, all the way to the city of Brassó. *Donau-Zeitung*, a periodical printed in Belgrade, announced this plan. A map that I saw in a school in Gschaid in southern Bavaria in 1945, when I was in a "Hungarist"[68] internment camp, also proved that this was the German plan. On this map, the entire region to the east, stretching all the way to the Volga River, was marked as German Lebensraum.

This also shows how gravely the people who emphasized the necessity of the closest possible relationship with Germany erred, people who could not have imagined that Hungary was capable of living as a self-reliant, independent state without the Germans.

Our leaders did not realize or did not want to realize that Hitler's Germany threatened to swallow Hungary just as it threatened to swallow the other small nations that lived in the territories considered theirs by the Germans and referred to by them as German Lebensraum and Kulturraum. They were incapable of seeing the danger posed by the Germans. True, the Germans, with Hitler at the vanguard, had done everything to prevent them from discerning this danger. They had blurred clear vision. Our short-sighted leaders thought that if they settled the so-called Jewish question, which had been raised violently and artificially, in accordance with right-wing visions, this would solve all of our economic and social problems, and in the meantime they failed to discern the real danger.

---

68 The Arrow Cross

Chapter III

War with Russia

Hungary was swept into the war against Yugoslavia because Germany had held out the prospect of support for our territorial claims against Yugoslavia. Our leaders thought that the powers that had emerged victorious from the World War in 1914–1918 would never permit changes to be made to the stipulations of the treaty that had come into being with their cooperation, no matter how unjust these stipulations might be. We would only be able to hold on permanently to territories that had been reacquired without their consent if Germany were to win the war. There was, however, no chance of this.

On 11 April, our soldiers set out, and they occupied Bácska, Muraköz, and the region between the Danube and the Drava Rivers. Only the rapid deployment force took part, for a short time, in the military operations in Bosnia, and working together with the German soldiers, they advanced all the way to Sarajevo.

With regards to the territories inhabited by Hungarians that had been severed from Hungary by the terms of the Treaty of Trianon, the government considered our efforts just. Even the treaty of friendship that had been signed with Yugoslavia had made specific mention of the possibility of a peaceful resolution. Later, I was asked what I thought of the attack against Yugoslavia. Many times I have heard the contention that Hungary stabbed Yugoslavia in the back and unjustly used armed force to recapture the territories that were annexed. On every occasion, I have explained that we sought and seek only to regain the territories that were ceded, in accordance with the peace dictate forced on us in Trianon (which I too believe was cruel and unjust), to Yugoslavia in which Hungarians form a majority. We attacked a Yugoslavia that had ceased de facto to exist by the time we dispatched our troops.

As I have already mentioned, the attack against Yugoslavia influenced Russia's decision to cooperate closely with the Western powers. The war against the Soviet Union began on 22 June 1941. Hitler justified the attack with the contention that he sought to ward off a likely and imminent Soviet attack.

On 26 June 1941, planes with Soviet insignia bombed the city of Kassa. Ádám Krúdy, a captain and commander of the Kassa airport at the time, informed Prime Minister Bárdossy, with whom he was on familiar terms, that he had established beyond all doubt that the attack had been carried out by German planes bearing Soviet ensigns.

Bárdossy, however, cautioned Krúdy to desist with this talk. Thus, it is quite clear that the air attack against Kassa was a German operation the goal of which was to make Hungary's declaration of war against the Soviet Union and its entry into the war on the side of Germany seem justified and understandable. A few hours after the air attack on Kassa, the Council of Ministers held a sitting. Bárdossy announced that on the basis of a report by the Minister of Defense and the chief of the general staff, the regent had decided, in response to the Russian air attack on Kassa, to enter the war against the Soviet Union.

Kristóffy, the Hungarian ambassador in Moscow, presented the declaration of war to the Soviet government. According to Kristóffy, Molotov[69] was quite taken aback by the Hungarian declaration of war. He even asked Kristóffy if the Hungarian government actually meant the declaration of war seriously, for there was no conflict of interest between the Soviet Union and Hungary. The Soviet Union desired of Hungary only that it remain neutral, in which case he promised that the Soviet Union would support Hungary's just claims concerning Transylvania.

He said that he would examine the circumstances of the air assault against Kassa, which allegedly had been carried out by Russian planes. If it turned out that Russian planes had carried out the attack—a possibility that could be excluded from the outset—then the Soviet Union would pay complete compensation. Molotov asked Kristóffy to tell Bárdossy that the Hungarian government should behave as if its declaration of war had never been made. In his reply, however, Bárdossy told Kristóffy that it was not the ambassador's job to give advice, but to follow the orders he had been given.

---

69 Vyacheslav Mikhailovich Molotov (1890–1986) was a prominent Soviet politician and diplomat. He served as the Minister of Foreign Affairs from 1939 until 1949 and then again from 1953 until 1956.

Chapter III

One on of the occasions when I was questioned by ministers about the military operations against Russia, I spoke with Horthy about the circumstances of the outbreak of war and our declaration of war. I informed the regent of what I had been told by State Secretary István Bárczy about the bombing of Kassa and Bárdossy's role in connection with it. I told him of the circumstances under which the declaration of war against Russia had been made. When we entered the war on the side of Germany—a war in which we had no interests—we had had every opportunity as a neutral state to wait and consider the further development of the war and to gain Russia's support in settling the Transylvanian question.

When I informed Horthy of the exchange of messages that had taken place between Bárdossy and Kristóffy, our ambassador in Moscow, and the statement that had been made by Molotov, to my astonishment he replied that this was the first time he had heard of this. Bárdossy had never made any mention of it to him. Bárdossy had said nothing of the possibility of withdrawing the declaration of war. Thus, Bárdossy had proceeded independently in this matter, as if he had been the omnipotent lord and commander of the Hungarian state. And it was hard to believe that Bárczy would have told me all this had it not been true. As a state secretary of the office of the prime minister, István Bárczy was present for almost all of the meetings of the Council of Ministers, and thus he was precisely informed of what took place there.

Bárczy also told me that at the meeting of the Council of Ministers at which the decision to declare war against Russia had been made Prime Minister Bárdossy and Minister of Defense Bartha had demanded a declaration of war against the Soviet Union. Bartha had threatened to resign if Hungary did not declare war against the Soviet Union.

On 27 June, the Hungarian soldiers crossed the Russian border, and our planes simultaneously launched an attack on Russian cities. The first serious problems began to arise after we crossed the border. The army leadership should have realized that the soldiers were neither properly organized nor properly equipped to fight a modern war. One of the brigade commanders recounted to me the experiences he had during the advance, and he contended that in his opinion, never had an army been sent into war with such insufficient equipment and supplies.

Fateful Years

In the military maneuvers that took place in 1941, the rapid deployment forces achieved initial successes, which I think was due primarily to the fact that initially the Russians slowly retreated. These successes, however, were soon slowed by the crippling effect of the tremendous expanse of the Russian lands. As the Russian forces retreated further to the east, the German soldiers faced an increasingly difficult situation because of the ever longer supply lines and the increasingly active partisan movement.

The hope that the war would come to a quick end as a blitzkrieg on the Russian front proved delusive. It was quite clear that the Russians could only be defeated through difficult and bitter struggle involving considerable sacrifice. In the meantime, Lieutenant General Ferenc Szombathelyi,[70] who had led the eighth army corps of Kassa, had replaced Henrik Werth as the chief of the general staff. The Hungarian soldiers fighting in Russia (as the Carpathian group) had been under his command.

Once the momentum of the advance had waned and it had begun to become clear that no more advances would be made in 1941, the Hungarian rapid deployment forces were withdrawn from the battles and transported home. Only a few light divisions remained in the Russian theater of war as an occupation force behind the frontline. They were charged with the tasks of safeguarding connections and maintaining peace in the occupied territory.

The Germans were beginning to realize that they had disastrously underestimated the strength of the Russians. They had also failed to take into consideration the increasingly intense efforts of the partisans. They needed reinforcements in order to be effective in the struggle, the end of which was nowhere in sight, so they demanded a larger contribution by the Romanian divisions and the Hungarian forces. While at the outset of the war against Russia they had emphasized that "if Hungary wishes to take part in the war at all costs, then it can take part," now they were demanding that Hungary support the German military as a duty, not a choice.

---

70 Ferenc Szombathelyi (1887–1946) was a Hungarian military officer who served as chief of the general staff from 1939 until 1944, when he was removed from his position following the German occupation of Hungary. He was placed under house arrest by the Germans and was arrested again in October 1944, after the Arrow Cross had come to power. He was deported to Germany in the last weeks of the war, but was later turned over to the Hungarian authorities by the American forces. He was put on trial by the Hungarian People's Court and was sentenced to life imprisonment and then extradited to Yugoslavia. He was executed in 1946 in Pétervárad (Petrovaradin). The sentence against him was annulled posthumously in 1994.

Chapter III

In early 1942, Ribbentrop, the German foreign minister, came to Budapest and demanded that the entire Hungarian fighting force join the war effort against Russia without delay. Field Marshal Keitel,[71] who was the Oberkommando of the Wehrmacht, also came to Budapest and called on the Hungarian government to mobilize and deploy an additional twenty-five divisions. After lengthy and difficult negotiations, an agreement was reached according to which Hungary would provide nine infantry divisions and one armored division, equipment for which would be put at the disposal of the Hungarian government by the Germans. Thus, the second army was formed, and it was put under the command of Colonel General Gusztáv Jány.

A light Hungarian division consisted of six battalions and six batteries. The Germans agreed to provide these divisions with up-to-date weapons and equipment and raise them to the same supply level as the German divisions. The chief of the general staff was of the opinion that if the Germans failed to keep their promises concerning the provision of equipment, the Hungarian divisions could only be used as an occupying force. When these questions were discussed, they were not yet aware of the weighty tasks that would fall on the shoulders of the occupying soldiers. In the course of the occupation, it became clear that our soldiers were poorly equipped in comparison with the partisans, who were using the most up-to-date weapons. Over the course of the rest of the war, the Germans mercilessly sent the Hungarian divisions to the frontlines with no regard whatsoever for whether or not they were equipped with the proper weaponry.

In the course of the military operations along the Don River, as the commander of the second army, Jány often resisted the inordinate demands of Hitler's high command. He asked the German military leadership to ensure circumstances under which the Hungarian soldiers would be able to perform their tasks. He urged them to shorten the frontline of the army and provide

---

71 Wilhelm Keitel (1882–1946) served as chief of the High Command of the German Armed Forces from 1939 until the end of the Second World War. During the war, he issued numerous orders infamous for their cruelty, for instance the so-called Commissar Order, according to which Soviet political commissars were to be shot on sight. After the war, he was put on trial in Nuremberg, where he was accused of war crimes and crimes against humanity. He was found guilty and sentenced to death. He was executed in 1946 by hanging.

suitable, up-to-date weapons and better supplies in general, and also to address the problem of inadequate reinforcements.

Jány was not favored among the Germans, who continuously made promises, but made only minimal efforts to keep them.

Chapter IV

In Retirement

The period from February until April, i.e. until my retirement began, passed quickly. The first days were a bit unusual. It was strange not to have any official matter to tend to and to have my time entirely at my disposal. The unpleasant part was first and foremost simply that my financial state of affairs declined drastically from one day to the next. As commander of the army, I had had a salary of 2,000 pengő, in addition to my housing stipend. As a retired general, I received 1,100 pengő, or 900 less than I had had before. The situation was exacerbated by the fact that, although I had had to move to Budapest, I still received my housing stipend on the basis of the allowances for Kolozsvár. These circumstances prompted me to mention my situation to Lieutenant General Sándor Bengyel, and he promised to help me find an appropriate sphere of work in civilian economic life. I even got some unexpected assistance. Lieutenant General István Náday put me in touch with József Hartmann, an old friend of mine who had enterprises in Szabadka.[72] Hartmann asked me, as a retiree, to accept the position of president of the joint stock company in Szabadka. After I had convinced myself that this post did not conflict in any way with my school of thought as a soldier, I accepted the position as president of the company, though just in case, in accordance with the rules, I asked for permission from the chief of the general staff. I was granted permission. I consider it necessary to mention this here because later, when the Arrow Cross men and the followers of Imrédy were attacking me as Minister of Defense, people in the parliament sought to call me to account for this. They contended that, by accepting this position, I had committed an offense against honor and patriotism. I will return to this later.

---

72 Today Subotica, Serbia.

I quickly got used to the quiet, peaceful life. On several occasions, I went to Szabadka to tend to the necessary tasks in the plant there. One could already tell at the time that the troubled state of affairs had caused challenges to pile up that hampered the smooth operation of the enterprise, making it impossible for the company to remain in private hands. Hartmann had already entered negotiations concerning the sale of the company when the city had been under Serbian rule. The change in the political belonging of the territory, however, had made this unnecessary for the moment.

This quiet life was interrupted by a summons that I received from the tribunal of the chief of the general staff. I was being summoned as a witness in the military trial against Lieutenant Colonel Gedeon Lejtényi, who had served as my orderly officer. The case was so characteristic of Werth's way of thinking (Werth had been serving as chief of the general staff at the time in question) that I feel it necessary to mention it, in spite of its insignificance.

At the office of the military prosecutor I learned that Lieutenant Colonel Lejtényi, who had been my orderly officer in the command of the first army, had been accused of disloyalty because he had sent one of my letters addressed to the chief of the general staff from Nyíregyháza-Sóstó (the seat of the command) by civilian post instead of military post. The antecedents to this were the following: I had received a letter from Werth in which he had mediated a request made by one of his acquaintances. In the letter, he asked me to enlist his brother into the army. This did not belong to my sphere of authority, but nonetheless, I agreed to try to arrange matters, and I managed to have the army corps command issue the conscription notice. I wrote Werth a letter to this effect so that he would be able to pass the news on to the person who had made the request. My orderly officer, Lieutenant Colonel Lejtényi had had the letter mailed without considering that perhaps it should be treated as a secret document. The contents of the letter, as is clear from its subject matter, were not a secret at all. At Werth's command, Lejtényi and the junior officer who had mailed the letter had been accused of having revealed the location of the army headquarters by using the civilian postal service instead of the military postal service to mail a letter that bore an official stamp. This information should have been treated as a secret. This idea was spiteful, petty, and baseless. Every day, thousands and thousands of people from Nyíregyháza had come

Chapter IV

to Sóstó to swim, and every day members of the army command had gone into Nyíregyháza. Since transportation between the city and the bathing resort was completely unobstructed, everyone could know and indeed did know that the headquarters of the first army was in Sóstó. I should also note, I received many letters addressed to Sóstó from the chief of the general staff, and he had not used the military postal service to send them either. I happened to have kept the envelopes in which they were sent, and I presented them at the military tribunal. This painted a more accurate picture of Werth's accusation of disloyalty. I told the judge-advocate who was conducting the hearing my opinion of the procedure, and I asked him to bring an end to the inquiry, for the whole comedy would turn into a scandal. For my part, at least, I would not simply let the matter rest. In response, the judge-advocate noted that he too found the whole case unusual, but that Lieutenant Colonel Lejtényi was not actually the real target... At this remark, I understood everything. This comment made the background of the whole case clear to me. In the course of my interrogation, it also came to light that I had given Lejtényi instructions concerning how to mail the letter. They wanted to prove that I had given the order to betray the secret. I observed that the idea itself was stupid and laughable, since any soldier worth his salt knew that after having signed a letter, an army commander does not concern himself with how the letter is mailed.

My interrogation came to an end with this. I was soon informed that the procedure had been terminated at the suggestion of the judge-advocate. The chief of the general staff, it seems, had been compelled to accept that he would not be able to bring me down in this manner.

In January 1942, raids were conducted in Újvidék[73] and the surrounding area with the consent of the government under the pretext of attempting to defeat the partisan movement. I was in Szabadka when I learned of the events in Újvidék, a few hours after they had begun. The events left the people in Szabadka in a feverish state. Panic-stricken, everyone spoke about what had taken place in Újvidék, and they feared that Szabadka was next. People listened, horrified, to the news. They said that everyone traveling on the rap-

---

73 Today Novi Sad, Serbia.

id train from Budapest to Újvidék had been taken to the waiting room in the train station and told to produce their identity papers. The Jews had been separated from the others and then taken to the riverside, where they had been forced, women, children, young, and old without exception, to strip and then been shot. The corpses had been thrown into the Danube River through holes cut in the ice. They also spoke about how the gendarmes and soldiers who had conducted the raids had gone from house to house and dragged the Jews from their homes. Even the elderly had been pulled from their beds and mercilessly murdered. One person claimed to have heard someone be dragged off from the neighboring room in one of the hotels. One colonel—a man who had once been under my command and who had happened to be in Újvidék—said he had heard people shooting in the streets. He had gone outside and seen cars piled high with corpses, heading for the Danube. He had ascertained what was taking place on the bank of the Danube River, and he had immediately rushed to find József Grassy,[74] a colonel who was staying in the city, and called his attention to the events. "Do you not hear the shots being fired?" he had asked. "And do you not know what is going on in the city? Innocent people are being dragged to the shore of the river and executed. Intervene immediately and put an end to this villainy!" Grassy had been drunk, and he had not wanted to give any credence to what the colonel was saying. He considered his words the product of a morbid delusion and he did nothing. Perhaps he was even pleased to hear that his soldiers were so thorough in their work, and in particular that they were dealing with the Jews so thoroughly.

A few weeks later, I was in Szabadka again. I found the garrison commander, who earlier had served under me, because I wanted to get reliable information concerning the events. He told me the following:

---

74 József Grassy (1894–1946) was a Hungarian military officer who served as an army commander in 1939–1941. He led the raid in Újvidék. At the initiative of Prime Minister Miklós Kállay, proceedings were launched against him. He was found guilty and condemned to death, but in early 1944, before the sentence was executed, he managed to flee to Germany, where he served in the Waffen-SS. After the Arrow Cross took power in October 1944, he returned to Hungary. He was made a lieutenant general and commander of an army corps. He used his newfound power to imprison the people who had passed sentence on him. In May 1945, he was captured in Austria by the American forces, who turned him over to the Hungarian authorities. He was put on trial by the People's Court and condemned to death, but given that the most grievous of the crimes of which he had been accused had taken place in Újvidék, which by that time was under the control of Yugoslav forces, he was handed over to the Yugoslav authorities. On 5 November 1946, he was hanged publicly on the main square of Újvidék.

Chapter IV

In connection with the arrival of the Hungarian soldiers in the southern lands, operations had been conducted to purge the area. Many people who had ties to the communist party, which, though illegal, was active underground, had fled from Bácska to Bánát, which the Germans had not turned over to Hungary. However, after things had returned to normal in the territories that were again under Hungarian administration, the communists who had escaped to Bánát, most of whom were Serbs, had snuck back into Bácska. In particular, many of them had gathered in the area around Zsablya.[75] When the Hungarian authorities had learned of this, they had decided to smoke out the farmstead where, according to the reports, the partisans were staying. A few gendarmes and one frontier sentry machine gunner squadron had been charged with the task of ransacking the farmstead. When this group was nearing the farmstead, they were met with gunfire. They responded by launching an attack against the farmstead. A few of their men had fallen in the first surprise volley of gunfire. The force which had been sent proved weak, so a machine-gunner platoon joined the operation under the command of a lieutenant. As a result of this attack, some of the Serbs hiding on the farmstead were caught and executed on the spot. Some of them, however, had managed to escape. This battle had been followed by a huge raid in Zsablya. Allegedly, some of the Serbs of the town supported the Serb partisans, and allegedly the town clerk had taken an active part in this. The Zsablya clerk was executed. Many of the inhabitants of Zsablya had been taken to a large depot and shot with a machine-gun affixed to the entrance, creating a pile of corpses.

According to their reports, the whole countryside was full of communist partisans. Three infantry battalions had been dispatched to search the area and, in particular, the shrubby territories along the Tisza River. They were under the leadership of Colonel Deák.[76] News had spread that some of the partisans had taken refuge in Újvidék, so they had decided to hold a raid in Újvidék.

---

75   Today Žabalj, Serbia.
76   László Deák (1891–1946) was a colonel in the Hungarian army who, like József Grassy and Ferenc Feketehalmy-Czeydner, participated in the massacres in Zsablya and Újvidék. The massacres sparked protests, and Feketehalmy-Czeydner was compelled to retire, but initially he was not otherwise punished. In 1943, however, a case was brought against him and others involved in the massacres. He was found guilty, but because he was not being held in custody, he was able to flee the country for Germany. He served in the Waffen-SS in Bácska and Bánát. After the war, he was extradited to Yugoslavia, where he was put on trial for war crimes. He was found guilty and was executed by hanging on 5 November 1946.

Fateful Years

The raid in Újvidék had been led by Colonel Grassy, an infantry commander, and Lieutenant Colonel Feketehalmy-Czeydner,[77] the commander of the Szeged army corps, had also been present. The raid had degenerated into a bloodbath. They had seized every Jew and Serb they had come across, and a couple of Germans and Hungarians too. Completely disregarding all legal procedures, they had then dragged them to the bank of the Danube River and shot them. They threw the bodies into the water through holes that had been cut in the ice. I shuddered upon hearing of these horrors. I could not have imagined that Hungarian officers and soldiers were capable of ordering and carrying out acts of such base villainy, or that commanders had not only tolerated these acts, but had themselves supported them. This awful bloodshed had lasted four days.

These atrocities were accompanied, not surprisingly, by organized pillaging and plunder. It is telling that in the course of the entire raid not a single soldier or gendarme was injured. They claimed that the whole bloodbath had been caused by the partisans, who had fired on the soldiers and the gendarmes, and the bloodbath had been a reprisal for this.

The outcry that swept the land and the remonstrations that were made in parliament notwithstanding, no inquiry was held. Later, however, the Kállay government was unable to avoid ordering an investigation into the matter. An inquiry was launched against Lieutenant General Feketehalmy-Czeydner, Colonel Grassy, Colonel Deák, Gendarmerie Captain Sándor Zöldi, several commanders and officers, and the soldiery. Much to the public's surprise, no judgment was reached in the case. At the suggestion of the chief of the general staff, the regent had given instructions to quash the indictment. Several people were given distinctions for the Újvidék purges.

---

77 Ferenc Feketehalmy-Czeydner (1890–1946) was a Hungarian military officer who held several important positions in the Hungarian army before being promoted to Lieutenant General in 1941. In 1942, soldiers under his command committed massacres in Zsablya and Újvidék. After a case was brought against him in 1943 for his role in the massacres, he was sentenced to 15 years in prison. In January 1944, however, he fled to Vienna. He then served in the Waffen-SS. He returned to Hungary following the rise to power of the Arrow Cross Party and was given the position of Deputy Minister of Defense. Like Grassy, he used his influence to have the people who had testified against him in his trial arrested, and he participated in the trials of people who had been accused of having tried to organize resistance to the German occupation. As the Soviet forces advanced on Budapest, he fled Hungary again for the west, but in May 1945 he was captured by American forces, who turned him over to the Hungarian authorities. He was condemned to death by the People's Court, but again like Grassy, he was handed over to Yugoslavia. He was executed on 5 November 1946 in Zsablya.

Chapter IV

The issue, however, did not end there. When I became the Minister of Defense, the supervisor of the gendarmerie suggested that I submit a proposal to the regent to quash the indictment in connection with the proceedings that were underway against the gendarmes. He justified his suggestion with the contention that it would give rise to bad blood if the gendarmes were to be punished for crimes for which the soldiers had been exonerated.

I asked for the documents, and having read them and again shuddered at the horrors of which I had known too well, I rejected his suggestion. I decided to present the case to the Council of Ministers and at the Crown Council to suggest to the regent that a thorough investigation be launched into the affair and the guilty be punished.

I read the document that had been submitted by Lieutenant General Feketehalmy-Czeydner, in which he protested against the accusations and, in particular, against the fact that the chief of the general staff, Colonel General Szombathelyi, as the commander with jurisdiction in the case, had launched proceedings against him. He contended that if they were launching proceedings against him, then the chief of the general staff should also be put on the bench for the accused. Czeydner thus was not going to give up, and he brought a counter-charge against the chief of the general staff, from whom, according to him, he had been given the command to be forceful in his execution of orders.

I should note, Lieutenant General Czeydner had not been given a command to be forceful in his execution of orders, but rather, as an army corps commander (the Szeged army corps) who was familiar with the circumstances on the ground, to provide support in accordance with the wishes of the organs of internal affairs.

From Budapest, several hundred kilometers from Újvidék, Szombathelyi could not have seen or known exactly how the raid had taken place. Indeed, he was even less informed than he might otherwise have been, because Czeydner, according to his own account, had provided him with false and misleading information. Szombathelyi said he had simply accepted the suggestions that had been made concerning the bestowal of distinctions and then submitted these suggestions to the regent on the basis of this information.

A few days later, a sitting of the Crown Council was held, at which, in addition to me, the prime minister and the Minister of Internal Affairs took part. I presented the case and revealed the situation to the regent. Horthy was very flushed and troubled, and he said that if this were the case, he had been deceived. They had even prevailed on him to bestow distinctions on several people for their roles in the purge. Scandalized and indignant, he rejected the very thought of quashing the indictment in the case that was underway against the gendarmes. He accepted my suggestion and ordered that the entire case, including the accusations against the officers, be investigated again. Prime Minister Kállay[78] and Minister of Interior Ferenc Keresztes-Fischer[79] completely agreed with my suggestion.

And thus, the tragic case of the raids in Újvidék again came before the courts. I was no longer a minister by the time the judgment was reached because in the meantime I had resigned. Indeed, the judgment was never pronounced in the presence of the accused, because the guilty leaders fled to Germany with the assistance of the Germans. Not only were they given refuge, they even served as officers in the German army until, following the rise to power of the Arrow Cross, they returned to Hungary and again became high-ranking officers in the Hungarian army.

---

78   Miklós Kállay (1887–1967) was a Hungarian politician who served as prime minister from 1942 until 1944. Although Hungary remained a German ally under Kállay and continued to fight in the war against the Soviet Union, his government refused German demands to deport the Jews of Hungary (though Kállay did not rescind the many anti-Semitic laws that had been passed by his predecessors; for instance, Hungarian men defined by law as Jewish continued to serve in forced labor units, in which fatalities were far higher than in the regular army). Fearing German defeat in the war and Soviet occupation of Hungary, Kállay made contacts with the Western powers and made offers to surrender to them unconditionally if their armies were to reach Hungary's borders. He was removed from office when the Germans occupied Hungary in March 1944. He was arrested by the Germans and sent first to the Dachau concentration camp and then to Mauthausen before being transferred to Tyrol, where he was liberated by American forces. He went into exile and eventually settled in the United States.

79   Ferenc Keresztes-Fischer (1881–1948), the older brother of General Lajos Keresztes-Fischer, held several prominent positions in Hungary's interwar governments and served twice, if for very brief periods, as interim prime minister, once after Teleki's suicide and once after Bárdossy's resignation. He served as Minister of Internal Affairs from 1938 until 1944, and he was a member of Kállay's political circle, which sought to establish ties with the Allies. In 1944, he was arrested by the Gestapo and taken to the Mauthausen-Gusen concentration camp. After the war the Hungarian government demanded that he be returned to Hungary for trial as a war criminal, but he was allowed to remain in Austria, where he died in 1948 of lung cancer.

Chapter V

At the Head of the Ministry of Defense

At roughly 9 o'clock on the evening of 20 September, the telephone in my apartment in Klotildliget rang. Colonel General Szombathelyi, the chief of the general staff, was calling me from Budapest. He hastily informed me that on the 21, the next day, the regent would be waiting for me in Gödöllő. The next morning, I took part in a celebration for a mixed battalion, and then I drove into the capital in a car I had borrowed from the battalion. At my apartment, I awaited the ministry car that had been sent by the chief of the general staff, and I traveled in that car to Gödöllő. I arrived at 4:30 on the nose, precisely when the regent had asked me to come. Naturally, the aide-de-camp on duty knew that I was coming, and a few minutes later he took me to see the regent.

The regent offered me a seat and then explained why he had summoned me. He informed me of his understanding of the military and other war-related problems. He emphasized the importance of maintaining discipline in the army. He also mentioned that recently it had become fashionable for people in the military to talk politics, and the deliberate refusal to follow orders from above was undermining discipline in the army. For the most part, he blamed Bartha for this, and so he had decided to relieve Bartha of his office. He asked me to accept the position as Minister of Defense. Interrupting himself, he asked me, almost as if an aside, "where do you stand with Imrédy?"

To this, I replied that I did not have and never had had any political ties to Imrédy. I was not connected with him in any way. It was suddenly clear to me that indeed I had been correct to have surmised, when I had been put into retirement, that my alleged ties to Imrédy were the reason I had been removed from active service, and it was also because of these alleged ties that, after my 35 years of military service, the regent had not even given me a final audience to bid me formal farewell.

Fateful Years

I accepted the regent's request. I proclaimed that as a minister I would make every effort to serve my homeland honorably. The regent informed me that naturally I would also have to speak with the prime minister, since I was becoming part of his cabinet. With this, my audience with the regent came to an end, and I bid him farewell as the soon-to-be Minister of Defense.

Adjutant-General Lajos Keresztes-Fischer, who had been a classmate of mine at the military academy in Vienna, accompanied me all the way to my car. He bid farewell, saying I had undertaken a great burden by accepting the portfolio of the Ministry of Defense, and I could not possibly imagine how many bitter minutes and hours the ministerial seat and ministerial power had in store for me.

I hurried back to Klotildliget. I informed my wife of the details of my audience with the regent, and I told her that a few days later, after having spoken with Kállay, I would be given my appointment as minister. My wife showed not the slightest trace of joy at the news of my appointment, for this new, burdensome sphere of work would bring an end to our intimate, peaceful family life. We would have to leave the solitude to which we had become accustomed and enter public life, and who knew what kinds of difficulties lay before me, difficulties which might throw my whole life off the rails.

Kállay received me on the afternoon of Tuesday, 22 September. On 24 September, I took my oath of office in the royal castle. Warmly written articles in the press announced my appointment. When I entered the Ministry of Defense, I took my place in the ministerial seat with the sense that I would easily execute the tasks that would now fall to me in the war. After the easy work of the first few days, however, came the more difficult tasks. After having been in the ministry for only a few days, I saw that one of the most difficult and most weighty problems was the Jewish question, which in the army arose in connection with everything. First and foremost, there was the issue of the people in the forced labor units. Since according to the Jewish Law people who were required to do military service but who were defined legally as Jewish could not be given weapons and could only be considered for labor-service, people who had served until then as officers in the Hungarian army could not be employed. Labor battalions consisting of Jews were formed, but the conscriptions were done not according to age-group, but rather with the

Chapter V

use of so-called "SAS" conscription notices, "siess, azonnal, siess" or "hurry, immediately, hurry!" This led to the most appalling abuses. If someone had an issue with a Jew, he would deal with it by having the person called up for service in the labor battalions, no matter how old the person was or what place he held in society.

This anti-Semitic spirit ruled in the Ministry of Defense. This spirit was made even more savage by the decree which regulated rotations in the field. According to this decree, no allowances were to be made for Romanians, Serbs, or Jews, and they could not be relieved. They were to remain in the field for the entire duration of the war, while the other soldiers, after six months had passed, had to be relieved. I immediately nullified the sixth point—the one that addressed this question—of this infamous 5000 decree. I did not wish to continue with this kind of cruelty. In particular, the heads of the personnel group and the nationwide mobilization division seized every chance to defy me on Jewish issues. Only with the greatest determination was I able to compel them and the divisions under them to implement and observe my orders concerning the people in the labor service.

I put an end to the practice of treating the people in the labor service as if they were prisoners.

I decreed that the people in the labor service be given proper provisions. We should not force famished human wrecks to complete the work that we sought to see done.

I ordered that people who had fallen ill or who were unsuitable for work immediately be discharged.

I prohibited maltreatment and the use of physical threats.

I launched the strictest possible investigations and severely punished people who had been brutal in their treatment of the conscripts in the forced labor battalions or had maltreated them, struck them, beaten them, or blackmailed them.

These measures, however, elicited antipathy towards me among some of the people in the officer corps in the Ministry of Defense. These men agreed with the Arrow Cross. Since I knew that there were many ways of obstructing the people who turned to me for help before they reached my room in the ministry, I made it possible for the petitions and requests to end up in my hands directly and without mediation so that I could arrive at a decision before these men interfered. By the time the document wound up in their hands, I had already written my decision concerning how it was to be settled on it.

I realized that I was surrounded by enemies. The complaints that were flooding in prompted me to take action. Many complaints came in from the front. In particular, I was besieged with requests from family members who had no idea where their loved ones were. There were people in the forced labor battalions who had been on the front for a long time, but their superiors had forbidden them from writing letters, so their families back home knew nothing about their fates.

The Jewish question was a constant point of contention between me and some of my colleagues. On this question, I found no understanding among the general staff either. I made sure the complaints concerning issues at the front made it to the general staff, and to Szombathelyi. In this matter, he had jurisdiction. The units on the front were under his command.

The other sensitive point, I could even say one of the most important and weighty problems faced by the Ministry of Defense, was the issue of providing supplies and reinforcements for the second army. The second army, which in the course of the big offensive advance in the summer had made it all the way to the Don River, had diminished considerably in number. Neither were the provisions adequate, nor was the supply of provisions continuous. The people in the field spoke of the army as if it were something about which everyone back home had completely forgotten. The members of the second army felt as if they had been sentenced to death. When I was brought to the ministry, negotiations were already underway to begin relieving the soldiers and giving them suitable reinforcements. I convinced the regent to accept the measure concerning this. He agreed to summon the necessary number of reserves in order to relieve and reinforce the soldiers of the second army. It proved necessary to reorganize the army divisions, but the hastily implemented mobilization caused a great deal of confusion among them. The intention of the leadership had been to place the same burden on each army corps by ordering partial mobilization. Thus, the divisions that were sent into the field were a mix. Not even by chance did it come to pass that all of the battalions of a given division or regiment were on the first line. This mix of the different formations, which were of different ranks and functions, made their usefulness in battle extremely uncertain.

On the occasion of my first report, I gave voice to my desire to inspect the second army fighting in Russia, because only then could I create a closer relationship between the home front and the army. The regent gave his consent. I informed the prime minister and the parties of my intention. My decision was received on all sides with joy. They approved of the fact that my first act as minister was to deepen contact with the army in the field. The inspection of the second army could be done in unison with my necessary visit to the German general headquarters.

We made preparations for the inspection of the second army. I announced my planned visit to the German general headquarters with the mediation of the Hungarian military attaché in Berlin and the German military attaché in Budapest. I soon received notification that they would be waiting for me. Hitler was postponing his move from Vinnytsia in order to meet with me. His doctors were of the opinion that the moist air of the Vinnytsia forest, where the headquarters was located, was not good for his health. The buildings of the headquarters were in a pine forest. So the headquarters was being moved to somewhere in Eastern Prussia, where Hitler would have more sunlight. General Staff Colonel Aide-de-Camp Kálmán Kéri and Lieutenant Colonel orderly officer Iván Gaál were part of my entourage. I was also accompanied by the German military attaché. We planned to travel by train to Ungvár. There, we would switch to a car and continue on to Kiev. From Kiev, we would travel by plane to the headquarters of the second army in Alexeyevka. Thus, the trip promised to be short. According to my calculations, I would have to be away from Budapest for approximately eight days.

Before I departed, when I bid farewell to Kállay on the morning of 14 October, the subject of my visit to the German general headquarters came up. In connection with this, the prime minister informed me of our relations with the Germans, and he gave me instructions concerning the questions I was to raise. He noted that political relations with the Germans had worsened significantly. There were several reasons for this. The first was that Hungary had not submitted in every respect to the German worldview.

Fateful Years

As a consequence of recent events on the battlefield, people's faith in the legendary heroism of the Hungarian soldier had faltered. Some of the units had retreated from the Russian attack. The most important thing was that in the eyes of the Germans, the Hungarian leadership was not on top of the situation. The Jewish question was another point of conflict. Hungary had still not resolved the problem of the Hungarian Jewry in accordance with the wishes of the Germans.

The relationship between Romania and Germany had evolved in a direction that was favorable to the Romanians… In comparison with us, the Romanians had been given a more positive assessment. In the eyes of the Germans, circumstances in Romania had been consolidated. At Germany's request, the Hungarian government had put an end to all irredentist stirrings and talk. In contrast, leading Romanian politicians were striking tones at public gatherings which were directed against Hungary. Antonescu[80] soothed the Romanians of Northern Transylvania, the territory which had been annexed by Hungary, with the contention that Romania was fighting on Germany's side in the war against Russia because in doing so it rendered clear services in the hopes that the Vienna Award would be revised and Romania's border would be pushed westward all the way to the Tisza River.

These circumstances continuously roused apprehension among the public, Kállay said. Thus, the Hungarian government had the duty to take every possible measure to ensure Romania not catch it by surprise. The Vienna Award, after all, had been reached at Romania's request. We would have been able to resolve the question of Transylvania successfully without the Vienna Award. Romania was not simply agitating against Hungary with the statements made by its leading politicians, it had also entered a military alliance with Slovakia, and it had done everything possible to draw Croatia into its caricaturesque "entente cordiale."

---

80 Ion Victor Antonescu (1882–1946) was a Romanian military officer and politician who served as Prime Minister and "Conducător" (the Romanian equivalent of "Führer") of Romania for most of the Second World War. Antonescu was an anti-Semitic, right-wing politician with authoritarian tendencies. Under his rule, independently of Nazi Germany Romania implemented measures that led to the deaths of some 400,000 people, most of them Jews and Roma from Bessarabia, what today is Sub-Carpathian Ukraine, and Transnistria. In August 1944, after Romania had sustained dire losses on the eastern front, Antonescu was ousted from office by King Michael I of Romania. The new government immediately declared war on Germany. Antonescu was arrested and initially turned over to the Soviet occupation forces, but he was later returned to Romania, where he was put on trial by the People's Court and found guilty of war crimes and treason. He was executed by firing squad in 1946.

Chapter V

With regards to the future, Kállay continued, the Serbian question had not been resolved by the alleged breakup of Serbia. The actions taken by the Croats to "establish order" notwithstanding, Serbia still represented a serious threat to Hungary. There was the almost certain threat of a second front in the Balkans. If this second front were to be opened, the Serbian forces, which for the moment were scattered, would unite and would join the enemies of the Axis powers. In this case, the standing of the entire Balkan Peninsula would be questionable. Thus, it was in Germany's interests to nurture concord between Hungary and Romania. The conflicts had to be smoothed over. Kállay thought the solution would be for Romania to expand to the east and content itself with Soviet-Russian territories.

Kállay also told me what to say in reply to some of the more important questions. Supplies and provisions in Hungary were in short order. In general, the harvests were poor. Industry, which had been put in the service of the Germans, took many people away from agricultural production, which was necessary to the country. In general, we had no surpluses.

He also spoke about the Jewish question. He was willing to implement radical measures. If necessary, he was willing to deport the Jews... Today, however, he was not capable of deporting one million people.

In dealing with the Romanian question, we had to keep a free hand. We had to emphasize clearly that there was no great enthusiasm in Hungary for the current war. Our real war threatened to come from the Balkans, because Antonescu was constantly agitating against Hungary.

In conclusion, Kállay called on me to speak resolutely on these matters with Hitler, Göring, and Field Marshal Keitel.

After having discussed the foreign policy questions, Kállay outlined the most important messages for the officer corps. The survival of the Hungarian people depended on the outcome of the war. We had to endeavor to arrive at a transformation of Europe in complete calm. People who spread rumors that could be used to disturb public order did a service for the enemies of our homeland... He acknowledged that, on the Jewish question, the officer corps was right. They should have faith in him to decide what would be the most suitable measure from the perspective of the situation as a whole.

Kállay used interesting reasoning to justify postponing the resolution of the Jewish question. Germany had long deviated from normal principles of finance, and in its new approach to economics it had the support of 90 million Germans. Hungary continued to adhere to a completely well-ordered, peacetime financial policy, because we would only be able to put the country back on its feet after the war if we stood on realistic economic foundations. The brutal and immediate elimination of the Jewish layer would imperil this economic consolidation.

According to Kállay, the relationship between the parliament and the army was perfect.

In the spirit of this conversation, on the train I broached the issue of the Transylvania question and our relationship with Romania to General Staff Colonel Pappenheim, the German military attaché. In connection with the entry of Hungarian forces into Transylvania the conversation touched on the difficulty of the railroad connection with the Székely Land and the question of how much it would cost to create such a connection. If the stipulations of the Vienna Award had dealt with this matter differently, today the solution to the entire Transylvanian question would be far simpler.

The more valuable territories of Transylvania remained in Romanian hands. The natural raw materials that were important in industry were also in their hands. The territory that had been returned to Hungary could only sustain the population if it were properly industrialized. The situation was also difficult because Romania did not regard the Vienna Award as permanent. The proclamations made by Antonescu showed clearly that Romania was taking part in the war with such a large force because it sought to revise the Vienna Award and push the western borders of the country to the Tisza River.

We had to seek compromise. Compromise was necessary if there were to be peace in the Balkans. Compromise was possible, but only on a foundation that was acceptable to both parties.

Colonel Pappenheim agreed with me, but he immediately added that Germany had to be a bit forbearing with the Romanians. We could not ask Romania to return additional Transylvanian territories now. According to Pappenheim, in the interests of compromise, the Germans would exert appropriate pressure on Romania "later, after the war."

Chapter V

It was clear to me at the time and is clear to me now that Pappenheim was merely the mouthpiece of customary two-faced politics. In his conversations with Hungarian leaders he affirmed Germany's loyalty to Hungary with vague, shrewdly formulated promises. At the same time, on the far side of the border another "Pappenheim" was assuring some Romanian minister of Germany's complete sympathy and in all likelihood painting a picture in fanciful colors for the Romanian minister of the territorial settlement that would be reached after the war in accordance with Romania's wishes and outlining the territories that were to be severed and taken back from Hungary. At the German general headquarters people soon heard my opinion, and thus they were in a position to know considerably more of my ideas and designs than I would have been able to explain in the course of my meeting with Hitler. I informed the military attaché that on the direct instructions of Kállay, I wished to speak with Hitler about these questions as well.

The next morning we arrived in Ungvár. We set out towards the Carpathians to reach our destination for the day, Lemberg.[81] I had made this journey several times. As army commander, I had traveled to the Uzhok Pass. In the First World War, from January until May 1915 I had taken part in the battles in the area as the general staff officer of the 79th infantry battalion of the Hungarian army. When we reached the pass, I saw that the enormous hotel that had been built under the rule of the Czechs had burned to the ground. At the border, we got out and visited the cemetery where soldiers who had fallen in the war were buried, where Hungarian and Russian slept in peace side by side, and perhaps in the fields of the next world hands were clasped in friendship which had once clutched at deadly weapons or pulled the trigger of the rifle, bringing death and destruction on an enemy on whom they had never even laid eyes. Now, Hungarians and Russians were fighting each other again.

As we crossed the border, we came across Jewish labor units that had been sent out by the Germans to do work on the roads. Jewish stars shone on the backs of the men. I could not suppress my contempt for people who cause their fellow man such humiliation simply because they were born Jewish. I felt an inexpressible compassion for these miserable unfortunates, who

---

81   Today Lviv, Ukraine.

clearly had lived under better circumstances until now, and now were being forced to work like slaves or animals.

As we continued onward, the highlands where we had been stationed in 1914–1915 came into view. The Magura, Scavinka, Oshtry, and the other peaks rose before me. The train station in Shiank, the villages of Butelka Visna and Wolosate. All old friends. In Turka, the marks of the war were clearly visible. The Jewish houses, which stood in the middle of the settlement, were all empty. Their inhabitants had been dragged off. The same picture unfolded in front of me in every village and city in Galicia. In Przemyśl too. We had lunch here in the German clubhouse of the local garrison. By the time evening had fallen, we arrived in Lemberg. The city had not suffered much from the battles. One or two larger buildings in the city center had burned down, but otherwise one hardly saw any other signs of damage.

The next day, we visited the governorship and the Hungarian clubhouse. I spoke with Hungarian soldiers who were returning from the front and going on furlough. Their conduct made a very favorable impression on me. In the courtyard of the Hungarian clubhouse we were welcomed by a group of soldiers, and I held a short speech for them. The liaison officer said that the Poles had a very hard lot, because someone who said he was a Pole was only given ration cards if he denied his nationality and proclaimed himself a Ukrainian.

After Lemberg, Proskurov,[82] a city in Podolia on the old Austrian border, was the next place where we spent the night. Here we ate at the Hungarian station command. This territory belonged to the sphere of the Hungarian occupying forces. There were Hungarian labor units in the city. In the morning, I saw a labor unit proceeding in an orderly, disciplined fashion to the work station in military uniform.

The German station commander commented that it was a shame that the Jewish workers of the city had been killed, because he would have had great need of them. He also said that the Hungarian labor units did very good work. He was completely satisfied with them.

In the morning we continued our journey towards Vinnytsia, which was not far from the German general headquarters. We were to meet with Hit-

---

82 Today Khmelnytskyi, Ukraine.

Chapter V

ler on the afternoon of our arrival. During the trip, I told the German military attaché that, in accordance with Kállay's wishes, during the audience with Hitler the conversation would include the question of Transylvania. I requested that he make this known at the general headquarters, because it would be more agreeable to me as well as to him if Hitler were to begin any talk on this question. Pappenheim promised to pass on my request and prepare the conversation with my wishes in mind.

Vinnytsia was an orderly Russian city. It had a nice and suitable hotel. The city had not suffered much from the war. The buildings, or at least the buildings near the main square, did not show signs of damage or wear. We were put in the finest hotel. After my arrival, the military attaché, General Sándor Homlok, reported. He was usually in Berlin, but he often had to be present at the German general headquarters too. Hitler did not live in the city, but rather in a small pine forest next to the main road to Kiev, because it offered a good hiding place from enemy planes and was well protected by the guards stationed on the surrounding farmsteads. I mentioned to Major General Homlok that I wanted to speak with Hitler about the Transylvanian question and that I had asked Colonel Pappenheim to make this known. Major General Homlok informed me that Kállay had raised this question on the occasion of his most recent trip in June. He had reason to believe that the Germans had called Antonescu's attention to this in July. He suggested that I not raise this question again, since by doing so I would only ruin the atmosphere. If we saw that German pressure had no effect on the Romanians, we would have to use the Hungarian Embassy in Berlin to take diplomatic steps, because only his would produce real results. I considered his suggestion and decided that I would not raise the Romanian question, my original intention notwithstanding. I would content myself with what I had essentially already shared with Colonel Pappenheim. When at 2:30 in the afternoon Colonel Pappenheim informed me before our departure that he had told the appropriate people at the general headquarters of my request, I informed him that I was not going to raise this question after all, but rather would postpone it for another occasion.

At 2:30, we departed for the general headquarters. We drove through strong wind and rain towards Hitler's quarters. I was accompanied by Lieutenant Colonel Baron Brockdorff, who had been assigned to the general headquarters. At roughly 3 o'clock, we turned off the main road onto a narrow asphalt road which led into a pine forest. The pine forest was perhaps half a square-kilometer in size. Farmstead peasant houses were scattered all around it. They were used as stations for the guards. I saw no one and no signs of motion anywhere. A barrier across the road in front of one of the houses indicated that one could not move freely here. The guard there must have known we were coming, because he let us continue on the road leading towards the forest without checking our identities. A bit further on we came across a military detachment. Probably they were being relieved. I asked if they were the guard force, to which Colonel Brockdorff replied that yes, they were, but the Führer was guarded by many others as well.

We continued on for about 300 meters at the edge of the forest before turning onto a narrower road. A few moments later we turned and came up in front of a forest house that differed in no way from a larger hunting lodge. A soldier opened the door to the entrance room for me, and I went from this room into a larger antechamber, where I was welcomed by Field Marshal Keitel. We introduced ourselves. Keitel said that he would see whether Hitler was ready to meet with us. We could speak with each other after our audience with him. A few minutes later, the orderly officer returned and informed us that Hitler was waiting for us.

We set out for Hitler's house. Behind us came the members of the escort and the staff of the general headquarters. A soldier in front of me showed the way. The house in which Hitler was lodged resembled Keitel's, and it was only about 100 paces from it. The exteriors of the two buildings were roughly identical. A net had been stretched above the house, concealing it so that even low-flying enemy planes would not espy it. In the antechamber I put down my overcoat and my holster. The holster was empty. Major General Homlok had informed me that one could not carry arms in Hitler's presence, so I had left the pistol in my apartment in Vinnytsia. I stepped through the door opening in front of me into Hitler's room.

As I entered the room, Hitler was standing in front of me. He allowed me to introduce myself and expressed his pleasure at being able to greet me, the new Minister of Defense. We then sat down at a large, round lunch table, where places had been laid for five people.

Chapter V

The room in which Hitler had received us was perhaps five by ten meters and some three meters high. Naturally, the room was covered with stained pine paneling. At the far end of the room there was a desk. In the middle of the wall on the right there was a fireplace. Logs were burning inside it. Not far from the entrance military maps were spread out across a long table.

We sat down at the table. The members of my escort remained outside. Hitler sat down in an armchair. I sat to his right, Keitel to his left. Another general sat down at the place to my right.

It would be difficult to repeat and recount all the details of the conversation, which lasted roughly one and a half hours, exactly as they were said at the time. I was not able to prepare notes, and without any record of what was said I would not able to relate the discussion completely accurately. Furthermore, I am of the opinion that it is only worth recounting the essential parts of this conversation, which are still important today.

Hitler began the conversation with the problem of the war with Russia. Only now can one see, he began, how fortunate Germany had been to have started the war against Russia instead of waiting for the Russians to attack. The confessions made by officers who were present on 5 April 1941 for the speech held by Stalin for students at the military school had laid bare the intentions of the Soviets. In this speech, Stalin had openly revealed his plans. He had proclaimed that he would not wait long before launching an attack against Germany. It was not hard to imagine what the consequences of this attack would have been. If the Russian attack had been launched without warning, neither Romania nor Hungary would exist anymore. Germany would have fallen. Although it still would have had plenty of tools in its defense, Europe would have been conquered by the Bolsheviks.

By coming to an agreement with Stalin in 1939, he [Hitler] had gotten a free hand in the west. Germany had been able to take care of Poland. Russia had even helped, because Stalin had sent in his troops. Thus, Poland, caught between two fires, had collapsed. True, some of the Polish spoils had had to be shared with the Russians, because Russia had taken control of the territories the inhabitants of which were Russian. With this, the eastern danger had been temporarily averted, and it had been possible to launch the attack in the West against the united French and English militaries. Then Norway had come, then Serbia and Greece, where the Italians had not been able to achieve anything. The Germans had brought about the overthrow, and in the meantime, Russia had been preparing for the war against Germany. They had done this in such secrecy that the state of Russia's military had surprised Germany. In the war against Finland, they had only used an old kind of tank, so later, the Soviet army had surprised Germany and the whole world with its enormous armored forces. "I [Hitler] had a good nose to know that we must beat Russia to the attack."

"I do not want to occupy all of Russia," Hitler said. "Under no circumstances would I follow the retreating Russian soldiers into Asia. The Russian soldier, as it so happens, puts up tremendous resistance. He fights like a cornered beast. He must be killed, for he will not surrender. In the previous world war, if the Russian was attacked from the side or the back, he immediately surrendered, but today things are different. This is why the battles are so bloody and the losses so high."

Hitler also spoke about the achievements of the Hungarian soldiers.

"I tremendously value the achievements of the Hungarian soldiers on the battlefield. The difficulties that come with the baptism into battle at the frontline arose with the German soldiers too. When the Russians attacked the German soldiers with the latest tanks and our soldiers saw that their antitank weapons were useless because the rounds from the German antitank canons bounced off the Russian tanks, in their initial surprise the German soldiers also retreated. This 'tank-terror' was present everywhere when the weapons used against the tanks were not sufficiently powerful and the soldier lost faith in the effectiveness of his weapons. The Hungarian soldiers also had had to get used to the enemy tanks. Now they were able to hold their own in every respect. They would be given the antitank weapons necessary to do battle successfully. The Hungarian armored division was already in reserve behind the second Hungarian army. In addition, measures were being taken to enhance the staying power of the army. The Italians were taking over a stretch of the right-wing. Thus, some of the forces could be taken from here. Furthermore, some 50 to 60 divisions were already being transported from the western front. They would also be stationed as reserves behind the frontline."

Chapter V

Hitler mentioned that the new divisions would be put to the south, behind the second Hungarian army. We would continue the fight against Russia without flagging until we had broken its ability to resist. In the case of such an enormous empire, this could not be done at a single stroke. Step by step, we had to deprive Russia of its resources, the resources it needed to survive. We had to cut the arteries that sustained it one by one. It had already lost some 60 percent of its arable land and more than half of its industrialized regions, as well as most of its iron ore deposits and manganese mines. It had also suffered great losses from the perspective of its supplies of oil. Of the five larger oil refineries, only one was still in operation. The others had been destroyed by German planes. Soon, German oil production would begin in the area around Maykop, because transportable refineries had been taken there.

Hitler also spoke about two sensitive points in the eastern theater of war: Moscow and Stalingrad.

"I could have launched an attack against Moscow long ago. I could occupy the city at any time. However, I do not wage war for such goals. Moscow is not a military target. As far as Stalingrad is concerned, it is essentially already in German hands. The Russians only have control of two big manufacturing plants. A few days from now and it will be completely ours. Stalingrad is not important anyway, for the Germans are already on the banks of the Volga River, and so the Russians cannot use the river as a supply line anyway."

"I always managed to get the necessary weapons in plenty of time. The 7.5 cm antitank gun and the hollow antitank grenade could penetrate any tank. The Hungarians had been given these weapons too. The air force units had also been given new planes, and if we later have enough such planes at our disposal, I will launch the attack against England too."

We then began to look at the military maps that had been prepared for discussion, and Hitler informed me of the military situation. He told me what he thought the Russians hoped to achieve with the Kharkov attack. If they were to be successful in the attack, the German troops near the Sea of Azov would not be able to retreat, because there was no bridge at the important crossing point on the lower Dnieper River.

"I annihilated the Russians in a battle in which I encircled them, and I managed to push the German soldiers in the middle forward to the Don River and in the south to the slope of the Caucasus. The battle is still being fiercely fought here, because the weather still permits it. In the area around Moscow the weather is no longer favorable, so I put an end to military operations there. Around Stalingrad the weather is fairly good. There, I am waiting for an attack against our left wing. I have taken every possible preparatory measure to defend against this Russian attack. I have stationed our strongest antitank forces here. This has already produced results: we managed to destroy thousands of Russian tanks."

Then, Hitler used a large map to familiarize me with the situation in Stalingrad. "If, however, the cold should set in, life in the land of the Kalmyks virtually comes to a standstill. The western and northern shore of the Caspian Sea freezes completely. The Sea of Azov is covered with ice. The Russians audaciously took advantage of this. Day after day, they launched attacks against the German positions on the western shore of the Sea of Azov. They traveled for two and a half days across the ice fields and spent the night on the frozen sea. Many of them froze, but those who did not still attacked." (I must pause to note that the massive Russian counterattack that was launched in 1942 and the encirclement of the German army in Stalingrad were successful precisely because the Germany army leadership was convinced that the right-wing of the German forces did not face any threat from the direction of the Caspian Sea. They focused only on securing the territory between the bend on the Don River and the Volga River. The right-wing towards Astrakhan and Kalmykia was protected by only a single armored brigade, and it was here, where in the eyes of the Germany leadership no human being could remain for the winter, that an entire Russian army had set out, specifically from Astrakhan, to attack in the minus 40-degree cold. They encircled the sixth Germany army.)

"It is now my intention," Hitler continued, "to occupy Astrakhan, Grozny, and Baku, as well as Tbilisi towards the south to prevent the Russians from getting reinforcements. It is possible, however, that this will only begin in 1943."

With this, our conversation came to an end. If I think back on those hours now, I have the sense that all of the things that Hitler said to me or that Keitel said to reassure me served only to lull the distrust I felt for the Germany

Chapter V

leadership. There was nothing about Hitler's appearance that suggested that he was abnormal. He made more of the impression of a high-strung, self-assured, aggressive man who wanted to appear self-confident. On the basis of his argumentation and the manner in which he imparted details, however, one could tell that the ideas were not views based on his knowledge as an expert, but rather were statements and ascertainments gleaned from his advisors, which in Hitler's mouth gave the impression that he planned and oversaw the strategic leadership of the entire Germany military.

We finished the discussion at roughly 5 o'clock in the afternoon, or rather, more precisely, Hitler finished his lecture. The questions that were important to us had hardly been mentioned.

By 6:00 PM, I was underway again, after having spoken with Keitel about some of the questions, in particular questions concerning the Hungarian army. I sought out the German chief of the general staff, infantry General Zeitzler. He struck me as a lively young man. He was forty-six years old. As Keitel had mentioned, he was an indefatigable, unmarried man who was devoted entirely to his calling as a soldier. At 8:15, he repaid my visit. He found me in my lodgings, and we spoke for about ten minutes about military questions. At 8:30, we went to the hotel restaurant on the ground floor, where Field Marshal Keitel was holding a dinner in my honor.

After dinner, Keitel, Zeitzler, Homlok, and I sat down at a small table. Our talk touched on a great number of things. Keitel said something interesting about the upcoming changes in command that would take place as people were put into retirement. He mentioned that some of the high-ranking German officers fighting on the eastern front were going to be relieved and replaced, and this would give many occasions to hold speeches. There was no reason, he said, to look for personal motivations in this or to think that the commanders were being replaced because he was not satisfied with them. All of these high-ranking soldiers did their jobs well, but they needed rest, in part because of their age and in part because they were physically broken. These high-ranking military leaders should not consider their departure from the military service a punishment. Nor should they even be put in retirement. Rather, they would be put at the Führer's disposal in order to make clear to them that Hitler was satisfied with them and would have need of their services in the future as well.

For the duration of the war, they would remain part of the active services. They would advance in position along with their fellow soldiers, and if they preferred to seek a position in civilian life, the state would use all its influence to help them.

The next day, we continued our trip, passing through Berdychiv on the way to Kiev. In Berdychiv, I inspected the army command headquarters. Before I had reached the headquarters, I passed by the living quarters for a Jewish work unit. The commanders were standing in front of the building. I got out of the car and acknowledged the commanders as they presented themselves. I then examined the workers' barracks. I could see that the workers were crowded together and poorly provided for, while the quarters of the skeleton staff was properly provided for and clean. I expressed my disapproval of this in the most resolute terms, and I said that if we wished the Jewish laborers to work effectively, we had to provide accommodations that were beyond reproach and feed them well. We had to take proper care of them in every way.

The soldiers were waiting in front of the headquarters. I went up and down the lines examining them. They made a good impression on me. I had lunch in the canteen with the officer corps, and in the course of a roughly thirty-minute speech I expressed my views on the questions of the moment. I spoke about the relationship between the officer corps and the rank and file soldiers, and also about the Jewish question. Again, I called their attention, in emphatic terms, to the importance of humane treatment. I informed them that I was making every possible effort to improve the circumstances of the officer corps and the soldiery. I told them that if any of them were facing an issue with which they needed my direct intercession they should turn to me with confidence for assistance. My door was always open to my comrades in arms.

We continued on our way to Kiev. We arrived in the city in the morning hours. On the outskirts of the city, one could see that many of the factories were not in use. In the inner city the buildings on the main road were almost without exception in ruins. This was the work of the Germans. When they had marched into Kiev, one of the army commands had taken up lodging in the hotel on the main thoroughfare, and soon after this, the whole

Chapter V

building of the hotel had been blown up. The entire staff of the division had been killed. In response, the Germans had blown up all of the buildings in the area. They said—and I had no way of determining whether or not this was true—that the Russians had put explosives in some of the apartments that had exploded when someone had turned a door handle or opened a faucet.

Kiev was a beautiful city. The court of the czar had had palaces in the city, and one could see from many of the buildings that had belonged to the court that they had spared neither space nor expense. They had expanded not up into the heights with their buildings, but rather horizontally. Most of the buildings had been built in the Baroque style. I was given a place in one of the buildings used for the members of the court entourage, not far from the palace, a place in which a commissar had lived before my arrival.

Szilárd Bakay, the station commander, was the commander of the Hungarian occupying forces. In the evening, he informed me of the tasks shouldered by the occupying troops and the conditions in which they lived. Bakay had six occupation divisions in the territory. The occupation units were charged with the task of securing the supply lines for the combat soldiers who were on the move by protecting the roads and the railway lines. The distances, however, were vast. The occupation soldiers were put in charge of stretches of roads and railways that were so long that they could not possibly be kept under constant watch. When the Russians had retreated, they had left men behind who were bold and fully prepared to sacrifice themselves. These men had been given the task of recruiting volunteers from the civilian population to fight in the struggle against the occupying forces. They had launched the partisan movement. Armed with the latest weaponry, they launched regular attacks against the guards and patrols watching the railways lines. The territories between the bases of operations defending the train lines could not be kept under constant observation, so the partisans were able to put mines between the tracks and detonate them when a train passed by, derailing the train. Bridges were frequently blown up and communication lines were frequently cut and damaged. The partisans attacked cars traveling in convoys and cars traveling on their own. They did everything possible to hamper the provision of supplies for the German troops and create as much confusion as possible in the supply lines. The continuous explosions on the railway lines slowed down transportation and made it unreliable. However, the most important accomplishment of the partisans was to draw significant forces away from the sphere of battle.

There was a very expansive and dangerous part of this territory: the Brianski forest. This tremendous forest extended along the back of the German frontline running immediately to the west of Moscow, and it was a major hindrance to the German fighting force and supply lines. It was roughly as large as Transdanubia. Bakay informed me that the soldiers in this territory faced greater difficulties than the soldiers on the frontline. They suffered great losses. The Russian partisans were armed with the most up-to-date weapons, and they were continuously resupplied by planes.

I spent one day in Kiev. I visited the famous Lavra monastery, which the Germans had blown up. Only the enormous bell tower and the smaller buildings around the church were left standing. Later, I heard, as an explanation, that the Germans feared that the Russian religious movement would be rekindled, because it was founded entirely on national sentiment and would serve the interests of the Soviet fighting forces.

I also visited the military hospital and the cemetery, and I then examined the bridge over the Dnieper River, to which repairs had been made. I had considered this river a considerably larger natural obstacle than it seemed, in reality, to be. However, if the enormous floodplains on either side of the river were to flood, then the forces attacking from the east would find themselves facing a veritable sea.

The next morning, we drove to the airport, which was tremendous and lay directly next to the city. The damage from the war was negligible. After the Russian retreat, the airport had still been fit for use. A Ju-52 passenger plane was ready for departure. Before I boarded the plane, I said goodbye to the leaders of the Kiev command: General Bakay and his company. A few minutes later, the engines began to rumble. They warned us that most passengers felt ill at takeoff. I, however, felt just fine for the duration of the trip, and I munched with delight on the bacon that they offered me.

We flew at only 400 or 500 meters. There was a strong wind. Watching the plane that was accompanying us, we could see it rise and fall in the winds. Obviously, our plane rose and fell too, but inside, we didn't feel it. We flew

Chapter V

low not simply because of the low cloud cover, but also because we did not have any fighter planes accompanying us. And since we were nearing the front, we could be quite sure to come across Russian fighter planes. We didn't really have any other way of defending ourselves from them than a rapid landing. There is so much open space in Russia, suitable for landing, that you can easily find space to land anywhere.

It was interesting to be able to observe the land and the people below from up high. You could easily discern the houses and the people working in their yards, as well as the train lines and the train stations. I think the train lines were the best guides for the pilots, not only because you could clearly see them, but also because, in comparison with the maps, they made it very easy to assess the situation rapidly.

Since we had to stop to get fuel for our plane, we did not fly directly to the command headquarters of the second army, but rather took a small detour and stopped in Kharkov. We did little more than deplane, and I greeted the commanders, who had come forward to report to me. After the plane had been fueled, we continued on our way.

We arrived in Alexeyevka at one o'clock in the afternoon. When we got out of the plane, I realized how strong the wind was and how unpleasant the rain. At the airport, Colonel General Army Commander Gusztáv Jány was waiting for me. We drove together to the quarters of the army command, one of the Nyikolayev plants.

The quarters were Spartan and very simple. No adornments anywhere, no comforts. The lodgings really bespoke the life of the soldier. The canteen was in one of the depots of the plant, which had been straightened up. The meal we were given was exactly the same as the meal for the rank and file soldiers.

In the afternoon, I was given the thorough report that I needed at the army command headquarters. Jány informed me of the following concerning the circumstances of the second army:

"The second army, with the third, fourth, and seventh army corps and the first armored division, is performing defensive tasks on the banks of the Don River running north and south.

The frontline is 210 kilometers long. The Cramer army corps is the only reserve force behind the army. He himself did not have control over this corps.

Hitler's consent was necessary in order to deploy them. The divisions of the army have between 6,000 and 7,000 guns. Considering their strength, the divisions have been given a disproportionately broad stretch of the frontline.

On the southern wing, the fourth Italian army corps will take over a stretch of the frontline some 30 km long, but the army will still have to defend roughly 180 km.

The armored car units at our disposal are not sufficient, and they are not properly equipped.

We do not have suitable antitank weapons.

We do not have adequate artillery or mortars.

We do not have sufficient reinforcements or supplies.

The Don River is not a serious obstacle. It is not suitable for defensive installations.

Our military positions should be withdrawn to the tips of the broad, flat hillsides alongside the river.

For the moment, the Russians seem to have no intention to attack, but were they to attack, they would break through the frontline."

I also listened to the requests that were made of me by the commanders of the formations. In their view, the provisions were not satisfactory. I promised to do everything in my power to address their complaints.

They complained about the inadequacy of the weaponry, first and foremost the antitank weaponry. They said that they did not have enough artillery, and they needed mortars of a higher caliber. They did not have adequate fodder for the horses, particularly grain. They asked that repairs be made to their cars and motorcycles more rapidly. I listened to all of their complaints and requests, and I promised that I would do everything possible to bring an end to the shortages and address the difficulties they faced as quickly as possible. After I had flown, on my trip homeward, to the quarters of Weichs, the head officer of the second army, in Byelgorod, I would strive to prevail upon the German commanders to address these problems as promptly as possible. I did not consider adequate the reduction in the frontline ordered by the command of the army group.

I also inspected the army hospital at the seat of the command of the second army. The care provided for the sick and injured left much to be desired. In particular, the accommodations provided for the sick and wounded members of the Jewish labor units were cramped and deplorable. Because of the lack of beds, people were lying on sacks of straw or, quite simply, straw that had been put on the floor of the room. I came across wounded who, having been sent into the territories in front of their positions, had been injured while clearing mines. The head of the hospital was medical officer Dr. Benő Rátz, who had performed an operation on me in Budapest in 1934. I knew him to be a conscientious, well-trained doctor who did everything possible in the interests of treating and healing those entrusted to his care. The circumstances, however, had tied his hands too, and sadly he was unable to provide the care for the sick and wounded that he would have liked to have provided.

The next day, I inspected the command headquarters of the fourth and seventh army corps. I spoke with Lieutenant Generals Csatay and Gyimessy. At both places, the commanders of the units also came to the station of the commands, and we had detailed conversations. I outlined the principles according to which I would act as minister, and I assured them that, as their old commander and comrade in arms, I would give them my full support. I explained my ideas concerning the proper treatment of the rank and file soldiers and the people in the labor battalions. I also instructed them to take care to ensure that the labor units had proper provisions and accommodations. I forbade any use of violence or unjust, harsh treatment, and I forbade them from tolerating any such treatment.

At one of the army corps command headquarters I saw one of the shelters for labor battalions. I saw that they were Jewish. I exchanged a few words with some of them. I spoke to several of the forced laborers, asking them about their fates and their pasts. I asked one of them which battalion this was. The reply he gave was characteristic and, under the circumstances, very brave: "I respectfully report that this is the twentieth century."[83] I could very clearly see that this was not to the liking of some of the commanders, who would have preferred me not to have talked to these people. If the higher-ranking commanders had inspected their lieutenant commanders, and the

---

83 This reply is based on a pun in Hungarian. The word "század" means both battalion and century, so the question "which battalion is this" could also be understood as "which century is this"?

lieutenant commanders had sensed that the leaders did not look on the laborers in the work battalions as people who had been condemned to die or pariahs who were to be treated like animals, then the cruel acts that caused the deaths of so many forced laborers in the Russian fields would have come to an end or never would have been committed in the first place. The unprecedented case that I describe below also never would have come to pass.

I was informed in a report that, in the course of the retreat of the second army after the defeat on the Don River, some 700 forced laborers who had fallen ill were put in the loft of a large stable in a kolkhoz. Most of them were sick with typhus. In the night, the barn caught fire, and the unfortunate laborers leapt from the burning loft like torches set ablaze to escape death by fire. On the ground, however, they were mowed down by machinegun fire. Later, I was told in reports that the people who were in flames had had to be shot, lest the other buildings catch fire. This was their idea of firefighting. Naturally, the building burned to ashes, and 400 people along with it.

According to the inquest, one of the sick had lit a cigarette, and the roof had caught on fire. This case reveals how strong the anti-Semitic mood on the frontline was, a mood against which no one, with the exception of one or two commanders, said anything. Most of them said that you cannot stifle general sentiment, instead of actually taking up the battle against this inhuman idea and these inhuman acts and striving to enforce the stipulations of the Army Regulations by using the strict tools that were available. This was one of the consequences of the fact that so much violence and villainy had been committed, and of the some 50,000 people who had been working in the forced labor units, only between 5,000 and 6,000 made it back alive.

I spent the night in the headquarters of the fourth command. The roads became considerably worse, because it rained in the night. Indeed in that area, even a slight rain made the roads almost unusable. However, if they're not used by cars, they quickly dry out and can be used again as if they were asphalt roads. I only inspected one unit of the armored army corps, because I did not have enough time to go everywhere. Lieutenant General Lajos Veress,[84] com-

---

84 Like Béla Miklós, Lajos Veress also used the title "Dálnoki," or "of Dálnok."

Chapter V

mander of the division, also reported to me in the army command headquarters. He reported on the state of his health.

The observations I made of the circumstances of the second army were not reassuring. Indispensable equipment and weapons were lacking. The equipment and weaponry could only be complemented or replaced if the Germans were to make good on their promises. As I have already mentioned, the greatest reason for concern was the fact that, given the actual number of armed soldiers, the army was too spread out along the Don River. According to Hitler, the occupation of Stalingrad was a matter of only a short period of time, and it appeared that the Germans would be able to fulfill the plans about which Hitler had spoken in his conversation with me. The general view was that the attacks launched by the Russians between the Don River and the Volga River in order to save Stalingrad would fail. According to Hitler, the Germans had set up tremendous artillery forces here, forces with which until now they had been able to stop any Russian attack. It did not seem likely that the Russians would launch any attack along the battle front of the Hungarian second army any time in the near future. In light of all this, I hoped that the situation of the army would improve a bit. I was mistaken in this.

The events took a catastrophic turn. The attack launched by the Russians between the Don River and the Volga River at the beginning of 1943 was successful. The mighty artillery forces and armored corps of the Germans, which they had considered undefeatable, were crushed. The Russians also launched a tremendous attack against the second army, breaking through the weak defensive line and almost completely annihilating the Hungarian forces.

Although my time there had come to an end and I had to hurry home, I nonetheless deviated from the original plans and stopped in Byelgorod, where I sought out Colonel Weichs, commander of the second army. It was my hope that if I could speak with him and inform him of everything I had seen during my time with the second army, I could prevail on him to address the lack of proper equipment and weaponry. In Byelgorod, the Germans had already taken possession of all the lodgings that were at least decent, so they provided quarters for me in a railway saloon car stranded at the train station. The car itself, as it so happens, had been ordered back in the day for the use of Poincaré, the former French prime minister. Since it was fairly cold, they heated one of the locomotives, and they used it to heat train, which consisted of two cars, for the night. At the command headquarters, I spoke to Weichs about everything, and he promised to help the second army. The next day, we continued our journey. At the train station in Kiev, the saloon car that we had left in Ungvár was waiting for us.

At 5 o'clock in the afternoon we departed from Kiev, returning home through Lemberg and Sátoraljaújhely. At the Eastern Train station in Budapest we were met by the officers of the Ministry of Defense and the German ambassador.

I recounted my experiences on the front to the regent. At a meeting of the Council of Ministers, I informed the ministers of what I had seen, and I held an account as a member of the unified armed forces committee for the two houses of parliament. I did not fail to mention the shortages and lack of equipment and weaponry, or the difficulties of providing supplies.

A great deal of work was waiting for me in the ministry. I was also beginning to familiarize myself with life in parliament. I seemed to have many supporters among the parliamentary representatives. It was only some of the officers who were unable to accept the fact that yet again I had come to the defense of the people in the forced labor units, and I was striving to impede abuses of power. I could sense that with every passing day there was more and more hostility towards me on the part of my division leaders when the question of measures pertaining to Jewish affairs was the subject of discussion. As part of his legacy, Károly Bartha had left me the plans for the implementation of the XIV law of 1942, which had only ended up in the form in which it was issued at the cost of considerable efforts. If I had accepted the ideas of the officials in charge, far more severe measures would have been taken. I based the treatment of people in the service on the stipulations of the Army Regulations, and I forbade any form of inhumane or unjustifiable severity. I took measures to ensure proper care be provided for the sick and the people who were unfit for service, and that they be properly discharged.

I had to replace the so-called "SAS" system of conscription which had been in use with a system based on conscriptions of class years, since this was more humane than the "SAS" conscription orders, which were sent out blindly and were based on mean-spirited denunciations. I justified this change with the contention that we would not cripple economic life as badly and we would be able to put the work of the Jewish conscripts to the use of the homeland more fittingly and more rationally.

After my return home, I had to begin my work with the submission of a budget. In the past, the custom had been for the civil service secretary to write the minister's budget speech for him. My secretary, a man named István Oláh, wrote the speech. However, in my assessment it did not faithfully reflect my thinking. I decided I would not read it as it had been written. The notion of pronouncing words with utter conviction that did not actually express my thoughts seemed absurd to me, so I wrote my budget speech myself.

In my speech, I pledged to make every effort to serve the good of my country as effectively as possible. The Hungarian constitution was sacred to me. My primary duty was to abide by it and to ensure that my every subordinate also abide by it. I would never permit anyone to use the Hungarian army in support of unconstitutional acts. I would strive bring the Hungarian nation out of the worldwide catastrophe with as few casualties as possible.

I spoke about assistance for the family members of the soldiers and the people who had remained at home, as well as the provision of care for the injured. And finally, I also mentioned the forced labor units. I emphasized that if someone was performing military service in a labor unit because according to the laws in force he could not perform any other form of military service, this should not be in any way degrading.

Discussion of the budget for the Ministry of Defense was scheduled for November 19. First, Dezső Beőthy spoke, a retired general and the official in charge of presenting the bill. When he had finished, representatives of the various political parties made their remarks concerning the bill. The parliamentary representatives dealt primarily with questions concerning military service and, more generally, national defense, and they made the most diverse array of proposals in their speeches. I had to pay close attention. Along with my state secretary and personal secretary, presenters of the individual specialized groups, who were seated in the journalists' gallery, also listened to the remarks. They immediately made notes, and they got their comments to me in the course of the sitting so that, in my reply, I would be able to answer them, as a kind of complement to my own notes. Almost all of the seats were full, because everyone was curious to hear my speech.

When I had finished my speech, the representatives congratulated me, irrespective of party. At the time, the right-wing still trusted me, and everyone who spoke concluded with the remark that they looked forward to me serving as Minister of Defense with a sense of calm and confidence, because both my past as a soldier and my humane and law-abiding personality were guarantees that the issue of national defense had been put in good hands. Members of the opposition explained that they had not voted in support of the budget only because, given their party affiliations, they did not trust the government.

My speech to the Upper House was a similar success.

Not long after this, Béla Lukács, a minister without portfolio and the president of the Party of Hungarian Life, sought me out and invited me to pay a visit on the party at any time so that I would have a chance to meet the representatives and they would have a chance to converse with me.

I was convinced that the Minister of Defense and everyone who was in a position of influence should be guided by the rational and sound thought that, in the interests of the defense of the homeland, it was not permissible to sever or exclude experts and specialists from economic, mercantile, and industrial life whose only "sin" was that they were not of Aryan descent.

At many enterprises, the Jewish workforce had already been dismissed in response to pressure from the organs of the military and, in particular, division 17/a of the Ministry of Industry. In the implementation of these measures, they had made use of the national mobilization division of the Ministry of Defense. As a consequence of these steps, there was a dearth of qualified individuals in every sphere. For instance, following my resignation, there was an eight month delay before the production of multi-barrel mortars began, because the Jewish engineers had been dismissed from the factories, and it had taken a long time to recruit and train new workers.

The case of the doctors was another example of this. Jewish doctors were called up for service without thought. Although according to the order, only one doctor could be assigned for every labor battalion (and a battalion numbered roughly 220 people), sometimes 10 to 12 doctors served in a single unit, doing everyday physical labor instead of lifesaving work. In contrast, there were no doctors in the villages. There was also a dearth of doctors in the military units. In times of battle, many wounded Hungarian soldiers did not get proper care and medical help in time and many died as a result of otherwise insignificant wounds because trained physicians were breaking stones, digging trenches, felling trees, hauling timber, pouring cement on train lines, or clearing mines in front of the battle lines.

Health care in the villages had declined tragically. On one occasion, the regent himself had complained to me that in the village of Kenderes, which had a population of 9,000 people, there was only one doctor. The Jewish doctor had been called up for compulsory labor service. Later, the Christian doctor had also been conscripted. The regent asked me to deal with this, as he could not simply sit by and leave the village without a single doctor. Similar measures were taken at the industrial enterprises, the banks, and in commercial life. The Jews were thrown out, and so in all of the institutions smaller staffs consisting in part of people who were new and untrained had to do work which, precisely because of the war, placed greater demands on them. The Minister of Defense should have seen this coming when the Jewish laws first began to cast their shadow on national defense. My predecessor, however, had let the wave of anti-Semitism swell, and thus I found myself facing a stormy sea. The people immediately around me continuously cautioned me not to fight against the prevailing mood, since no good would come of it. I, however, was convinced that with hard work and impartiality I would manage to change this frame of mind, which had run wild, and I would be able to convince my colleagues that we must not give in blindly to theories of racial superiority. Rather, we must do what is humane and, furthermore, what is rational and in the interests of the nation. I believed that this was the only proper course of action.

I also often called people's attention to the fact that with our violent and inhumane treatment of the Jewish question we were exacerbating our situation on the international stage, and we would pay the price for this when the peace treaties were signed.

Perhaps this is why people starting saying that I had lost heart and was thinking of resigning. At the swearing-in ceremony of Baron and Keeper of the Crown Albert Radvánszky, Mrs. Kállay, the wife of the prime minister, addressed me: "For God's sake, you don't want to resign? Do not do that. You are the regent's favorite." I reassured her that I had not yet come to that point. For the moment, I did not want to resign. I began to grasp that one must pay close attention to what one says in the company of others, for there are those who will rush to trumpet one's most confidential avowals to the world. At the time, I had not thought of resigning, but I could not remain silent in the presence of those I trusted about the fact that many difficulties towered before me, and sooner or later things would come to a head, because I would not compromise my principles. I also realized that I could not work together with the people who had been confidants of my predecessor, and I gradually had to begin replacing them. This applied first and foremost to the eighth division of the ministry, the department of personnel affairs. I asked the chief of the general staff to dismiss the head of the national mobilization division of the general staff.

Lieutenant General Littay, my former schoolmate, was my deputy. When the regent had chosen me to serve as Minister of Defense, he had felt slighted. He told me as much the first time we met. He had expected the regent to ask him to accept the portfolio of Minister of Defense. In compliance with an earlier resolution of the Crown Council, soon after assuming office I informed him that as of November 1 he would have to retire, since he belonged to the class of 1905 the members of which should have gone into retirement in 1941, when I had been compelled to retire.

Littay asked me to allow him to continue to serve as head of his office, even though from 1 November until February 1943 he would have been able to have gone on leave. I agreed. As Littay's replacement, I had had my eye on Lieutenant General Ruszkiczay-Rüdiger, who at the time was the commander of the first army corps of Budapest. Before this, he had been at the head of the financial group of the Ministry of Defense, so he would be able to take some of the burden off my shoulders when it came to these kinds of affairs.

In the Ministry of Defense, I had occasion to see how strong people's trust was in the Germans. This was particularly true of the heads of the general staff. Almost everyone was convinced that the Germans could not possibly lose the war, and indeed they would emerge from the struggle the decisive vic-

Chapter V

tors. There was one leader who continuously insisted that the German defeat was foreseeable and inevitable: István Náday. Náday had even made this contention when he had been working as a member of the inner circle of the chief of the general staff. I confess, at the time I too was skeptical of his claims. This fine soldier was already saying back then that he had no confidence in a German victory. He had not kept his view a secret even from Henrik Werth, the chief of the general staff at the time. And later, on another occasion, he shared his views with Werth's successor, Colonel General Szombathelyi.

I am writing a memoir, so I must be sincere when writing about myself as well. I confess, at the time, I did not see the military situation this clearly. As far as I could tell, the military might of Germany, Italy, and Japan was unbreakable. Both in equipment and weaponry and in their ability to kindle and sustain the fighting spirit they had shown themselves to be superior to the Anglo-Saxons. Another factor in this was the fact that Hitler had succeeded in reaching an agreement with Russia. Only much later, when I had observed the front as minister, did I see the insurmountable difficulties with which the German military leadership was grappling, and only then did I grasp that the scales of war were beginning to tip, even if only slowly, in favor of the allies. When Náday had first begun making his prescient auguries concerning the outcome of the war, I had not yet had the benefit of these experiences, so I thought that he saw the future in overly somber tones.

Náday, however, stuck unflappably to his view, and now, when as minister I found myself working closely together with him again, he informed me that his assessment had not changed. Now I too began to see that his explanations were not eccentric at all, and that the Blitzkrieg, which had left people looking on in amazement, was over.

I was convinced even then that from the perspective of Hungary, a German victory would be catastrophic, because it would so bolster their pride and increase their appetites that they would do openly what until now they had only done with restraint and pretense: they would swallow Hungary. If Germany were to emerge from the war victorious, the empire's economic and political bullying would know no end. If, however, the allies were to win, then in all likelihood they would impose another grave peace on us, and perhaps more Hungarian territories would be whittled off the trunk of the country. Our survival as a nation, however, would not be endangered. I sensed that Slovakia and Romania, though they were fighting at the side of the Germans, would establish ties with the enemy camp in time. We Hungarians, alas, had let the moment slip!

Romania had provided significant military support for the Germans. Antonescu's circle had held a rally in Brassó over which a university professor had presided. German officers had been present for the gathering. They had said, as if proclaiming a resolution, that Romania would not give up Transylvania, and it demanded the return of the territories in northern Transylvania that had been given back to Hungary. Indeed, they sought to annex the stretch of Hungary all the way up to the Tisza River. The German officers had listened to the bellicose outbursts. The German military leadership provided the newly organized Romanian military units with weapons, planes, and tanks, and in addition, it provided Romania with every possible form of support. The support that had been provided for the Hungarian army, in contrast, had never been adequate. Indeed, it had been completely neglected. The Germans considered the Hungarian units fighting forces in the hinterland, so they put neither up-to-date weapons nor planes at the disposal of the Hungarian army. The Romanian soldiers constituted a greater force, so they provided incomparably greater assistance to the Germans than we did.

Now I see how flawed and how disastrous for the Hungarian people the policy adopted by the government was, a policy that tied Hungary to the Axis powers and, by doing so, swept it into a war against the Soviet Union and the Allied powers the failure of which was now clearly foreseeable.

The various political parties had an array of views concerning the possibilities available to us in the war. In general, they were confident in a German victory. Only a few of them understood that Hungary should not throw itself into the struggle with all its might. It must strive to remain prepared, with the bulk of the army, to defend the homeland against the aspirations of the Romanians, including with the force of arms. Imrédy's circle and the other right-wing parties contended that the Germans had not given us the same support they had given the Romanians because, in contrast with the Romanians, we had not put our entire army at their disposal. For this reason, Hitler and the army leadership were distrustful of Hungary.

Chapter V

Clearly, emphasis was placed on these claims with the intention of getting Hungary to interfere even more, and it served merely to help the right-wing parties ensure that they would have the support of the Germans and, in the end, that they would be put into power.

Christmas was approaching. Since during a meeting of the Council of Ministers several ministers had raised the question of providing modest bonuses for Christmas, I insisted that as far as the Ministry of Defense was concerned, bonuses would only be given if every officer and junior officer in active service were included. I did not request any additional funding for this from the Minister of Finance, as I had the available funds. Minister of Finance Lajos Reményi-Schneller nonetheless was late giving his consent. Thus, the payment of the bonuses dragged on for so long that in the end I had to drive my ministerial colleague into a corner. I told him that apparently he was opposed to my officers and junior officers being given Christmas bonuses. In response, however, he immediately gave in. Thus, it became possible for me to help a bit and mitigate the already difficult circumstances faced by the officer and junior officer families. Every married officer was given 300 pengő and every single officer was given 200 pengő. The families of the junior officers were also given appropriate assistance. At the time, I had also entrusted Major General Jenő Röder to check the general conditions of the labor units. I instructed him, among other things, to investigate and address complaints concerning the treatment of the forced labor units.

Before Christmas, a plan came according to which I would travel to Berlin as the representative of the Hungarian army for Göring's 50th birthday. I wanted to take advantage of this occasion to get from Göring, the main coordinator of the German air force, the airplanes without which Hungary's air defense was inadequate.

After the appropriate preparatory diplomatic measures had been taken, on 9 January 1943, I traveled to Berlin, accompanied by General Fütterer, the military attaché of the German air force. General Hellebronth, the head of the air force group in the Ministry of Defense, was also traveling with me, since we would be dealing primarily with questions concerning airplanes and anti-aircraft defense. I was accompanied by Aide-de-Camp Colonel Kálmán Kéri and orderly officer Lieutenant Colonel Gedeon Lejtényi. Near Pozsony, we were joined by a high-ranking officer of the Slovak Ministry of Interior, who accompanied us until we reached the Slovak-German border. He spoke Hungarian perfectly.

We arrived in the Anhalter train station in Berlin on the morning of 10 January. At the train station, we were welcomed by Lieutenant General Haase, commander of the Berlin garrison. Döme Sztójay, the Hungarian ambassador to Berlin, and his military attaché, General Sándor Homlok, were also waiting for us. I was given a suite in the Adlon Hotel. When we had retreated to my room, Sztójay immediately warned me not to speak too loudly, since it was entirely possible that our conversation was being recorded. I discussed our plans. I told him that I wished to speak to the German secretary of foreign affairs about the incidents on the Romanian border. I wished to inform him of the circumstances on the border, which were untenable, and of the fact that the German-Italian committee in charge of investigating the incidents had not been impartial in its dealings.

After Sztójay left, the first thing I did was to check the clock above the fireplace to see why it wasn't working. I have a weakness, as it so happens, when it comes to a clock that is standing still. I don't like to have one in my room. Inside the clock, there was no trace whatsoever of the mechanisms of a timepiece. Rather, I found a microphone. This, then, was what Sztójay had been thinking of. I pulled out one of the plugs, making it impossible for anyone to eavesdrop. I must concede, however, that the Germans had been thorough. There was a similar clock in the bedroom too, and it too was not running, but rather presumably was working perfectly as a microphone. Naturally, I "disabled" it too.

With Sztójay, I paid a visit on Weizsäcker, the secretary of foreign affairs. In the course of our talk I brought up the conduct of the Romanians, and I mentioned the most recent border incidents. In every single case, it could be quite clearly ascertained that the atrocities had been committed with the approval of the higher Romanian commands. The Romanians were completely unwilling to accept the situation that had been created in accordance with the Vienna Award, and they made every effort to express this and to sustain among the Romanians in the territories that had been returned to Hungary the belief that the situation was not permanent and soon would change. I also said that at the

Chapter V

gathering that had been organized by the Brassó "Liga Culturala," in which German officers had also taken part, draft resolutions had been passed according to which the border would be pushed to the Tisza River. Weizsäcker replied diplomatically and irresolutely. I could tell that while he did not doubt the truth of our claims, he nonetheless did not wish to give any critical assessment of the conduct of the Romanians. He spoke as if he were in completely agreement with us. I had hardly expected him to give an opinion on the spot. But I did my duty and informed him of the view of the Hungarian government.

On the 11, a tremendous crowd had gathered in the inner courtyard of the Ministry of Aviation for Göring's birthday. We too were there at the head of the delegation in order to give Göring the presents that had been sent by the Hungarian government. The regent had sent a Grand Cross of the Hungarian Order of Merit, and the prime minister had sent a beautiful, old, valuable painting. The Hungarian army had sent a complete hunting outfit: three rifles, a suede fur coat, a cap and an arm muff, and a golden aviation badge. By the time we arrived at the palace, a throng of people had gathered to hail the marshal. There was an Italian and a Slovak delegation as well. The Romanians had not yet arrived. In front of me, the Italian ambassador went into Göring's chamber. A few minutes later, we were led into his study.

Once everyone had introduced themselves and paid their respects, I asked Göring to set aside time the following day for us to speak at greater length so that I could present my requests, which I considered necessary in the interests of the further development of the Hungarian air force. He promised to have me informed of the time at which we would meet.

The reception was followed by a brunch. Field Marshal Keitel came into the dining room. We greeted each other. We had heard the news that the great Russian attack, of which there had been signs weeks earlier, had been launched. More detailed reports concerning the circumstances had not yet come in, but apparently Keitel thought it necessary to reassure me. He said that he was rapidly moving the reinforcements of which he had spoken at the general headquarters to the front. He was providing reserve forces and proper equipment and supplies for the second Hungarian army. *Clearly, he thought it necessary to reassure me because of the continuous urgings of Colonel Gusztáv Jány, the commander of the second army.*

Fateful Years

Before I had departed, Colonel General Szombathhelyi had informed me that the Germans wanted Jány to be replaced. After my arrival in Berlin, I immediately asked Major General Homlok, our military attaché, what he knew of this. He was of the opinion that the Germans did not wish to work with Jány anymore because they found it unpleasant that Jány was continuously asking for reinforcements and equipment. Jány had also said that if he did not get the implements of battle that he had requested, he was no longer willing to accept any responsibility for what happened.

Clearly, this is what had come to mind when Keitel had spoken to me, and now that the Russians had launched their attack, he had told me the things I mention above in order to reassure me.

The lunch was a wartime meal. Germany is not famous for its cuisine, and we Hungarians, who are used to flavorful cooking, had trouble getting used to the salted fish, the unsalted cabbage soup, and other, similar German delicacies.

In the afternoon, I sought out Colonel General Milch in the Ministry of Aviation in order to speak with him about the details of the issues that would come up in broad strokes in the course of my conversation with Göring. I was given many promises.

It was interesting that in Germany an officer of Jewish ancestry was at the head of the very important aviation office. They had not striven to rid themselves of him, but instead had made good use of his expertise until the very end. They say that when Göring had been reproached for leaving Milch, a man of Jewish ancestry, in his position, Göring had said, "in Germany, I decide who is a Jew."

In the evening, we were invited to dinner at the Hungarian embassy. Sztójay, the Hungarian ambassador in Berlin, had invited several leading German soldiers in order to introduce them to me. The reception rooms of the embassy opened onto the dining room. The whole place was shaped like a horseshoe, and there was a single larger room. The guests took their seats in the different saloons, which were of varying styles, as if they were all in a single room, but were still able to form separate groups. The walls were decorated with works by Hungarian painters. In the last years of the war, the palace would burn to the ground.

Chapter V

I received the invitation to my meeting with Göring the next day. The meeting was scheduled for 12:30 in the afternoon. We had planned to speak for only half an hour, but the meeting stretched to an hour and a half. First, Göring thanked us for the presents he had been given for his birthday. They had arranged a veritable exhibition of the presents that had been sent for him. The many gifts filled four rooms, one for furniture and interior design objects, one for silverwork, one for art treasures, and one with a model of his dwelling and vacation home.

Göring thanked me for the gifts, and he said he was particularly pleased by the rifles. He asked us, please, not to shoot at the Romanians. "We should not shoot at the Romanians?" I asked him. "There is no question of us shooting at the Romanians. We have no feelings of hostility towards them." Then our conversation took a different turn, and only later did we return to the question of the Romanians and Transylvania.

We discussed the questions concerning the development of the air force in detail. I brought General Hellebronth into the conversation as an aviation expert. We asked for anti-aircraft batteries and searchlights, which we had been promised many times, but these promises had never been kept. I asked him to put at least one or two batteries of the 10.5 centimeter anti-aircraft cannons at our disposal, because we did not have enough up-to-date cannons in Budapest, and thus in the case of an air raid the city was essentially defenseless. Göring told me that he would only be able to give me some of the old 8 centimeter cannons. He could not give me any of the news ones, because the Germans themselves did not have enough.

I also asked him to put some of the new Messerschmidt planes at our disposal, because otherwise we could not possibly train our pilots. He said that he would provide everything for the army fighting on the front, but he could not send implements of war to Hungary because he knew that we were preparing for conflict with Romania, and we wanted to use the weapons in an attack against Romania. He had precise reports indicating that we had put units on a full footing for war along the border, while the Romanian units, in contrast, were only at a peacetime standing.

"Pardon me," I replied, "that I am compelled to use words that are unusual in diplomatic talks." I told him that not a word of this was true. The sketch that he had offered painted a false picture of the situation. I would send him a map showing the real situation. It would make very clear that the contentions he had made had been drawn out of thin air. The accusation that we were preparing for conflict with the Romanians was absolutely baseless. On the contrary, the very opposite was true. Antonescu had said that Romania was fighting and making sacrifices on the side the Germans because it wanted to secure Germany's support in order to reacquire the territories in northern Transylvania that Romania had lost because of the Vienna Award. We wished to live in peace with them. The Romanians were unwilling and unable to accept the new situation. "You are giving the Romanians everything," I told Göring, "planes, tanks, and you are also training their soldiers, but you are suspicious of us and you do not give us the necessary support."

Göring was very surprised by my candor, and I could tell that I had caught him a bit off guard, because he replied very quietly: "Actually, your Excellency is correct."

He then said the following: "the Hungarians can only expand to the east. The Romanians have Bucovina and Bessarabia. They can take their people eastward without obstacle. They can expand to the east as they please."

Göring had no grasp of the enormity of the change that had been brought about in the circumstances at the front by the Russian attack. He thought that there was no obstacle to Romanian expansion into Bessarabia.

The most interesting remark he made, however, was the following: "The Romanians should not assume that the Führer will change the Vienna Award, because the Führer doesn't haggle!"

Essentially, I had performed the task with which I had been entrusted by Prime Minister Kállay by speaking at the German general headquarters about the conduct of the Romanians and the Germans in connection with the issue of Transylvania. I knew that this detail of the conversation I had had with Göring would be passed on to Hitler and the German military leadership. Perhaps I had revealed a bit too much of my understanding, and perhaps I had been too sincere, but the very obviously two-faced approach that the Germans had adopted with regards to Transylvania had brought me to the end of my tether. In my opinion, we had always made the mistake of being too cautious and negotiating politely with the Germans. I thought that my candor might have helped.

Chapter V

I was mistaken! The Germans needed Romanian oil badly, so badly that they had no intention whatsoever of doing anything that might offend Romanian sensibilities. Thus, my candor was merely one of the reasons that the Germans considered me someone who was "too difficult." I was too Hungarian in their eyes. My greatest failing was my stance with regards to the Jewish question. The fact that I was not willing to give in to every request they made of us also contributed to the chilling in our ties. But I will address this in more detail later. I should note, signs of this disaffection were already apparent. The Germans had bestowed no distinctions on me, and I bore this with a very light heart. Indeed, in other cases this was legal custom.

In the afternoon, I looked at the Sports Stadium where the Olympic Games had been held. The next day, we took an excursion to Potsdam. I had a chance to see the old royal palace and the famous garrison church, and I also observed training for work in propaganda and military correspondence.

With this, my time in Germany came to an end. The next day, I bid farewell to the German capital after an array of ceremonies that resembled the formalities that had been held to mark my arrival.

As I have mentioned, during the proceedings in Berlin we had gotten the first reports indicating that the Russians had launched their attack on the entire stretch of the eastern front. By the time we arrived in Budapest, more detailed reports had already come in. The Russians had broken through the frontline at the section under the fourth Italian army corps, to the south of the second Hungarian army. An attack had also been launched against the wings of the sixth German army, which was attacking Stalingrad. To the northwest of our position, a decisive attack had begun against the second German army.

The battles had taken an unfavorable turn. A few days later, we were getting news according to which the frontline of the second army had been broken and the army had been cut in half.

While the wreckage of the seventh and eighth Hungarian army corps were retreating, our third army corps, which had joined the second German army, managed to maintain its positions for a few days under the leadership of Lieutenant General Marcell Stomm. The army corps was completely encircled by the Soviet tanks. The army commander was captured with the troops.

Only a few groups of the army corps were able to get through to the west, so only a few thousand people survived.

The battles that were fought during the retreat were hard and brought many losses. In the bitter cold, with temperatures at roughly 40 degrees below zero, people froze outside. Even handheld weapons didn't function properly. The second army was almost completely annihilated. Most of the effective force was killed. At precisely this time, some of the soldiers who were on the front, twelve battalions, were supposed to be relieved. The troops who were going to replace them had been sent to join the second army in October, but they had been sent without weapons. Weapons were not being produced quickly enough to enable us to address the shortages that had arisen as a consequence of the fact that the second army had needed more guns because the troops on the railway lines had needed to be better equipped in order to fight the partisans. The army command first consolidated the additional supplies and weapons that were sent in the training camps behind the army lines, and in these training camps the soldiers were given training suitable for the unusual conditions in the eastern theater of war. They were made familiar with the conditions in Russia. It was believed and hoped that the soldiers could be inured to the Russian winter. It was a tremendous mistake, however, to have ordered the change of troops in spite of the imminent attack, in spite of the fact that news had been coming in for a long time concerning the preparations being made by the Russians for attack. Thus, the Russian attack swept away not only the army corps on the frontline, but also the relief units that were behind the frontline.

There was no chance for any counterattack or any attempt to prevent the Russians from gaining ground, because no reserve forces were available. The only reserves were the Cramer army corps and the Hungarian tank division.

The promised German tank divisions did not arrive. Another catastrophic mistake was made that was the fault of the German military leadership. When Colonel Jány had wanted to send the reserves in immediately, he first had to get the permission of army group commander Weichs. It turned out that Weichs also did not have the authority to use the reserves, but rather had to get permission from Hitler himself. In other words, in order for an army commander to use reserves in order to even out a battle taking place nearby, it was necessary to get permission from Hitler.

Chapter V

And yet, a break in the front can be the most easily defended if it is followed immediately by a counterattack. In other words, the counterattack must come quickly, in order to ensure that the enemy does not have time to make the split larger and take control of the territory it has occupied. Jány had wanted to take immediate measures. Twice he had urged that the reserves be put at his disposal. In vain! In the end, he tired of the delays, and without waiting to be given permission, he ordered the reserves to launch a counterattack. His deployment of the reserves came too late. But the reserve forces were not strong enough to have been able to turn back the Russians, which had attacked the seventh Hungarian army corps in the back, coming from the south, from the direction of the fourth Italian army corps. The army commander's bold step was in vain, in vain did he himself sit in a tank and try to stop the soldiers who were retreating. He failed, and the battle was lost.

The Russian tanks also encircled Alexeyevka, where the quarters of the army command were located. The units that found themselves trapped had to cut through the ring. Only a few planes managed to take off from the nearby airport. The others had to be destroyed on the ground. The airport commander was killed on the spot.

The entire eastern front was reeling. I knew that the Germans did not have any more reserves, and as I followed the advances and gains made by the Russians on the map, it was easy to imagine that they would take Kiev in a single burst. For a stretch of some 200 kilometers in that direction there was not a single soldier, but rather only a gaping space.

The Russian military leadership, however, did not hurry the advance, because they did not want to take the risk of separating tank units sent far in advance from their supply formations. The supply lines were hard to maintain already because of the horrible cold and the terrain. Thus, the pace of the advance slowed. The Germans brought in army corps from other fronts, and it seemed as if they were going to succeed in stopping the Russians. Nonetheless, the Soviet army continued to advance. Hitler failed to hold the line of the Dnieper River, and he even had to give up Kiev. He quickly had to evacuate forces from the Caucasus too. Taganrog, Krivoyrog, Kharkov, and Odessa were all lost. The counterattack that was launched on the southern wing was also not successful for long. It was clear that the Russians had gained the upper hand.

Fateful Years

The winter war had disastrous consequences for the Germans. In the Crimea, they held their positions, but one could see that even there they did not have sufficient forces to ward off the attacks that presumably would soon come. They had only staved off complete defeat by not waiting for any official decisions. In their reports, they tried to assuage the public with reassurances that they were fighting "preventative battles," and the enemy had not managed to hamper their breakaway maneuvers. These statements, however, didn't even fool laymen, and they were only taken seriously by people who wanted to believe that no matter what happened, Germany and Hitler would triumph.

The remains of the second Hungarian army were withdrawn from the direct area of the fighting with great difficulty and at a cost of such losses that it was no longer possible to speak of it as if it were a battle-ready army. The Germans ordered that the remains of the army gather in the territory to the west of the Dnieper River. They retreated here, along with the remaining labor units.

Some 60,000 to 70,000 people were left of the second army, which had numbered 200,000 men. Of the 50,000 forced laborers, some 5,000 to 6,000 had survived. The others had died in battle, frozen to death, or been taken prisoner. The artillery had been destroyed, along with the heavy weaponry, the supplies that had been stockpiled near the frontline, and a considerable amount of train cars and equipment. The material losses came to some 300 million pengő.

The public was shocked by the news of the catastrophe on the Don River and the enormous losses. The loss of nine divisions deeply touched the country. Difficulties in production and the lack of raw materials (which was already felt) made it impossible to compensate for the losses.

I reported the news of the losses on the front to the regent first. The regent was devastated by news of the defeat. However, he continued to hope that the Germans would succeed in stopping the Russians. I gave an account of the events to the Council of Ministers as well. I also had to inform the political parties, and I reported on the events at a confidential sitting of the armed forces committees of the two houses. I spoke quite openly of what had happened on the battlefield. I made no attempt to gloss over the truth, nor did I

Chapter V

omit anything, so when I had finished my account, some of the representatives asked indignantly whether I was afraid to speak the truth. "No," I replied, "because the parliament should know the truth."

I gave voice to my view that the reason for the defeat on the banks of the Don River lay first and foremost in the failure of the German leadership to reduce drastically the extent of the frontline covered by the second Hungarian army, in spite of the urgings and demands of the army commander. Considering the size of the army, it had been too long.

I also noted that the German leadership had not put the reserves at the disposal of the army commander in time, and they had never given us the armored units for which the army commander had pleaded, and which Keitel himself had promised me. The defeat of the Hungarian second army was thus to be blamed entirely on the German leadership. They had not believed the reports of the Hungarian command headquarters, though reconnaissance had ascertained considerably earlier that the Russians were making preparations for a large-scale attack. The Germans had not believed these reports. They had not taken appropriate countermeasures in time in order to ensure that the necessary reserves, both men and materials, be ready behind the parts of the frontline that were threatened.

I told them that I did not consider the German efforts to hold on to Stalingrad at all costs militarily justified, and I faulted them for leaving the sixth German army in the Stalingrad sector and thereby sealing its fate instead of withdrawing it in time.

I told them that I had no faith in the success of the counterattack that had been launched to save the German army in Stalingrad. The forces that had been amassed for the counterattack were not sufficient to be able to carry out the rescue operation. I explained that the counterattack launched by the Germans from the southwest would only succeed if the encircled sixth German army were also to launch an attack. The army of General Paulus, however, no longer had the strength for an attack.

I was unable to express my concerns regarding the further developments of the war, because I knew that there were representatives present who were unconditional followers of the Germans, and they would immediately report my pronouncements to Hitler's military leadership, even if these pronouncements were made in the course of a closed sitting. There had already been cases of this kind of informing and denunciation. I had even mentioned this to the committee members present for one of the closed sittings.

Though I was well aware of the fact that my every word would be passed on to others, I nonetheless informed them of the unheard-of violence and brutal conduct of the Germans. Reports had come in according to which some of the German commanders and soldiers had been merciless with our soldiers in the course of the retreat. If Hungarian units had taken up lodging in the villages and the Germans had then arrived, the German soldiers had been capable of using violence to drive the Hungarian soldiers from their quarters in the night.

I informed the committee of the unbelievable and inhuman German practice of forbidding the Hungarians from using the roads because they, the Germans, were using them for their retreat. The Hungarian soldiers had to drag themselves across farmlands, swamps, and bogs.

Hungarian wounded were not picked up by the German cars. The Germans were the most lacking in any show of camaraderie specifically when dealing with the Hungarians.

The chief of the general staff called the attention of the German leadership to these questions in a transcript and ask that they be addressed.

The right-wing parties in Hungary, and in particular the Arrow Cross party, regarded it as a mistake not to have the Hungarian army take part with all its forces in the battles on the eastern front. I also learned that according to the Arrow Cross, I was to blame for the catastrophic fate of the second army, because I had prevented more soldiers from going to Russia. If these reinforcements had gone, the Arrow Cross contended, the second Hungarian army would have been able to withstand the numerically superior Russian forces, and thus they would have been able to prevent the defeat. According to them, Germany would win the war if Hungary were to throw itself into the struggle and sacrifice what little it had managed so far to save from the futile bloodshed.

Beginning with the defeat on the Don River, relations between the Hungarian and the German leadership continuously worsened. I could sense that the Germans did not trust me. The entire government had begun to seem unre-

Chapter V

liable in the eyes of the Germans. In February 1943, something unprecedented took place. The regent was invited to the German general headquarters. The Hungarian head of state was not accompanied by a single minister, because the Germans wished only to see Szombathelyi, the chief of the general staff. Hitler reproached Horthy for the conduct of Prime Minister Kállay, and he accused Kállay of failing to pursue politics that were friendly to the Axis. When I spoke with Szombathelyi about this after the trip, I asked him whether or not the Germans had made any remarks concerning me. He said they had not. In his opinion, Kállay could no longer do anything other than resign. At the meeting of the Council of Ministers Kállay had not informed the ministers of the purpose of the regent's trip. On the basis of this, I concluded that the reports I had received in connection with the trip had been true. Kállay had not resigned because the regent had not been willing to dismiss him, Hitler's threats notwithstanding. He remained at the head of the government.

The annihilation of the second army raised the question of the extent to which Hungary would take part in the rest of the war. I was of the opinion that what remained of the second army should be brought home and nothing should be sent to replace it. The six divisions that had taken care of the occupation behind the German forces should remain where they were, under the command of Lieutenant Colonel Bakay. I did not think it right, after the losses we had suffered, to bring the second army back to full number only to make new sacrifices at the altar of the lost German cause.

The chief of the general staff, who had forces which had taken part in the military operations at his disposal, discussed this question separately with the Germans as a problem that did not demand a new resolution. He agreed that we would bring home the remains of the second army, but in their stead we would leave six divisions behind, responsible for the tasks connected with the occupation.

I took cognizance of this agreement. If the Germans were only going to use them for the occupation tasks, then at least the Hungarian soldiers would not be in the maelstrom of the battles. The Germans, however, did not keep their promise this time either, and in the summer of 1943, in order to fend of Russian attacks, they threw the poorly equipped Hungarian occupation units into the struggle without hesitation.

Fateful Years

Following the retreat of the second army, there were only four and a half divisions that could be mobilized in the hinterland. I made the following statement to the Supreme Council of National Defense: "We can achieve nothing with this force. If there are no problems with industrial manufacture and production, then we can set up nine new divisions by the spring of 1944 and eighteen divisions by the end of the year." I said that we must not send any of these forces to the front. We needed them to secure and protect the borders of the country. Minister of Agriculture Dániel Bánffy was particularly supportive of my views.

In February 1943, the Germans asked us to take part in the occupation of Yugoslavia with three divisions. The manner in which I learned of this question was not an everyday story. The head of the military operations group of the general staff brought a document to me and informed me that it had been sent by Szombathelyi, chief of the general staff. He asked me to sign the file and acknowledge its contents. This document concerned an agreement that had been reached by the chief of the general staff and the Germans—a matter of no small consequence: Hungary would put three divisions at the disposal of the Germans. Because of the increasingly threatening events in the eastern theater of war, the Germans had been compelled to transfer divisions from their forces in the Balkans to the Russian theater, and they wanted to replace these soldiers with Bulgarian and Hungarian troops. An agreement had already been reached between the Germans and the Bulgarians, and on 1 June 1943, we were supposed to send our divisions. I informed the general who had brought the document that I could not simply acknowledge its contents, because the chief of the general staff was not authorized to arrive at such an agreement with the German military leadership without the knowledge and consent of the Hungarian government. We were speaking of deploying new Hungarian soldiers outside the borders of the country, and furthermore, in the Balkans, which in my view was not at all in our interests. I told him that I would take the issue to the Council of Ministers, and if the Council gave its consent, then and only then could the question be discussed with the Germans.

Szombathelyi immediately called me on the telephone. He tried to explain, in a voice first measured, then exasperated, that indeed he was authorized to reach such an agreement. If the government was not content with him, then it should "toss him out," but it could not treat him in this manner. I explained to Szombathelyi that this was not personal. Rather, it concerned a problem that was much higher and much more important. It was not the chief of the general staff who bore responsibility before the parliament and the entire nation, but rather me. As I was the minister responsible to the government, I had to present the question to the Council of Ministers.

I presented the question of sending the three divisions to the Council of Ministers on 10 March 1943, and I expressed my view, according to which the suggestion should be rejected. The government was unanimously opposed to sending the divisions, and it rejected the chief of staff's proposal.

This was my first major clash with Szombathelyi and the general staff.

The annihilation of the second Hungarian army and the labor battalions did not have the effect on the general staff that I thought it would have. They did not see the tremendous losses as a great tragedy. They suggested replenishing the labor units. They wanted twenty new labor battalions to be put at the disposal of the command of the second army to compensate for the losses. I replied that I was not going to send new units anywhere where workers were not valued and so many worker units had been so readily left to die. The army should perform its tasks using its own strength and its own forces.

I had to impress the importance of this upon the second army in part because, after his return, the army's technical inspector, who had inspected the army before the retreat, had reported back to me on his experiences. He informed me that on one occasion he had come across a Jewish labor battalion trudging on foot from one work site to another in negative 15 degree weather in summer clothes and rags. There were people whose naked shins could be seen through their summer trousers. In his eyes, they looked like the remains of Napoleon's defeated army trudging westward through snowbanks in 1812. This was the report made to me by Lieutenant General Kassay-Farkas.

Not long after this, Horny, the national supervisor of the labor service, reported that the Germans were requesting 10,000 workers to labor in the copper mines near Bor, Serbia. (As it so happens, I had just gotten a report calling my attention to the conditions in Bor.)

I presented the request to the Council of Ministers, and I indicated that I did not recommend giving our consent. I summarized the report that had come in and the situation it described in Bor. First, we had to reassure ourselves of the circumstances in Bor, but whatever the case, I did not think we could permit ourselves to send 10,000 workers to Serbia when we needed Hungarian workers at home.

The Council of Ministers accepted my proposal, and so we moved on to the other items on the agenda. A few weeks later, following a report from an official working under me who had been sent to Bor, the question again was raised before the Council of Ministers. The report that had been submitted by my delegate only partially confirmed the information in the first report. However, I nonetheless remained in favor of rejecting the request of the Germans. The Minister of Industrial Affairs and even Kállay himself challenged my view. They said that we could not completely reject the wishes of the Germans, and opposition would be an unfriendly gesture. We should agree to send 2,000 workers. We did not reach a decision at the time, however, because I did not recommend it. Following my resignation, however, the question came up again, and then the government agreed to send 10,000 workers after all.

Until then, Colonel General Lajos Keresztes-Fischer had served as the head of the regent's military office as adjutant-general. One day, the regent surprised me by informing me that, while he had complete faith in Keresztes-Fischer, he nonetheless was considering putting someone else at the head of the military office. Many people had criticized his adjutant-general, and when one has heard these kinds of criticisms many times, in the end one comes to think that something should be done to change the situation. He had decided to replace István Uray, the head of his cabinet, and Lajos Keresztes-Fischer, his adjutant-general. He asked me to suggest someone to replace Keresztes-Fischer.

I consulted the chief of the general staff about this, and he suggested General Jenő Major as the person who, in his assessment, was the most suitable for the position. I, however, decided in favor of General Béla Miklós. I knew he was a good Hungarian, and I would have been glad to have seen him at the regent's side. I was firm in my support of Béla Miklós. I presented my propos-

Chapter V

al to the regent concerning Colonel General Keresztes-Fischer's retirement, and I recommended General Béla Miklós as his successor. The regent accepted my proposal, and not long after this he appointed Béla Miklós adjutant-general and head of the military office.

My relations with the right-wing parties continuously worsened. I must mention one of the antecedents to this, something which took place in January 1943. Margit Schlachta had written an article in one of the issues of the religious periodical *Lélek Szava* ["The Word of the Soul"]. She wrote, among other things, of the sufferings of the workers, and she called on Hungarian mothers and girls to think of the unfortunate people who had been dealt so much undeserved suffering and indignity. She alluded with thanks to the Minister of Defense, who had boldly dared to proclaim that the Jewish forced worker was a human being as well, whose work should be honored every bit as much as the work of the soldier in battle. She was referring to my budget speech, in which I had taken a clear stance in support of the workers in the labor units.

Complications arose concerning the burial of Colonel Dezső Mokcsay, a right-wing representative in parliament. At one o'clock in the afternoon on the day of the funeral, the head of the office of the president reported and asked me to decide: could a delegation of officers attend the funeral, and could the orchestra of the river guard be ordered to play? The family had requested both. At the time, given the wartime conditions, we could not provide the funeral procession that usually would have been offered according to the Army Regulations for the burial of retired officers. Since I knew that earlier, at the funeral of Infantry General Árpád Tamássy, the Arrow Cross had organized a demonstration, and this had been very unpleasant for me as the Budapest brigade commander, I did not want there to be a similar scandal again, in the presence and indeed with the collaboration of a delegation of officers. I received an unambiguous report according to which the Arrow Cross wanted to stage a political demonstration at the funeral. In order to ensure security, I called Adjutant-General Béla Miklós, the head of the military office, and informed him of what was afoot. I told him that I gave the officers permission to attend the funeral only as private citizens, and I did not authorize a delegation of officers to attend.

Not long after this conversation, Béla Miklós called me back and reported that the regent had supported the measures I had taken. He had also heard word of the demonstration that the Arrow Cross had been planning, and he knew that the Arrow Cross regarded Mokcsay as a fallen soldier of their party. This only reassured me in my conviction that I had been right to take the measures I had taken.

The people around me, however, did not approve of my decision. They all contended that it would not have a good influence on the right-wing parties, and the measures I had taken might have unpleasant political consequences. Nonetheless, I did not waver in my resolution. I instructed the army command to persuade the family to drop their request for an official delegation and a military funeral procession. They did.

Suddenly, a new figure came into the arena: László Baky,[85] a former gendarmerie major and now an Arrow Cross representative in parliament. He wrote a letter to me after the funeral in which he protested against my decision not to send an official delegation to the burial. I replied to this when he reported to me for questioning. He seemed to be convinced by my argument, and he behaved as if he had accepted my reasons. In truth, however, he did something very different. He began to gather information against me, and he started working to undermine me and bring about my dismissal from office.

I soon received a report from the police headquarters indicating that the right-wing parties had joined forces against me and had decided that if they couldn't bring down the entire government, they could at least compel some of its representatives to resign. In their view, the two greatest obstacles to complete support for the Germans were Minister of Interior Ferenc Keresztes-Fischer and me. We had to leave, and then the path would be open to the right-wing parties. And this path was the path to power.

---

85   László Baky (1898–1946) was a prominent member of several right-wing groups in Hungary, including for a time the Arrow Cross Party. After the German occupation of Hungary in March 1944, he was made state secretary in the Ministry of Internal Affairs, and he actively took part in the coordination and implementation of the deportation of the Hungarian Jews. In the summer of 1944, Baky participated in a failed coup against Miklós Horthy. He was arrested, but after the rise of the Arrow Cross to power in October 1944, he was again given a position of influence as the head of the Office of National Security. As Soviet forces advanced on Budapest, he fled the country, but he was captured by American forces and returned to Hungary. He was put on trial and found guilty of crimes against the state. In 1946, he was executed by hanging.

Chapter V

At all of the gatherings held by the right-wing parties, people spoke about me as if I were an enemy of the Axis powers and a patron of the Jews. In particular, they condemned every measure I had taken to improve the lots of the workers in the labor units, and they continuously praised the former chief of the general staff, Jenő Rátz, and my predecessor, former Minister of Defense Károly Bartha. I knew that eventually things would come to a head.

I had initiated proceedings against Imrédy in a case involving an affair of honor, and this stirred up the right-wing parties against me even more. There was a libel case against Imrédy in connection with the selection of the vice regent, because a journalist had accused him of breaking his word. The case ended, however, in the acquittal of the journalist. According to the military code of honor, however, in a case like this an inquiry had to be launched, even in the case of a reserve officer. Since Imrédy was a parliamentary representative, I had signed the order initiating the inquiry, even though the chief of the general staff, as the responsible commander, had to institute the proceedings. I could have had my deputy sign the order, but I didn't, because I didn't want to shirk the responsibility.

I took similar measures in the case of representative Ferenc Rajniss too, who had been accused by the court of the chief of the general staff of having defamed the regent.

These cases were like pouring oil on the fire, and they fanned the feelings of hatred that the right-wing parties had for me. Thus, I became the "great traitor" in the eyes of extremist civilians and soldiers. I also learned from private channels that Imrédy's supporters and the Arrow Cross were snooping and sniffing everywhere in search of information that could be used against me in an interpellation, in the course of which they wanted to make all my "sins" public.

In the meantime, there was no pause in the work to be done in issues involving Jews. The many instance of brutality committed against the poor workers in the labor units and the measures that I took to address them led many people with complaints to seek me out. In tears, they spoke of the sufferings endured by their loved ones, and they presented evidence to me and asked for my assistance. Thus, it was necessary to launch an inquiry. I passed the cases involving incidents in the theater of war on to the chief of the general staff, since he had jurisdiction in these cases. When I personally urged him to address these cases, because they were growing in number, Colonel General Szombathelyi told me not to be impatient, because "you must deal with these cases very gingerly." I, however, was outraged by every injustice, abuse, and use of force, and I felt that if I did not treat these cases as if they were my responsibility, if I did not take immediate measures, then I was little more than an accessory of the criminals. This attitude further inflamed officers with right-wing sympathies, i.e. the people who thought the acts of cruelty committed against the Jews and other violent measures were not only permissible but desirable, and the measures I had taken were not only unpatriotic, but also an affront to the interests of the Hungarian nation. Nonetheless, I entered the fray, for I did not wish to turn back simply to escape the web that was being woven around me. If I had to fall victim to the hunt led by fanatics and people who had lost their way, then so be it. I would not compromise my principles. I would not work in the service of foreign goals that stood in stark contradiction with the interests of the Hungarian nation. I bore the expressions of hatred for me with a clear conscience.

I also bore the accusation of being an enemy of the Axis powers with a clear conscience. Hungary could not and should not sacrifice its own interests in the service of the Germans, and it must not defy the command of the Hungarian past, according to which we must do everything in the name of the complete independence of the Hungarian nation and a free and independent Hungary.

In March, I learned that two members of Imrédy's political party were going to enter questions against me as part of an interpellation. One of the interpellators was Antal Incze, Prime Minster Kállay's secretary. The other was Ferenc Rajniss. The accusations that they wanted to bring against me in the parliament were so laughable and meaningless that at first I did not concern myself with them at all. However, after I had spoken with my friends in politics about them, I nonetheless resolved that I would challenge them.

When I learned of the accusations that were being brought against me, I sought out Prime Minister Kállay and informed him of the news. Kállay knew the whole case because Imrédy had already spoken to him about it.

Chapter V

Kállay did not speak with me about the accusations that were being brought against me. Indeed, he did not attribute any particular importance to the whole case, at least so he claimed. When I offered to submit my resignation, he assured me that that was out of the question. We would remain together, because his views harmonized entirely with the measures I had taken in my dealings with the Jewish question. He completely understood my conduct, and he saw no reason for me to resign. He told me that he would speak with Imrédy, and he would convince him that there was no need to give voice to the accusations, nor was there any foundation for them. Indeed, he himself had already cautioned Antal Incze to desist, and Incze had stood down.

A few days later, I spoke with Kállay again following a sitting of the Council of Ministers. This time, he was not as reassuring. He said that Imrédy and Rajniss had sought him out, and neither had been willing to give in. Both were going to raise questions against me. I replied that I had prepared my reply, and I would give it to him so that he would immediately be able to respond to the questions put to the government if necessary.

The attack that was being prepared against me stirred up a big cloud of dust in the Party of Hungarian Life. Several politicians informed me that they would stand resolutely beside me, and if the right-wing politicians really wanted to hold their speech, they would drown them out. I asked them please not to do this, since it was hardly in my interests to create a scandal. I could defend myself. I wanted to gaze on these underhanded attacks with the visor to my helmet up, as it were.

Before my second exchange of words with Kállay, I requested an audience with the regent on 2 May so that I could inform him of the attacks that were being prepared against me and offer to submit my resignation if, by doing so, I could help the government.

In the course of our talk, I informed the regent of every detail of the attack that was being planned against me. I summarized the whole thing in a memorandum, and after the conversation I gave it to the adjutant-general, Béla Miklós. In this memorandum, I wrote the following:

"I have learned that, months ago, acting in unison, the right-wing parties resolved to compel me to resign by putting me on the pillory and bringing accusations against me in parliament.

Fateful Years

In their view, my conduct in connection with the Jewish question has harmed the general interests of the Hungarian nation, and since I am not willing to fulfill all of the military demands of the Germans, I am an obstacle to complete and perfect cooperation with the Germans.

I knew quite clearly, on the basis of information from confidential and trusted sources, that the campaign that had been launched against me by Imrédy's group was not the work of individual parliamentary representatives, but rather a plan that had been hatched long ago by a party block that aimed to bring me down. In this effort, the members of Imrédy's group were joined by all of the right-wing elements that had labeled me a "Jew-lover."

As I was told by one of the people who belonged to Imrédy's party, Imrédy's group considered the regent, the Minister of Interior Ferenc Keresztes-Fischer, and me all enemies.

In their view, the Hungarian government at the time rested on our shoulders. The efforts of their block in parliament would be futile as long as we remained in our positions.

The most important precondition of their block coming to play a more important role in the future was our removal.

The campaign that had been launched against me was one chapter in a carefully planned and centrally implemented movement led by the unified right-wing party block. In this movement, the representatives who had brought up questions against me had only been playing the role that had been assigned to them. Béla Imrédy was behind the conspiracy.

Imrédy and his followers sought to win the favor of the Germans. The leaders of the party block made no secret even in Hungary of the fact that they would provide a far larger contribution in the service of the shared struggle than the current government.

They presented the attack against me as an effort on the part of the party block to thwart the political attitude that was hampering Hungary's complete mobilization on the side of the Axis powers.

Certain signs also showed that in the attempts to influence public opinion against me there had been either a concrete agreement or at least tacit consensus between the two national socialist camps.

On the question of who would serve as my successor, there was disagree-

Chapter V

ment. On several occasions, at the district meetings of the party block the presenters and the officials made derisive remarks concerning the measures taken by the Minister of Defense, and all to the continuous cheers of the members. In particular, they scoffed at the measures concerning aid for the family members of the people in the forced labor units, the treatment of the laborers, and the Jews who had been granted exceptions from conscription. At the meetings, they consistently praised my predecessors, Károly Bartha, and Jenő Rátz.

Of the members of the Arrow Cross party, it was primarily Gábor Vajna, Károly Máróthy, and László Baky who stoked sentiment against me.

I saw the explanation for László Baky's conduct in the fact that when they had wanted to send an official delegation to the funeral of Colonel Dezső Mokcsay, a supporter of Imrédy and member of parliament, the order to send the delegation had been disregarded by the city command because of my intervention.

I had learned that the Arrow Cross had planned to use the funeral to stage a demonstration.

Since I myself had witnessed a similar demonstration at the funeral of Tamássy, I did not consider it permissible to allow members of the officer corps to be present at the demonstration that was planned for this funeral, so I instructed the city command to persuade the family not to insist on a military funeral. They did not insist.

Baky wrote a letter to me in connection with this in which he protested against the measures I had taken and asked me to provide an explanation for my conduct. I gave him an explanation in person in my office. At the time, he appeared to understand and to accept my reasons.

When I had first arrived at the ministry, the prevailing conditions under which the people in the labor units worked were so appalling that it had only been with superhuman effort that order had been restored in this sphere among the units in the hinterland. In December 1942, I entrusted Major General Jenő Rőder with the supervision of the people doing forced labor in the units in the hinterland. In the order concerning his appointment, among other tasks, I made him responsible for investigating and addressing the complaints concerning the poor treatment of the people and, in particular, the Jews in the forced labor units. Rőder performed his task very conscientiously and with thorough consideration of humane concerns."

I strove to improve the situation that had been created by the 1942 XIV law. Until then, the people in the labor units had been easy prey to cruel, brutal, I could even say brutish treatment. There was nothing terribly surprising about this. After all, everywhere people were proclaiming that it was a patriotic duty to torture, ruin, and murder Jews. The workers who were sent as part of the labor units to Ukraine took their death sentences with them in their bags. When Jews were conscripted, the most arbitrary and despotic abuses were committed. If people said of someone that he was harmful to the country, they were in effect sentencing him to death.

Day in, day out, I received reports concerning the brutal treatment of the Jews. In many places, the skeleton staff of the labor units who had gone wild and, I am sorry to say, reserve battalion commanders introduced such inhuman forms of treatment that even decent Hungarian soldiers got fed up and reported them. As a consequence of the beatings, the overly burdensome work, and inadequate nourishment, many of the workers died. In the course of military inquests, it was verified that these atrocities had been committed, and I strove to ensure that they would come to an end.

It was also determined in the course of official inquiries that many of the sick workers in the labor units were not admitted to hospitals. People with consumption, heart ailments, and stomach ulcers suffered in the camps, and none of the commanders did anything to address this, since according to the instructions that had been issued by my predecessor, they were not allowed to grant the workers in the units any benefits whatsoever. Some of the leaders even regarded humane treatment as a benefit. Out of greed and as a form of vengeance, they conscripted people who were completely useless as workers because they were old and exhausted. For this reason, I had to bring an end to the "SAS" conscriptions and introduce a system of conscription based on age group. The treatment of the labor units had to be regulated according to the Army Regulations, which applied to every member of the Hungarian army. I did not permit any kind of unusual severity, and I demanded that the people whose working hands we urgently needed be treated humanely. I launched a campaign to eradicate the blackmail and extortion of the people in the labor units and their family members.

I also settled the issue of the use of physicians, pharmacists, veterinarians, and engineers who were among the people in the labor units.

Chapter V

I explained the view at which I had arrived concerning the proper function and use of the Hungarian army in what was to come. I was of the opinion that we could not allow our battle on the side of the Axis powers to go so far as to bring about the destruction of the Hungarian nation. For my part, at least, I was not willing to take my nation into this suicidal struggle. Since Hungary had already taken part in the war against Russia to an extent beyond what its strength would have permitted, we could not further weaken the country in this final act.

I also asked the regent under no circumstances to give his consent to send any more of our forces to the Russian theater. We only had four and a half light divisions in the country. It was possible that the Anglo-Saxon forces might land somewhere in the Balkans, but it was also possible that some other military-political turn of events would force us to revise our military-politics completely. In this case, we would face a completely new situation in the Balkans. We had to prepare for this eventuality.

If the Anglo-Saxons were to land somewhere in the Balkans or the military situation of the Germans were to worsen, the Romanians might immediately turn their backs on Germany and join the other side, and then we would have to prepare for the possibility that Romania would attack Hungary and reoccupy northern Transylvania. We would have to prevent this from happening.

We could not provide forces for use beyond the borders of the country. For this reason, I considered the offer that Imrédy had made to the Germans not only a sign of military ignorance, but also a sinful assault on the interests of the Hungarian nation. As a constitutional minister, I could not take any other position on this question.

It was also important to keep in mind that the Hungarian army was very unprepared—I did not seek to know whose fault this was. There was a great deal to replace, since the second army essentially had been completely destroyed. And yet we had to have this army prepared for battle by the spring of 1944 with at least 10 to 12 divisions.

This was how I reported and described my work and my conduct to the regent. Though I felt that I had not deviated from the guiding principles that the regent himself had emphasized, I still had to ask whether or not, after all this, I could count on his trust. In other words, I offered to submit my resignation.

Horthy reassured me that he had complete faith in my efforts. With regards to the Jewish question, I had also conducted myself in accordance with his view and his intentions, so he had no reason whatsoever to have lost his trust in me. He only regretted that I had found myself in this position because I had acted in accordance with his wishes.

At the sitting of the parliament on 4 May, the interpellations that had been recorded against me were supposed to be read out. Instead of Antal Incze, József Piukovics, a representative who supported Imrédy, agreed to read aloud the interpellations. At 10 o'clock on 4 May, the prime minister summoned all of the ministers to the parliament for an urgent Council of Ministers. I had no idea what the subject of the council would be, and perhaps no one else did apart from one minister from the Ministry of Internal Affairs. During the hastily summoned council, Kállay explained that the conduct of the opposition parties had taken an extremist turn that could no longer be tolerated. He could not allow the opposition to issue dictates to the government in the work of making law, and so he had suggested to the regent that he prorogue the parliament. He had been prompted to do this in part by the fact that the opposition had wanted to read interpellations against the Minister of Defense which were impermissible in a time of war. At the last sitting of the parliament, which had been on the previous Friday, when the representatives had been setting the agenda, representatives Rajniss and Jaross had spoken in an extremist tone that was similarly impermissible. The events that had taken place in the parliament had convinced him that at the moment it was not possible to do any work of any merit with the parliament.

If the attack against me had been the only thing at stake, then it would not have been necessary to prorogue the parliament, but he could not allow the opposition to issue dictates to the government. He announced that he had obtained the handwritten order of the regent to prorogue parliament, which he would read immediately after the sitting had been opened.

He did just this.

This move on Kállay's part surprised the opposition, because it nipped all their further plans to bring down the government in the bud. To be honest, I was not pleased that parliament had been prorogued. True, I had been spared an unpleasant half hour, for I was prepared, if necessary, to challenge the as-

Chapter V

persions made against me myself. If the head of the government had considered it necessary, I myself would have refuted the accusations made by the opposition and exposed their secret plans. However, I was thus deprived of the chance to defend myself openly, and the efforts to undermine me continued. Since they could not launch an attack against me in parliament, they wrote the interpellations down and circulated them, without any signature, among the other representatives. (Later, this document was printed in the 27 April 1944 issue of *Esti Újság* ["Evening Newspaper"] as a memorandum send by Imrédy's party to Prime Minister Kállay. Since the article contained slanderous accusations that I could not have left without reply, I launched a libel suit against *Esti Újság*. Because of the events that ensued, however, the case was never held.)

The storm died down, but the embers continued to smolder beneath the ashes, and I could see that in the end I would be forced to resign from my position as Minister of Defense. During an audience with the regent on 20 May, I again spoke of the efforts of the right-wing to undermine me, and I asked the regent to relieve me of my post. The regent again declined to accept my resignation.

In the meantime, I was forced to confront the fact that the prime minister sought to create political peace by sacrificing me. Several times, Kállay had tried to persuade the regent to accept my resignation. Horthy, however, had not given in. After a confidential discussion, however, which took place in the Ministry of Internal Affairs, Ferenc Keresztes-Fischer cautioned me not to trust the prime minister, because he was playing a double game. Eye to eye, he might reassure me of his friendship, understanding, and support, but behind my back he was working against me.

I even got documentary evidence of this. I happened to obtain a telegram sent by Anfuso, the Italian ambassador, to Mussolini. It revealed that the Italian ambassador had spoken with Kállay about sacrificing me, "the Jew-lover, who is not working in the interests of the military goals of the Axis powers," in order to improve relations with the Germans. Anfuso had also advised Kállay, in addition to sacrificing the Minister of Defense, to take other steps and make concessions to the Germans, because by doing so he could improve the situation and thus, in his own way, help strengthen the Axis.

Fateful Years

Kállay had spoken at length with the Italian ambassador. In the end, these discussions led Kállay to persuade the regent to accept my resignation, and in his report to Rome the Italian ambassador characterized this as a gesture on the part of the Kállay government in support of the Axis.

By then I knew that I could not have remained in that government, nor should I have. On the basis of all this, it was clear that the head of the government was simply striving to strengthen his position. Instead of speaking openly and honestly with me and telling me that my unwavering opposition in military questions and my humane conduct with regards to the Jewish question were not appropriate to the position of subjugation in which the country found itself with respect to the Germans, and instead of informing me that the humane measures that I had taken were not to the liking of the unhinged people with abnormal inclinations, who because of the weakness our leadership had shown now essentially held power, so instead of straight talk, the prime minister had chosen the twisted, diplomatic path. He had softened the regent until he had achieved his goal by referring directly to the wishes of Hitler and Mussolini.

Hungarian independence had sunk so low that that the governments of foreign powers interfered in the question of who would be the Hungarian Minister of Defense. Thus, we were only seemingly independent, we only appeared to be our own masters. We took orders from Hitler and Mussolini, and these orders were passed on by political brigands who joined with the right-wing and cast grime and aspersions on anyone who still had a spark of self-respect as a Hungarian. Whatever the poor Hungarian might want, he was not the master of his household. He had to dance to a German melody and jump when the Germans whistled. Under the circumstances, I realized that it would be better to step aside as quickly as possible and not take part in the machinations that were leading my nation into servitude and annihilation!

On 2 June 1943, Kállay informed me that the regent had sent a message according to which he had accepted my resignation. I must include one sentence from the message here: "The regent does not have the heart to deliver this message in person, so the prime minister is relaying Horthy's message."

Since I had announced weeks earlier that I would examine the eastern border of Transylvania, I did not want to cancel this trip. We traveled by train

Chapter V

to Marosvásárhely, and I went on from there to Parajd. I visited my father's grave, the site of which in the meantime had been found. The people of Parajd knew how important it was to me that my father's grave be properly tended, so they had searched for it. An old woman of the village had also taken part in these efforts, and in the middle of the tiring work of looking for the grave site she had sat down on an old, moss-covered gravestone to rest. She had happened to poke a little at the thick moss covering the stone and suddenly she had seen the name Nagybaczoni.[86] She was sitting on my father's gravestone. The women of Parajd had completely straightened up the site. My heart was suddenly free of all the bitterness that the events of the previous days had kindled in me. At peace, I bit farewell to the grave. Perhaps forever!

Nagybacon,[87] Sepsiszentgyörgy, Kézdivásárhely, Bereck,[88] Sósmező,[89] Tusnád,[90] Csíkszereda, Gyimesbükk,[91] and the mountain peak of Csülemér were the points where we stopped so that I could examine the work that had been done to fortify the border. From here we went to Beszterce,[92] and from Beszterce I traveled to the stretch of the border to the north of the Maros Valley. In the area around Visó Valley and Kosna[93] I examined the points that I had not yet seen, points the sight of which I wanted to take back with me among my memories. I completed the inspection at Óradna.[94] At one of the stations before the trip back I informed my Aide-de-Camp General Staff Colonel Kálmán Kéri that upon arrival in Budapest I would submit my resignation. He was surprised to hear this, but he realized that this was the only proper path I could take.

Soon after I had arrived in Budapest, the head of the press division of the prime minister's office, ministerial advisor Häffler, called me and asked why I was resigning. Surely I was sick, he said, giving me a pretext, and that was why

---

86 This name could be translated into English as "of Nagybaczon." The letter "i," in other words, makes a proper name out of the name of the settlement, Nagybacon (the "cz" in the proper name is an archaic feature of Hungarian spelling).
87 Today Bățani Mari, Romania.
88 Today Brețcu, Romania.
89 Today Poiana Sărată, Romania.
90 Today Tușnad, Romania.
91 Today Ghimeș-Făget, Romania.
92 Today Bistrița, Romania.
93 Today Coșna, Romania.
94 Today Rodna, Romania.

I was resigning. Clearly this was what he wanted to tell the press. However, I told him that I was not sick at all and I did not want them to tell the public that I was. I was just fine. I was not leaving for health reasons, but rather because I did not suit the Germans or the Italians.

On 8 June, I wrote two letters to Prime Minister Kállay. In one of these letters I formally requested that he present the document of my resignation to the regent. I wrote the following:

"Your Honor informed me on 2 February that the Italians and the Germans did not want me to continue as head of the Royal Hungarian Ministry of Defense. Your Honor also informed His Honor the Regent of this. Since the situation of our country also makes it desirable to restore the old, good relations with the Germans, the Regent accepted Your Honor's report.

I therefore request that Your Honor present my resignation from my position in the Ministry of Defense to the Regent."

In my second letter to Kállay I wrote the following:

"On the fourth of last month, the Hungarian national assembly was prorogued. According to the contentions that you made at the hastily convened Council of Ministers on 4 May in parliament, the principal reasons for this were the events that had taken place in the national assembly on 30 April, during the discussion of the agenda. The press release that was issued in connection with the adjournment also suggested this when it stated that the government would not permit the opposition to function as the leading and decisive force.

The interpellations that were entered against me cannot have been the sole reason for the decision to prorogue the parliament.

In the meantime, however, the situation has changed. Now the contention is being made that the interpellations that were entered against the Minister of Defense are preventing the parliament from recommencing its work. The situation has also changed because the contentions that were made against me and spread in writing by the right-wing Arrow Cross opposition are circulating among the public without having been refuted and thus in a completely one-sided form, and they have probably have been passed on in this form by the Arrow Cross to the German and Italian embassies.

As a consequence of the spread of these allegations, which were not refuted or, rather, were left unanswered, the Italian ambassador asked you to dismiss the Minister of Defense in the interests of improving the situation with the Germans.

On 2 February, you also informed me that the Germans and Hitler himself wanted me to leave my office.

I do not with to begin a debate concerning the reasons behind the wishes of the Italians or the Germans, because I consider it beneath me to defend myself from the claims of these kinds of meddlers or to attempt to justify myself by giving the reasons for my acts. There is one thing, however, on which I cannot remain silent, and it is the following: from the perspective of the Hungarian state, I regard it as an extremely dangerous precedent to allow the governments of foreign states to select the person who suits them for the position of royal Hungarian Minister of Defense.

Since the Council of Ministers has not yet concerned itself with the interpellations that were going to be brought against me, but the ministers have quite certainly received anonymous leaflets that were sent out several times with the substance of the interpolation, I ask that you be so kind as to have my observations concerning the claims made against me read aloud before the Council of Ministers and submitted to the party conference."

In my resignation, which I submitted to the regent through the prime minister on 8 June, I wrote the following:

"Your Honor!
In connection with Your most recent meeting with the German head of state, the Hungarian government has found itself in a difficult position.

The reason for this, as far as I know, is that our efforts have not met with the approval of the Germans.

On 2 February, the prime minister informed me that the Hungarian government had to take steps to improve relations with the Germans, and that now not only the Germans but also the Italians wanted me to turn over my seat in the Ministry of Defense to someone else.

Although on the occasion of my audiences with You on 2 May and 20 May, Your Honor assured me of Your complete confidence in me, I nonetheless feel that in light of the above I must ask Your Honor to relieve me from my position as Minister of Defense, even if I have not lost your confidence."

The regent accepted my resignation.

On 10 June 1943, at the audience held to mark my formal leave, the regent expressed his regret concerning my departure. He said that now not only the Germans but also Mussolini wanted me to withdraw. He did not explain why they were demanding my resignation. I then made my last request. I pleaded with them not to send a single soldier to the eastern theater of war. Eventually, the regent embraced me and bid me an emotional farewell, saying that we were not parting ways for good, for we would still work together! He mentioned that he thought I should take the position as president of the Danube Airplane Factory, as he considered it important that a soldier be at its head. Later, I did indeed accept this position.

My successor was Colonel General Lajos Csatay. I asked Csatay to come to see me so that I could complete the necessary transfers and exchange a few words with him before I left. He came to my office on Friday, 11 June. I openly explained the reasons for my departure, and I asked him not to agree to send any more Hungarian divisions out of the country. I also told him that there was no chance whatsoever of Germany winning this war, and thus it would be reprehensible for Hungary to send more troops to fight against the Soviet Union, a state against which we had no claims. The Hungarian government should try to loosen its ties to the Axis powers, and it should consider how to get out of this struggle with the fewest sacrifices possible. I informed him of my stance on the Jewish question and the measures I had implemented in an effort to make the circumstances of the people in the labor units more humane. I emphatically asked him not to bend to the school of thought that sought to send thousands of people to their deaths.

On the afternoon of the 11, I bid farewell to the officer corps and the staff of officials. I said several things, including the following:

"Over the past few days, I spent time in Transylvania, my homeland, more narrowly understood. I walked to the top of not the tallest peak in the Csík

Chapter V

Mountains, but I might say one of the tallest peaks, and one of the peaks that offers the most beautiful view. The climb to the top of the mountain, which is almost 1,700 meters high, was difficult and tiring. We had to stop many times, and every time we stopped, we looked back on the spot in the valley of the gently winding river from which we had begun our climb and then our gazes turned back towards the peak that rose before us, and we looked at the climb that was still left. You see, my friends, life is like this!

In our youth, we seek goals that lie in the heights. We stop here and there in the course of our hard climb, consider our past, and then continue onward towards the goal we have set ourselves. I am doing just this today. I have reached the apex of my path in life. I have run my race… And I have arrived at a spot from which I can only look back on the path that brought me here, to the place at the head of the Ministry of Defense. In front of me lies only the stretch of my path that leads to respite. I did not seek power. I believed that in this position I could serve my homeland as my history as a soldier and my Hungarian heart ordered me to do. I wished to serve my comrades in arms as well. I wanted to help the fallen whom no one had helped. Now, as I turn over my place and leave the ministerial seat, I feel, *opinions to the contrary notwithstanding, that I proceeded down the right path, for it is my sacred conviction that this was the only proper path within the framework of the law that was just, straight, humane, and honest, even if it did not always overlap with the ever-shifting interests and views of everyday life*. I told my colleagues that respect for the law and for justice is a Hungarian virtue. Many people smile and say with disdain that the Hungarian nation is a nation of lawyers. Well, yes: and good that it is, for this means that the Hungarian stands guard over his rights, but at the same time deals justly with everyone he meets in life. I always preached justice and respect for the law, and I preach them today. This is the foundation of military discipline and the supporting pillar of our homeland. I demanded this of everyone who wore the uniform of the Hungarian army.

I also preached that one cannot live without honor. I preached and continue to preach today that the concept of honor includes standing with conviction on the path that our laws and our rules prescribe. One must never deviate from this path for anyone or any interest. Honor demands steadfastness, endurance, and straightforward, sincere acts.

The soldier can only stand his ground if he firmly fixes his foot in the arena of integrity. He must demand integrity of himself and everyone else. For almost nine months, I managed the defense of the Hungarian homeland here and in political life. It was not easy to do the right thing in difficult times, when the war put us on the frontline before we were properly prepared.

I experienced every tense moment of the difficult battles of the second Hungarian army, and I sensed that we had arrived at a turning point in our fate. Our armed forces were not always blessed with good fortune. We lost a great deal, men and materials alike, but in spite of this, we must not lose faith in the Hungarian future. With all our strength and all our talent, we must strive and we must manage to recover from our losses, and we must ensure that our Army, reorganized and retrained on the basis of experiences gleaned on the battlefield, is ready for the tasks that await us, Hungarians, in the future.

Difficult times lie before us. If I now leave the sphere of active work and turn the task of leading the Ministry of Defense over to someone else, do not forget that the Hungarian future will be decided by our brave willingness to shoulder sacrifices.

I thank all of you for your support, and I ask you to stand firmly beside my successor on the path that leads to a more beautiful Hungarian future!"

In the name of the ministry, Lieutenant General Ruszkiczay-Rüdiger offered simple words of thanks for the work I had done as a minister in the interests of the homeland.

My departure caused quite a stir in public opinion. Long articles in the dailies offered praise for the work I had done as a minister. *Népszava* ["The People's Voice"], the newspaper of the social Democratic Party, wrote on me with recognition that was rare in political life at the time. I will cite this interesting article here, in part just to show clearly that I do not follow party politics, but rather offer my fellow countrymen of every order and rank the same support.

The 16 July 1943 issue of *Népszava* contained the following:

"The minister who is leaving his post in general does not stir up big waves in public opinion and does not touch on unusual sentiments. A few

Chapter V

thoughts may linger concerning the minister who is now leaving his post, and perhaps a few words of farewell, but then he will be forgotten within a day or perhaps a week.

And yet we are living in unusual times, and these times give rise to unusual phenomena.

Vilmos Nagy's resignation and departure from his place at the head of the Ministry of Defense have collided with circumstances that have been familiar. The farewell, which in general accompanies a departure, has been an occasion for the expression of very understandable and clear signs of respect, recognition, and appreciation.

The former Minister of Defense was at the head of the ministry for nine months. This period of time, or even simply the first third of this period, was enough for the public to get to know him and gather and affirm impressions of his person. In particular of his person and his mentality, which in his management of his unusually important office he expressed boldly, consistently, and with forceful conviction. Vilmos Nagy is a soldier from head to toe, and as a soldier, he was distant from the widespread notion according to which the politician, and in particular the politician of everyday affairs, is different from the figures of public life. A few rare cases from history, Hungarian political history, prove that someone who is a soldier, who is fully a soldier, is fully a man as well. The man who is fully a soldier bravely adheres to conviction and the mentality he has espoused. Whether we are speaking of his office or the many concerns that tie him to public thinking and the dominant big questions.

If possible, the speech with which Vilmos Nagy, Hungary's former Minister of Defense, bid farewell to the officer corps and the staff of officials at the ministry presented him in an even clearer light to the public. In this speech, the true soldier spoke, the true soldier and the true man: he was straightforward, sincere, and bold. He has every right to say of himself that he leaves with his head held high. And when he spoke of the path on which he has traveled, at the same time he spoke of the path on which those who accept great responsibilities must travel under trying circumstances.

'The only proper path,' he said, 'within the framework of the law that was just, straight, humane, and honest, even if it did not always overlap with the ever-shifting interests and views of everyday life.' When he proclaimed that he has 'always preached justice and respect for the law, and [he preaches] them today,' he was only making a gesture to the public, which recognized his respect for justice and the law long ago, and valued and esteemed it.

The minister who has now bidden farewell was very sincere, which is natural given his personality as a soldier. He was sincere when he called attention to the losses we have suffered in the war, and he was particularly sincere when he emphasized how—by what path and by following and showing respect for what mentality—we can recover from our painful losses and gradually fortify the army until it is at full strength.

In light of all this, it is clear that not only the minister who is now assuming his post, but also the minister who is departing has earned the right to establish a platform. A platform in the sense of how people who have accepted responsibility and duty should live, and the mentality according to which they should work, but also how everyone who lives in this country and belongs to this earth with every nerve should live and work if he wishes to remain on the path which, in the words of the minister who is now bidding farewell, 'leads to a more beautiful Hungarian future.'"

Endre Bajcsy-Zsilinszky[95] also spoke up. He candidly called the regent's attention to the harmful consequences that my departure would have. He sent the memorandum that he submitted to the regent to me, as if to prove that the Hungarian national opposition had not joined the right-wing politicians for whom my resignation had been a source of joy and who now must have felt that they were one step closer to taking power.

I would like to put down in writing here sections of this document, which was of historical significance and which shed considerable light on the do-

---

95   Endre Bajcsy-Zsilinszky (1886–1944) was a Hungarian populist politician and outspoken opponent of Hungarian cooperation and collaboration with Nazi Germany. Bajcsy-Zsilinszky was drawn to theories of national and racial purity, and in 1923, together with Gyula Gömbös (who later served as prime minister), he formed the Hungarian National Independence Party, also known as the Guardians of Race Party (Fajvédő Párt). He later distanced himself from Gömbös, and in 1930, he founded the National Radical Party (Nemzeti Radikális Párt). He served as the editor-in-chief of several anti-Nazi periodicals, and he was vocal in his insistence, during the war, on the importance of defying German expansionist aims. In 1944, he put up armed resistance to the Gestapo, who arrested him in his home. He was released in October, only to be arrested again after the rise of the Arrow Cross to power. He was put in the prison in Sopronkőhida (where Vilmos Nagy was also held), where he was executed by hanging on 23 December. Many streets in cities and towns in Hungary bear his name today, including a major thoroughfare in Budapest.

Chapter V

mestic political situation in Hungary and Hungary's role with regards to the Axis powers. In this memorandum, which was submitted on 10 June 1943, Endre Bajcsy-Zsilinszky wrote the following:

"The national assembly was prorogued, and thus the well-intentioned, national minded opposition had no opportunity to make its voice heard on the fundamental questions of the governing of the country. And yet, in the unusual times we face today, situations may arise in which the voice of the opposition that was against this war from the outset may be of some gravity to Your Honor, the opposition that considered this war hopeless from the perspective of the Axis from the start and even forewarned the Hungarian prime minister of the grave losses which we—sadly—now already face. It is my conviction that in the future this opposition must fulfill its duties with redoubled strength within the frameworks established by the Hungarian constitution, duties which derive from its conviction and its situation, duties which may save the country. For this reason, I took the bold step of turning once more to Your Honor, representing without having been entrusted to do so the view of the entire national opposition on this question, which is incredibly important considering the grave and delicate situation of our country today.

Your Honor! As tremendous as the relief and hope was with which Prime Minister Kállay's most recent speech was met both by the parliamentary opposition that has not been led astray by foreign ideas and, one could rightly say, the whole enormous majority of the country, which still thinks in Hungarian and feels itself to be Hungarian, similarly tremendous was the bitterness with which the news was met that Minister of Defense Vilmos Nagy of Nagybaczon was leaving and allegedly Lieutenant General Gusztáv Jány will take his place.

The question of who serves as Minister of Defense, who leaves and who comes in his place, is a question of domestic politics under normal circumstances. Today, however, it has far-reaching foreign policy implications as well. It is precisely these foreign policy implications to which I wish to call Your Honor's attention.

Vilmos Nagy unquestionably brought a new understanding and new style when—alas, very late—he assumed his position as minister. I could put it like this: he brought the old, truly Hungarian military spirit back to the office. His humane and elegant mentality is the mentality of the genuine Hungarian, the genuine Hungarian soldier. His god is clearly not the foot-soldier Wotan! And his acts, with which he cried out 'stop!' to the lawlessness and atrocities—symptoms of a foreign frame of mind that had spread—against Jews and the national minorities, how he strove to arrest the civil war-like symptoms of petty-monarch lording over subordinate elements. How he was the first to recognize the fateful inadequacies of our supplies and equipment on the front and boldly endeavored to draw the conclusions: all this, Your Honor, we now see was a historical effort.

He represents the most purely and the most clearly the political frame of mind that is the most profoundly Hungarian and that exclusively serves the interests of the nation and the country. Precisely for this reason it is not hard to understand why those on the outside, who seek to drag our unfortunate homeland even further into their doomed fate (which has already been sealed), and those on the inside, who, spurred on by the selfish desire to assert their will, encourage Hungary to undertake even greater risks both in political and in military affairs, are hostile to this outstanding man.

We have arrived at a moment at which Hungary's existence is at risk, when more clearly and resolutely than ever before we must express in our politics, including our military politics, the independence of our nation, the independence of our state, and the interests of Hungary, which are not the same as the interests of any other people. I would even dare to say that the importance of Prime Minister Kállay's speech could easily miss its mark if now, with the dismissal of Minister of Defense Vilmos Nagy, the suspicion were to gain the upper hand in world public opinion that the speech remains talk, while acts say something very different. Vilmos Nagy's fall could create the impression in Hungarian domestic politics that Kállay was compelled to back down under certain pressures from both the outside and the inside, pressures which seek to bring down Vilmos Nagy!

The House of Representatives had to be prorogued in order to prevent the Arrow Cross from trying to stir up a scandal with organized, completely unfounded, and unjust attacks Minister Vilmos Nagy, attacks which could have been easily rebutted. But now, it seems that the departure of the Minister of Defense is indeed the mark of their success. Indeed, Imrédy's men are spread-

Chapter V

ing rumors everywhere, even in Transylvania, according to which Vilmos Nagy's fall is only the first detail of a series of successes for them, soon to come. But even the German claims, according to which Hungary is not providing adequate support, can consider this ministerial crisis, which will soon follow the Arrow Cross attack, proof of their success, both politically and militarily.

The supposition could quite easily take root, not just among the Anglo-Saxon public, which is quite restrained in its unfriendliness to us, but also among the public in friendly neutral states (for example, Turkey, Switzerland, Sweden, and Portugal, which are very important to us) that Hungary is not in fact ruled by its own will, but rather grants considerable influence to completely unjustified foreign intervention, and this would not be at all desirable for us.

No Hungarian loyal to the Hungarian constitution would ever think for a moment, in the difficult times we face today, of allowing unjustifiable interference from anywhere to encroach upon the sovereignty of the Hungarian state or the basic rights of the army. And yet, in the eyes of the well-intentioned opposition, if the appearance of effective pressure coming either from the allied side or from the Arrow Cross (which has dwindled to an insignificant factor in domestic affairs) were to weaken the regard in which the Hungarian state is held by public opinion abroad and at home, this would constitute precisely such an encroachment on these jealously guarded Hungarian rights.

But to fill the seat of the minister of defense with a general who was in any way responsible for our entry into the war or for the pogroms in Zsablya or Novi Sad or any other atrocities, or for the equipment with which our military was provided or the blunders and failures of our military leadership so far would means a serious risk equivalent to the removal from his post of Vilmos Nagy. It is thus in no way in the interests of the country in the moment in which we find ourselves today to have a minister of defense laden with such odium, whether real or seeming!

But let me call your Honor's attention to one other consideration. The fact that, among our generals, so few are Hungarian by blood has a truly devastating effect on national public opinion. From this perspective, Vilmos Nagy of Nagybaczon's appointment as minister was a genuine national celebration in Hungary. His appointment was met with particularly tremendous joy by our excellent Székely people. The Székelys welcomed the distinction bestowed on this fine soldier, one of their own, by the highest leader with overwhelming fervor. Now Vilmos Nagy is leaving, allegedly in response to German and Arrow Cross pressure. I would never call into question, even with a single doubt, the good patriotism of the Hungarians who are not pure Magyar by descent or their spiritual identification with the fate of our poor Hungarian nation. But a Magyar man who is pained by and grappling with the fate of his nation is nonetheless shocked if he considers the fact that not enough of our own people, world-famous as soldiers, can make it to leading military positions, and precisely at a moment of decisive crisis everywhere people of foreign blood fulfill the highest military functions, doubtlessly with less military talent and less natural instinct than people who are Magyar by birth. A throng of high-ranking, vigorous, wondrously talented and prepared generals are in retirement. And if, amidst the great jubilation of the Hungarian nation, a man Hungarian by blood were to come to the head of the Hungarian army, then it should be him, the talented and warm-hearted Hungarian who finished Ludovika first in rank, who as minister earned historical distinction and who is not laden with any of the odium which happens in this country to the detriment of our nation, whether with regards to politics or the military.

Your Honor! I ask your forgiveness for my perhaps unusual outspokenness. I was guided only by my identity as a Magyar and my concern for the fate of our poor homeland. And I feel that, if perhaps with less ability and more modest aptitude, I nonetheless wrote my Tiborc complaint[96] in the spirit of the old Hungarian patriots, who always accepted the burden, like a bitter duty, of telling the truth in hard times, even to their superiors.

With my profoundest respect,
Endre Bajcsy-Zsilinszky
Balatonrendes, 10 June 1943"

---

[96] Bajcsy-Zsilinszky is alluding to the play *Bánk bán* by nineteenth-century Hungarian dramatist József Katona (1791–1830). Tiborc, a fictional character in the play (which is loosely based on historical sources), is a faithful servant to the viceroy, Bánk. Indeed, he saved Bánk's life in battle many years before the action of the play. Tiborc warns Bánk of the intrigues of Queen Gertrude, a foreign ruler, and of the dire conditions faced by the Hungarian peasantry. Thus, Bajcsy-Zsilinszky casts himself as someone who is warning the leader of the country to beware the machinations of foreign powers and show concern for the conditions in which his people live. The play is available in English translation entitled *The Viceroy* by Bernard Adams.

Chapter V

When I bid farewell to Kállay, I cautioned him not to consent to send new forces to the Russian front. I told Kállay in no uncertain terms that the Germans could not win the war. Kállay interrupted me: "They have already lost!"

One of the most difficult periods in my life, a period in which I had born tremendous responsibility, had come to an end. I had spent nine months in the minister's chair. In many ways, my departure was a relief to me. I again could be my own master. My situation, however, was hardly free of concerns. The fate of the country continuously made me fret and brood. In every hour of the day, I watched the shadows gathering ever more densely, shadows that clouded our homeland's future. I met with friends and acquaintances, and every conversation culminated in the same question: what will be the fate of the Hungarian nation after the lost war?

I was caused great concern and anxiety by the question of the fate of the Jews who sought me out again and again in the belief that I still had some way of helping. I helped whenever I could. I endeavored to bring about some improvement in their difficult fates by appealing to my successor, Lajos Csatay.

Later, the news that I had been made an honorary citizen of Marosvásárhely was like a cheerful ray of sunshine among the many clouds that had filled the sky of my life. In the letter sent to Budapest, the mayor of the city at the time informed me of this and asked me to tell him when and where the delegation from the city could give me the honorary citizen's certificate. The troubled times that came and the arrival of the Germans on 19 March 1944 upset our plans. Thus, the presentation of the honorary citizen's certificate could not be held, because the people who would have had to come to Budapest with the certificate disappeared from the stage of public life. For me, only the pleasant memory remained that in my native Székely Land people had not forgotten about me, even after my departure from the ministry.

Chapter VI

Again in Retirement

My departure from the position at the head of the Ministry of Defense created quite a stir. They could not figure out what had made my departure from the ministry necessary. Naturally, I could not share the circumstances of my departure with everyone. I could not openly tell everyone that the German and Italian governments had demanded my resignation because I had not been willing to accept military, political, and economic obligations the fulfillment of which would have been in sharp contradiction with the interests of the Hungarian nation.

One cannot speak of Hungary's independence when foreign powers have a say in the selection of the Minister of Defense. Neither could I inform everyone of my belief that the Germans had already lost the war, nor could I tell them that I considered Hungary's continued participation in the war pointless and I felt it necessary to do everything in the interests of stepping out of the war as soon as possible.

Among certain layers of the officer corps of the army the mentality spread by the right-wing became increasingly dominant. In the eyes of the right-wing I had been an obstacle to the realization of their endeavors because I had not been willing to make sacrifices on the altar of a cause that I did not consider just.

In the eyes of members of the officer corps and, in particular, the general staff who were infected by the Arrow Cross ideology, the fact that I had not been willing to turn a blind eye to the atrocities that were being committed against the workers in the labor units and on more than one occasion had used the military courts to try to stop these atrocities at the roots and punish the perpetrators had been a great sin indeed.

In the course of what came to pass following my departure, I was compelled to confront the fact that when I turned to one of the people who had worked under me in the interest of helping the persecuted who had turned to me, more often than not they fulfilled my request only reluctantly. In many cases, they shirked the task. More and more often, my intervention yielded no results. Sometimes, they clearly informed me that they had not dealt with the matter favorably specifically because I had supported the case.

My ties to politicians were not completely cut. The politicians who knew and valued the work I had done in the interests of the nation and the actual circumstances of my departure sought and managed to establish a relationship with me. Endre Bajcsy-Zsilinszky, Károly Rassay, Zoltán Tildy, retired General Staff Colonel Jenő Tombor, retired Lieutenant General János Kiss, Lajos Zilahy and many other Hungarians who feared for the fate of our homeland sought me out in my dwelling.

There was mention of my departure on the Moscow radio. On one occasion, the radio broadcast the text of a memorandum which I allegedly had presented to the regent. According to the Moscow radio I had suggested that, since the Germans had lost, Hungary immediately withdraw from the war.

When Prime Minister Kállay learned of the news broadcast on the Moscow radio, he sent General Géza Vörös, the leading secretary of the Supreme Council of National Defense, to ask me whether or not this was true. General Vörös brought the mimeograph from the Hungarian Telegraph Office, and I read the announcement myself. I informed him that I had not given a memorandum with this text to the regent, but the contents of the memorandum were very close to the statement that I had made to the regent on 2 May 1943, and I had given the text of this statement in writing to Adjutant-General Béla Miklós. In this, I had indeed noted that Hungary had to plan for a German defeat. I had asked the regent to avoid all further sacrifices. General Géza Vörös mentioned that the prime minister was enraged, and he had said that if this was true, I should be arrested.

After General Géza Vörös had left, I began to ponder how the substance of my discussion with the regent and the memorandum could have gotten to Moscow. I considered it out of the question that they could have reported the news on the basis of the document that I had submitted to the military office. Among friends, I had spoken about this memorandum, and I had even read the entire text aloud to a few of my friends. Perhaps through them it had

Chapter VI

come to the knowledge of people who had spread the details abroad, though with some distortions. I had read the memorandum to Endre Bajcsy-Zsilinszky, among others, and he had completely agreed. I was quite amazed that Kállay had flown into a rage. He himself had told me when I had bidden him farewell that the Germans "had already lost" the war.

I must note that Kállay did not handle the issue in the manner in which an issue involving a former minister should be handled. If he had had doubts and had wanted to determine what I had said to the regent, he could have summoned me to meet with him or he could have sought me out and asked me directly everything he had wanted to ask. He knew perfectly well what I had told him on the occasion of my farewell audience. He also knew well that I had warned him that the Germans would not win the war, and so he should not permit a single soldier to be sent beyond the borders of the country. He himself had replied that "the Germans have already lost this war." This took place on 12 June 1943 in the office of the prime minister. Thus, he was perfectly aware of my opinion concerning a German victory. At the time, he had agreed with me on this. Regrettably, he had not worked bravely enough or resolutely enough in accordance with these declarations. He had not wanted to come into open opposition with the warmongering fomenters, and although he was convinced that the Germans had lost the war, he nonetheless acted as if he were a faithful adherent of the Axis powers. He may have feared that if he had dared openly state his conviction the Germans would have demanded his immediate resignation, and they would have forced the regent to allow politicians and parties to fore which were unconditional in their support for the Germans and had blind faith in something in which perhaps even Hitler himself no longer believed: final victory!

And yet if at the time, with bold resolution, he had poured clean water into the glass and had openly taken a stand against the senseless war, he could have saved Hungary's future, and perhaps we could have kept the territories that had been regained in accordance with the two Vienna Awards. Kállay only worked in secret. He sought to establish ties with the west, but at the same time he feigned friendship with the Germans. He sacrificed Hungarian blood and Hungarian belongings, and in the end he still had to flee. After 19 March 1944, he took refuge in the Turkish Embassy. The Germans were continuously distrustful of him. Every time the regent met with Hitler, the dictator complained and accused Kállay. The regent continuously had to defend his prime minister. Then would it not have been better and more useful for Kállay to have revealed the situation openly and sincerely and openly to have spoken his mind? Perhaps after he had been forced to resign, the Germans would immediately have insisted on Szálasi taking over as leader, but most of the Hungarian people would have stood by Kállay. But the regent's proclamation of 15 October 1944 would not have caught the country unprepared.

But if he had not had the courage to do this, the other path had always been open: he should have resigned.

Endre Bajcsy-Zsilinszky sought me out many times in my home, and on each occasion, he mentioned new, unprecedented acts of violence that were being committed against the Jews. I discussed with him the memorandums with which he was besieging the regent and the prime minister. In these memorandums, he demanded, among many other things, that the leadership of the Hungarian army be put in the hands of officers of the Hungarian descent. He objected to the fact that even the chief of the general staff was of German descent, and thus it could not be expected that he would take into consideration only Hungarian interests. I agreed with him on many things, because I myself had observed that some of the people of foreign blood had never sensed what the real interests of the Hungarians were. Some of the people of German descent were inclined to think of something that was purely a German interest as a Hungarian interest. They had always been admirers of Germany, and they had always overestimated German accomplishments in contrast with the accomplishments of the Hungarians. Those of us who were Hungarian by blood, even with our flaws, were better able to love and honor our people than they. Naturally, this judgment did not apply to the people who were not of purely Hungarian descent, but who declared themselves Hungarian in every respect and acted accordingly. They were preoccupied by the thought that we must now cut ties with the Germans without delay. We must avert the foreseeable Romanian attack, and we must occupy Transylvania before the war comes to an end. They had put together a study on this, which they gave to me. The study had been written by Lieutenant General János Kiss, who was executed, along with Colonel Jenő Nagy and General Staff

Chapter VI

Officer Vilmos Tarcsay, for having organized the resistance movement and having served as its military leader. Concerning the study, I observed that however desirable the recovery of Transylvania was in my eyes, during the war that was currently underway this was quite impossible both for political and military reasons.

After all, one could not even consider, at a time when the German military was doing battle with the Soviet Union in of the east, launching a separate war against the Romanians. The Germans themselves would prevent this, for they would not simply look on passively as a separate war began in the territory behind the German army against Romania, a cooperative German ally.

The first question of the people who came to see me always concerned my view of the possibilities for the further continuation of the war. I told them again and again that the Germans had lost the war. We must loosen our ties with the Germans, for if we are not careful Romania will beat us to it. Romania will withdraw from the war and will attack us. People must be made to understand this, in the widest possible circles. However, the official propaganda said something very different. Many of the people who had heard these things from me did not believe them. They imagined that this was merely the voice of disappointment and wounded pride. Wondrous weapons were coming, weapons the introduction of which was only a question of a short period of time. And yet, the situation in Germany was continuously deteriorating. When I got a closer glance into the German war machine, I saw that the support they had given us had not been adequate and they had not kept their promises not simply because they did not want to, but rather primarily because they were not able to. With regards to the production of airplanes too, I saw that they could not fulfill the plans they had set. As a consequence of enemy air attacks, the Germans were not able to make the parts that they needed to deliver to us for the planes in time. I saw that German industry was progressing only haltingly, and anyone who traveled in Germany with his eyes open could see that the German people were tired. They did not dare do anything against the system, but only because of the immeasurable reign of terror. Thus, I consider it completely natural that the right-wing felt, on the basis of my declarations and my acts, that I hampered the complete expenditure of force on the side of the Germans.

Fateful Years

Retired ministerial advisor Artúr Vákár visited me in my home several times. He passed on a request from a painter named Gyula Hatvani-Perlusz, who wanted me to open an exhibition of his paintings of landscapes in the Székely Land. I accepted his request. One evening, Hatvani-Perlusz sought me out in my home. He was happy to learn that I was going to open the exhibition. He left, and then about a half hour later he returned, and, very distraught, he said that he had forgotten to mention something very important. He had not informed me that he was not of Aryan descent. I reassured him that I was not interested in his ancestry. In the arts, literature, and all other spheres of life I respect values and not anyone's descent. Shedding tears, he thanked me.

I opened the exhibition, which gave clear proof of the artist's remarkable talent and deeply Hungarian spirit. I admired the many beautiful, fresh paintings, which seemed to breathe Székely air. Standing among the paintings, I felt as if I were looking directly at the mountains of Csík and Háromszék and the scent of the forests that rise on the Tusnád and Borszék mountains were wafting towards me. I felt at home among these paintings.

The papers also wrote on the exhibition with considerable appreciation. A few days after the opening, I received a letter from retired Colonel Antal Hellebronth, Deputy Captain of the Order of Vitéz. Hellebronth asked me to come to his office because he wanted to speak to me about an important issue. Since I was traveling to Ipolyvisk[97] that day and I was not able to postpone the trip, I asked him to allow me to contact him after my return. To this, he replied that he himself would come to the Western train station in order to speak with me in person. To my surprise, he brought up the opening of the Perlusz exhibition. He informed me that at the last meeting at the seat of the captaincy someone had reported me for having opened an exhibition of works by a Jewish painter as a gesture of protest. He asked me not to do anything like this again. I thanked Hellebronth for having taken the trouble to come to the station, and I informed him that I had not been guided by any kind of political consideration when I had agreed to open the exhibition, because I do not concern myself with the artist's race, but only with the question of whether his work is artistic and valuable or not.

---

97 Today Vyškovce nad Iplom, Slovakia.

Chapter VI

I bid Hellebronth farewell and boarded the train, which was ready to depart. As the train rolled down the tracks with me aboard, my thoughts returned again and again to this question. So this was where we stood. The members of the Order of Vitéz have nothing better to do other than bash Jews, and they call me to account, their former Minister of Defense, and demand an explanation concerning an artist for whom I, as a private citizen, hold an exhibition opening. So ancestry is the only thing that matters to them too? Where will this lead? And how will all this end? This continuous incitement, towards what precipice is it thrusting our homeland? Certainly no good can come of it!

Chapter VII

Another Attempt to Occupy Serbia by Hungarian Soldiers

The worsening situation on the eastern front demanded more and more German soldiers. The Germans were compelled to weaken the occupation forces in the Balkans and, in particular, in Serbia. Since they considered the occupation of Yugoslavia with a force of the same strength as the one that had been on the ground absolutely necessary, the German military leadership wanted to send in Bulgarian and Hungarian soldiers to compensate for the shortage that had arisen because of the forces that had been removed from that theater and the withdrawal of the Italians. In February 1943, the Hungarian general staff had tried to send three divisions to support the Germans. However, as I have already mentioned, I thwarted this attempt during my tenure as minister. The chief of the general staff had informed the German government of my decision to reject their request through the German military attaché. He had informed him that there were equipment shortages, because we had sent arms to the second army, and we did not have equipment for new formations. Thus, for the moment, we could not provide army corps for the occupation of Serbia. In May, we might be able to, but only if we were given equipment for them by the Germans.

It is thus understandable that the Germans raised the question of Hungary providing army corps for the occupation of Serbia again, in August 1943, following my resignation, when my successor, Minister of Defense Csatay, had an audience with Hitler. The Führer could no longer deny that, as a consequence of the Russian attack that had begun in January, the situation on the eastern front had become grave indeed. As he told Csatay, the general situation was serious, but we must endure, because fortunes are always shifting, and a people which abandons the struggle when faced with such a grave situation does not merit victory. He spoke of Frederick the Great, who had only 4 million people left, whose war industry was not functioning, and who had lost most of his country. His enemies had 52 million people, and their industry was functioning without interruption. However, he did not lose his faith in his final victory. He saved his country and made it great. He compared the example of Frederick the great with the situation at the time, and on the basis of the turn in the Seven Years' War, he drew the conclusion that Germany must not lose heart, for if the German people were to lose their faith in victory, even he would not be able to pity them for their downfall.

Hitler declared that he deplored the deaths that had been caused by the air attacks, but he did not regret the loss of the material wealth that had been destroyed, and he did not consider the buildings that lay in ruins a loss at all, since most of them would have had to have been demolished anyway. Before the war 380,000 apartments had been built in Germany every year. After the war, 2 million apartments would be built every year, and thus within two years of the end of the war there would be no trace of the devastation that had been suffered.

What Hitler thought of the strength of the Russians was interesting, as was the question of why he lulled himself with hopes of victory when he himself saw and admitted how serious the situation was.

According to Hitler the offensive strength and momentum of the Russians was gradually declining. He thought that there was a lack of men in Russia, and so even 16-year-olds were being drafted. They did not have any manganese. The weapons and equipment produced by their military industry were of increasingly poor quality. Their machine tools had been used up, and they were unable to replace them. With the acquisition of new territories, their transportation situation was becoming increasingly worse. The Russian military leadership had to bring increasingly expensive territories into its transportation network, and thus their rolling stock was being used up. They could not compensate for this. Since the harvest in America had been bad in 1943, the deliveries of foodstuffs from there would not come. Hitler tried to prove that his hopes for victory were justified by referring to the deterioration of the situation of the enemy. However, he made no mention of the situation in Germany, which was being hit with continuous air attacks.

He thought it necessary to emphasize that Germany had launched the war against the Russians in the interests of all of civilization. It did not occur to him that others were also observing the events with open eyes, and that German expansion within Europe was a fact that could not be kept secret, a fact that meant a continuous threat for every nation of central and eastern Europe. Hitler was of the opinion that if he were to withdraw the German occupying forces from France, Italy, Norway, or the Balkans, the civilian governments would not be able to maintain control and the communists would come to power. He was certain that the German submarines and airplanes would again play a role and would deliver decisive blows against the Anglo-Saxons.

In the course of the time he spent in Germany, Csatay also met with Ribbentrop, who expressed his view primarily in connection with Italy's withdrawal from the war, which had taken Germany by surprise. He condemned the people who had stabbed Mussolini in the back (in Ribbentrop's view, quite treacherously), thinking that as a consequence of this the Allies would give them better peace terms. The Germans had been surprised by the events in Italy. They had not counted on such a turn of events at all. The loss of Italy was not a big problem. The English fleet had sailed into the harbors in Syracuse and Augusta unimpeded. The German government had asked where Mussolini was, but neither the Italian king nor the government had wanted to say. They avoided answering by saying that they did not know where he was staying. Ribbentrop told Csatay that they must persevere and that Germany was the only barrier to Russian bolshevism. If Germany did not hold out, Europe would perish, and Hungary within it. Thus, we must not consider following Italy's example.

The German military leaders did not properly assess the situation. Field Marshal Keitel spoke of the necessity of shortening the frontline in order to free up forces to address the tasks that the Italians had performed until then. For the Germans now had to take over from the Italians the defense of the Balkan seashores. For this reason, he was asking to use Hungarian army corps in the Balkans.

Infantry General Zeitzler, the German chief of the general staff, painted a very interesting picture of the situation for Csatay. He explained that in his view it would be a good thing if the Russians were to continue their attack so that, in the course of the battles, they would be worn out, and they would have no strength to attack in the following winter.

In the interests of the foreseeably successful military campaigns, they were giving up territories, and so we should count on evacuations of additional territories. Many defensive positions had already been prepared where the Russians would be stopped. Oryol had been evacuated. The entire population had been removed, along with all of their personal belongings. He gave a very reassuring assessment of the situation on the Russian front, and he was certain that Russian moral resolve and material strength would dwindle. Every day, 300 deserters fled to the German side. Shortages were beginning to appear in the Russian production of war supplies.

Thus, every leader tried to dismiss concerns with reference to the decline in the situation of the enemy, and it was amazing that the Minister of Defense, whom I knew to be a soldier with clear vision, was made dizzy by the self-confidence of the German leadership and did not discern the foreseeable German failure. He could not come to a decision concerning the direction of Hungary's fate. He failed to sense that the step Italy had taken was a cautionary example to us, and an example to be followed. He should have brought the leadership to its senses, and he should have stopped the German fanatics. But this did not happen! Lajos Csatay was not of the opinion that one would have expected, and he stated the following:

"On the basis of what I have heard and seen," Csatay reported after his trip to Germany, "I have the impression that at the moment the Germans are indeed in a grave situation, but they are firmly committed to continuing the fight. They consider unconditional perseverance the only way to emerge from the difficult situation they face now and again get the upper hand. Trusting in their strength, they are convinced that the continued struggle will not be in vain, but rather it will lead to victory.

They want to ensure control of the Balkans by replacing the Italian forces and continuing to defend the seashore. They can only provide this defense if Hungary cooperates by sending Hungarian soldiers to take control, as an occupation force, of the territories and the supply lines in Yugoslavia."

On the basis of the above, he suggested that we accept the duty of maintaining order in Croatia, with the consent or rather at the request of the Croatian government. In order to do this, we would request that the second Hungarian army be sent home, after which it would be sent, following the necessary rotations and reinforcements, to Croatia as an occupation force to secure connections for the German units defending the Adriatic coast and maintain domestic order.

He offered several political and military reasons in the support of this suggestion. Among other things, he said: "This is the only solution that will make it possible for us to bring back our occupation forces from the Russian theater of war and use them for direct defense of the country's borders. In the difficult situation faced at the moment by the Germans, it would be hard completely to avoid providing the support that has been requested. This solution would constitute serious help for the Germans, and for us it would not mean any more or any greater sacrifices."

The suggestion and the plan proposed by the Minister of Defense were not met with an enthusiastic response by the ministers. Rather, they stirred up indignation and opposition. In February 1943, when I had submitted a similar proposal made by the chief of the general staff to the Council of Ministers, the government had rejected the proposal to send Hungarian troops out of the country on the basis of my contrary opinion!

The chief of the general staff adopted the most resolute stance in support of the occupation plan suggested by Minister of Defense Csatay. He explained his standpoint at a sitting of the Supreme Council of National Defense on 4 September 1943. Since his stance on this question sheds clear light on the attitudes of the leading military figures and in many respects offers an explanation for the events of October 1944, I consider it necessary to deal with it in detail.

In his presentation, Colonel General Szombathelyi explained the general strategical situation, and he observed that "the Axis powers have conquered enormous territories, which they are now keeping under occupation. They can use the enormous sources of raw materials in these territories, but the occupation of the territories has compelled them to scatter their forces.

The Axis powers have indeed achieved great successes, but they have not managed to squeeze out a final victory. They have not annihilated the enemy forces. Russia is protected by its tremendous expanse and England by its position as an island and its superior navy. As a consequence of this, they won time to catch up with and even overcome the advantage that the Axis powers enjoyed at the beginning of the war in armaments.

In 1942, the Allied powers seized some of the initiative themselves, and they attained smaller and larger successes. In Africa, the English pushed back the Germans and the Italians. In the course of the offensive that was launched in the winter of 1943, the Russians delivered serious blows to the military forces of the Axis powers. The Axis powers not only were compelled to give up enormous territories, they also suffered painful losses."

In the opinion of the chief of the general staff, in mid-April, when he had accompanied Regent Miklós Horthy on his trip to see Hitler, the situation of the Axis powers had not given any cause for concern. Slowly, the initiative had ended up in the hands of the enemy, and as a consequence of this, the prospects for the Axis powers were increasingly unfavorable. But it also seemed beyond doubt that the Germans were prepared for anything, and even if they didn't triumph, they could avoid the worst, their own defeat, or at least they would not soon be vanquished.

"Germany is putting up a ferocious battle on all fronts," the chief of the general staff said. "Their soldiers are doing battle in a manner beyond reproach, and they have a considerable tactical and strategic advantage over the Russians."

In spite of this, the chief of the general staff said, we cannot count on an Axis victory. There is no prospect of the Germans attaining decisive successes.

Perhaps sensing the approaching collapse of fascism, on the occasion of his spring visit, which he made to the German headquarters not long before Horthy, Mussolini had sought to persuade Hitler to reach a negotiated peace with Russia. Following his discussion with Hitler, he returned home strengthened in his confidence in the future, and with renewed strength he continued the struggle, in spite of the fact that the Italian army was not in a proper state to achieve any major results.

All things considered, initially, 1943 had not promised to bring any decisive results, and it seemed that all organizational and planning solutions could be implemented and that the Axis powers would be able to attack again on all fronts, though the complete show of strength was more likely to come in 1944 than 1945. It also seemed that Hungary would be able to implement its military plans, since it was not yet necessary to plan for an Allied attack in the Balkans. It would be possible to transport the second army, which had suffered such terrible misfortune in the military campaign in the winter of

1943, back home, additions could be made to compensate for the losses, the military forces could be retrained, and, finally, we could hope that it would be possible to bring our occupation forces home.

The Germans promised not to force the Hungarian military to participate on the eastern front or in the Balkans, since in February 1943 their request concerning the latter question had been denied.

"However, 1943 unfolded very differently than one would have thought in April of that year. The first major surprise came in May 1943, when the German submarines suffered losses so devastating that they had to be called back from the seas, and since then, they have not gone to distant waters. As a consequence of this, the number of enemy boats that have been sunk has dropped considerably, indeed almost to zero. Transportation on the seas has become safer for the Anglo-Saxon powers.

The biggest surprise, however, has been the collapse of fascism and the fall of Mussolini. The traditional strategy of the Anglo-Saxons, or rather the English, the essence of which is to break the will of the enemy country to fight and thus squeeze out a victory by compelling the enemy military force to lay down its arms, again has brought essential advantages in the offensive against Italy, even if it did not lead to complete success. The intensification of the bombings has so depleted the already frail resolve of the Italian people to resist that they have rid themselves of fascism. In the 1914–1918 World War, the English used the food blockade as a weapon, and it contributed significantly to their victory, much as it had in the Boer War. In the war we are fighting now, they have been given a more powerful and more effective weapon: the airplane, which is more suitable for bringing about rapid results than the food blockade was. It makes it possible for the English approach to warfare to unfold in its entirety. The mercantile spirit, which has brought this otherwise hard people a great economy, finds complete expression in their approach to warfare too. The principal, according to which one makes the greatest possible use of a small investment, has also proven effective in warfare. This mercantile strategy is in sharp contrast with the annihilating, heroic strategic principles of the Axis powers, namely the Germans. This strategy always seeks to achieve victory through grand and devastating battles, into which it mercilessly throws its crowds of millions. The English never seek battles that they know from the start will be bloody. Indeed, they try to avoid them. They only go into such battles when they are unable to attain their aims with other, less costly tools."

Before we continue, let us stop for a moment and consider what has been said. I consider it essential, in the interests of furthering an understanding of the measures taken by the Hungarian military leadership and the general staff, to shed some light on how the elite of the Hungarian officer corps, the general staff, was raised.

"Mercantile military strategy" and "heroic military strategy"! According to the assertion made by the chief of the general staff there was a sharp difference between these two tendencies in military leadership. The German school, the teachings of which the Hungarian general staff had been breathing in for decades, sought to defeat the enemy by throwing great masses into battle, creating a local preponderance of arms, and using its devastating impact. Out of this attitude grew the so-called heroic view of life, according to which, in order to achieve victory, it was absolutely necessary for every soldier to fight to the end, with no regard whatsoever for whether or not there was any point to the bloody sacrifice or not.

According to the German school of thought, the enemy must be annihilated with brutal blows by mercilessly throwing all forces into battle to attain the goal at any price, with no consideration of one's own bloody losses. The translation of this theory into practice gave birth to Hitler's notion of "persevere and fight to the last man." The consequence of this military leadership, which insisted on "perseverance," was the tremendous devastation that struck not only Germany, but all of the countries that, guided by their misinterpretation of this "heroic" strategy, had fought until the "mercantile strategy," which in their eyes was not valiant, had gotten the upper hand and smashed their poorly used militaries.

Thus, according to the chief of the general staff, Germany had lost the war. The question arises, if indeed this was how the chief of the general staff and his colleagues saw the situation, why did they not reach the only possible conclusion: that under the circumstances Hungary must immediately withdraw from the war.

Regrettably, instead of taking determined steps to seek peace, they turned again and again to self-consolation and self-delusion. They thought that the differences among the Allies would deepen, and as a consequence of a conflict that would break out among them, somehow we would extricate ourselves from the war, along with Germany. Drawing on history, they arrived at the false conclusion according to which, if Frederick the Great had managed to gain the upper hand in the Seven Years' War because he had shrewdly exploited the discord that had broken out among the allied powers which were fighting against him, the German Reich today would also manage to negotiate an acceptable peace, exploiting the alleged conflict between the Anglo-Saxons and Russia. The must have consoled themselves with the thought that they were not facing any major problem, since the situation of Germany today resembled the situation faced by Frederick the Great, who had lost a great deal of blood in the long war, and Prussia, which had been exhausted by battle, had also been forced to adopt a defensive position, and so it had waited for a bit of good fortune and, as a consequence, had arrived at an acceptable peace. Now, however, this had not come to pass. Hitler had waited in vain for a bit of good fortune. His enemies had not quarreled with one another for his sake, but rather, remaining united from first to last, they had defeated Germany and its allies and destroyed Hitler's German empire.

"In the eastern theater of war," the memorandum continued, "Germany is withdrawing defensively. Perhaps it will stop at the Dnieper River, and if there are still reserves left when the Russian attack begins to stall, it could even make a counterattack. Today, however, there are no significant reserves left. The enemy's numerical superiority has left Germany in a tight corner. The Hungarian military leadership wishes to help Germany out of this tight corner by sending occupation soldiers to the Balkans, and, by providing this support, it also seeks to prevail on Hitler to 'turn over' the Hungarian divisions serving in Russia as an occupying force, divisions which could then perhaps be used to defend our native soil."

As I noted earlier, the government did not give its consent to use the three divisions in the Balkans. It rejected the proposal.

On the basis of an accurate assessment of the situation, the chief of the general staff himself no longer had faith in a German victory. Yet one can justifiably raise the question: why did he not seek a way out, and why did he propose sending Hungarian soldiers to the Balkans?

Again it was quite apparent that with this war we had become entangled in something for which we had neither the forces nor the material capacities. As a consequence of the constraints of the Treaty of Trianon, we could not develop our war industry as would have suited the circumstances. Its ability to perform was therefore inadequate. We were not able, using our own strength, to equip, reinforce, or train the Hungarian army properly. It was my personal conviction that we could not even think of taking up the battle with our neighbors in the hope of restoring the millennial borders.[98]

And Germany just kept making promises. In spite of the fact that the experts that we had sent to Germany could clearly see that these promises could not be kept and that quite possibly there would have been little point in trying to improve the armed forces anyway, since now we should have been considering the prospects for peace, not war, the hope for victory nonetheless clouded the vision of the military leadership. The military leadership strayed into the slippery field of politics. It took such a firm and resolute stand in support of continuing the war that anyone who dared to consider that Hungary could finish the war without the consent of the Germans and indeed even against their wishes was branded a traitor.

The chief of the general staff ascertained that in the east the Germans no longer had any substantial reserves because they had been compelled to send all the forces at their disposal to Italy and the Balkans. The numerical superiority of the enemy had left Germany in a tight corner. This was why the Hungarian military leadership wanted to support Germany by sending occupation soldiers to the Balkans. By doing so, they hoped to prevail on the Germans to agree to send the Hungarian occupation divisions in Russia home in exchange. However, only a layman could have hoped that the Germans would give up the Hungarian divisions on the Russian front when there were no other forces available that could have been used in their place.

Thus, this notion, which was the only argument which could have been taken seriously and might have offered some justification for sending occupying forces to the Balkans, also came to nothing.

Szombathelyi continued:

---

98   In other words, the borders of the medieval kingdom of Hungary.

Chapter VII

"The withdrawal of the second army would make our situation easier, but it should not prompt us to soothe ourselves with the thought that the war has lost its seriousness for us, and now our only task will be to watch the events unfold and indulge in speculation. Speculation always lures people towards the thought that it is not necessary to make sacrifices. The essence of speculation, thus, is shirking the duty to fight. This will take us to a slippery ethical slope! If we are not careful, then the Hungarian will be in a position of inferiority to every enemy and in every combat duty. He will fear everything, thus he must be given to understand that the respite that the second army has been given with this withdrawal from battle is only temporary, and we must prepare for difficult new tasks, tasks which we will have to fight in order to accomplish.

We cannot speculate. Whichever side wins, neither will see to it that we prevail in our mission. Rather, we must fight to achieve this ourselves. We must awaken the nation, lest it fare as it fared in 1918. It may now well come to pass again that half the nation does not wish to fight because the Germans will be defeated anyway, so now everything is in vain anyway. The other half will not fight because the Anglo-Saxons will triumph anyway, so now justice, human rights, and international law will triumph, and we can all take comfort in this. The fact that these were the victors in 1918 no one seems to remember.

This must not happen, for a large layer of the nation is still imbued with a sense of honor and the fighting spirit. They wish to remain Hungarians and heroes (!) under all circumstances, and if they cannot help in any other way, then they would prefer to die as heroes than accept the cowardly servility and compromises of 1918 and 1919. This brave layer, this fighting spirit merits our protection and support, lest it be ground down by continuous wariness and caution. Thus, it would be a sin not to give them the chance to redeem the reputation of our nation in heroic battles and offer a shimmering example for later generations, an example of which there is dire need precisely because of 1918–1918. Ever since Trianon, generations have stood in line, valiant men and war-ready Hungarian souls, who have sworn their loyalty to the Hungarian cause and the Hungarian nation, and who were always preparing to step forward and take a stand when the hour struck, and now, precisely in times of crisis, they should subordinate themselves to the layer that always shunned duty, that always speculated and feared, that was never able to save anything, but rather had even lost its honor. They were the people who, though perhaps well-intentioned, gnawed at the roots of the living nation and destroyed its crown."

The military leaders who gave voice to these thoughts espoused the same principles and views with regards to the continuation of the war as the people who planned and committed the takeover of power in October 1944, who in the autumn of 1944 branded those who had not been willing to continue the pointless war traitors—those who, having assessed the situation with foresight, had not bellowed empty slogans or incited anyone to play the hero, but rather had boldly accepted that our paths, the Hungarian and the German, were now splitting, and although regrettably until now we may have proceeded down them together, we could not follow Hitler into national suicide. The fanatics who proclaimed these ideas had forgotten that we were no longer a member state of the Austro-Hungarian Monarchy, and we must be guided not by imperial interests, but rather solely by the interests of the Hungarian nation.

Then there were the foresighted people, the people who "indulged" in "speculation," of whom I consider myself one. Szombathelyi attacked me as well, in a veiled manner, because in February 1943 I had foiled the plan to occupy Serbia and the agreement he had already reached with the Germans concerning this. In the course of our work, we always kept the interests of the nation in mind first and foremost. We were not cowardly or servile.

The "professional and non-professional soldiers" who had been misled and the "war-ready" Hungarian souls had been the ones who, on 15 October 1944, had not wanted to submit themselves to the order given by the regent, with which he had sought to bring an end to the war, and had proclaimed—relying on the German bayonets and forgetting the interests of the Hungarian people—that they wanted to fight for a specter, a cause already lost, and then had labeled anyone who had tried to lead them to the path of sober reflection a traitor. "Crucify him," they had cried out, a sentence they proclaimed for anyone who wanted to proceed on the path of common sense. They were the military and political leaders who ran into the

Chapter VII

wall headfirst, who sacrificed untold quantities of Hungarian blood on the German altar and who squandered billions in Hungarian assets. They destroyed human lives and fortunes simply because they did not want to subordinate themselves to the stratum of the nation which, according to them, "always shunned duty, that always speculated and feared, that was never able to save anything, but rather had even lost its honor," though in reality this stratum was working to save the nation.

There is an interesting section of the memorandum in which Szombathelyi insists on the necessity of remaining on the side of the Germans and resolutely speaks out against any and all efforts to break ties with the Germans. According to Szombathelyi:

"Unquestionably, the Germans are in a tight corner today, but we would misperceive the situation if we were to think that we can simply withdraw from the alliance and abandon them. The resolve of the German military is unbreakable, its sense of discipline unflinching, and while it may be fighting hard, it can still fight and do battle, and it can deliver merciless blows to those who rise up against it.

For precisely this reason, the idea of simply abandoning the Germans, even at the risk of a German occupation, is particularly dangerous. Indeed, many people even think that a German occupation would be desirable, because it would make us look better in the eyes of the Anglo-Saxons and, furthermore, it would not last long. Anyone who thinks this has not thought the idea through, or otherwise he would soon have recoiled in fear. First and foremost, we would be occupied not by the Germans, but by the Romanians and the Slovaks, and even—the miseries they have suffered notwithstanding—by the Croats, who would soon take back the territories that were theirs according to the Treaty of Trianon, and indeed even more, and they would plunder and pillage these territories of all their wealth. As far as what this might mean, it suffices to refer to the 1919 occupation, which lasted only a few months. But in addition to this, they would do everything to destroy the only pillar of our sovereignty and our ability to defend ourselves: our military. They would disarm it, and they would steal our weapons. Our officer corps and junior officer corps would be interned, much as they were in 1919, but now they would use the method used in Katyń. Germany would perhaps take hold only of Budapest, and they would bomb any place where the resistance was stronger. Naturally, in response, the Anglo-Saxons and the Russians would also bomb us. A few months would suffice for them to destroy us completely. Hungary would lose its sovereignty, and the land which its neighbors took from it would be lost forever.

Today, Germany is the only barrier left against Bolshevism. The Anglo-Saxons will not be able to erect a defensible barrier against the flood of Bolshevism for a long time, but in my view they do not even want to. We bore witness to this in 1918. Today, our interests still put us at Germany's side. We can still defend our interests at their side, and we can prepare for the events of the future and create a position for ourselves if we walk in their shadow. Honor also binds us to Germany. Of course, this does not mean that we will serve them without thinking. Let us not embark on adventures, but if necessary, let us make every sacrifice in order to maintain our armed forces, and if necessary, lead us not shrink back from accepting a mission in the Balkans. Perhaps the Germans will lose this world war too, but this does not mean that we will lose it, as happened in 1918, when, powerless, we collapsed, because a peaceful spirit, whose primary goal was to avoid battle and bloodshed, undermined the military strength of the nation."

Thus, the memorandum came to the conclusion that it was not only in Hungary's interests to remain at Germany's side, but also its duty, a duty dictated by honor, and no one should dare think that it might be possible to abandon them or "rise up" against them.

Many of the leading politicians were of the view that Hungary had to break ties with Hitler's Germany. Endre Bajcsy-Zsilinszky was one of them, along with the entire parliamentary opposition, with the exception of the Arrow Cross, and even István Bethlen. These parliamentary representatives were convinced that the Germans had lost the war and that there was therefore no point in continuing the fight. At a sitting of the armed forces committee of the Upper House, Bethlen insisted that we must take this step even if it meant that the Germans would occupy the country. That would do less harm than continuing this battle and joining Germany in its fall. The general staff, however, protested against this idea tooth and nail, because they could not imagine that we could turn against the German empire.

Chapter VII

It was perfectly natural that, after the stern warning that had been given by the chief of the general staff, the Hungarian government did not dare openly support taking action, because no one wanted to risk the dangers that would come with a German occupation and even possible arrest. Kállay, however, remained faithful to the resolution the government had reached in February, and he rejected Csatay's and Szombathelyi's proposal. On this occasion as well, he did not give his consent to send Hungarian occupation forces to Serbia.

In a letter addressed to the chief of the general staff on 15 September 1943, the prime minister wrote the following concerning Szombathelyi's trip to Germany:

"Having attentively studied the memorandum submitted to me by your honor, I wish to inform you of the following:

I share your reasoning and your view in every way concerning the military, military political, and even military and national spirit and ethics. However, I do not see any causal relationship between these things on the one hand and the acceptance of a mission in the Balkans on the other. Indeed, from the perspective of the survival of the Hungarian nation, I consider such an undertaking a devastating and irremediable mistake. Under no circumstances can I give my consent."

Kállay asked Szombathelyi to try to prevail on the German leadership to put the Hungarian troops in a position in which, if necessary, they could be used to protect the Hungarian borders. They had to avoid giving even the slightest hint that Hungary wanted to withdraw from the battle in Russia. He also asked the chief of the general staff to see to it that the German deliveries avoided the train lines that pass through industrial centers.

"These are the guiding principles," Kállay wrote, that I ask Your Honor always to keep in mind, and the Hungarian government cannot accept anything that deviates from these principles. If you see, in the course of the negotiations—in which I agree with your honor's intentions when I recommend the greatest possible caution—that it will not be possible to attain any results, I consider it preferable that we not attempt to bring about any change in the situation at the moment, endeavoring under all circumstances to obtain whatever relief is possible in the interests of our soldiers.

With regards to this question, the letter that was written on 29 August 1943 by Andor Szentmiklóssy, permanent Deputy to the Minister of Foreign Affairs, to the chief of the general staff is interesting. Szentmiklóssy wrote several things, including the following:

"At the request of the prime minister, I enclose a copy of the transcript that was addressed by Minister of Foreign Affairs Ghyczy to His Excellency Kállay on the questions that arose in connection with the Minister of Defense's trip to Germany.

The standpoint of the Minister of Foreign Affairs completely addresses every aspect of the question; in this fight of this, however, with reference to our last conversation, allow me to make note of a few perspectives which must be given full consideration before a decision is reached:

So far, in the war between the great powers, Hungary has only taken part in the campaign against Russia, because after the air attack against Kassa Hungary felt it had been attacked. This attitude was reinforced by the fact that the government at the time, true to its traditionally anti-Bolshevik frame of mind, saw participation in the Christian military campaign as an ethical duty. This is as clear to the Germans as it should be to everyone.

There was never any direct conflict of interest between the Anglo-Saxon powers and Hungary. As long as the war concerned only the conflict of interest between Germany and the Anglo-Saxons, Hungary strictly maintained its neutral, or non-belligerent, position. The state of war between the Anglo-Saxon powers and Hungary was not a matter of any solidarity of interest, but rather was only a consequence of external circumstances. The Germans are well aware of this as well.

England, after all, only declared war on Hungary because of Hungary's participation in the war against Russia and as a consequence of the English-Russian alliance.

We ended up in a state of war with the United States not as a consequence of a literal interpretation of our obligations according to the Tripartite Pact, but rather as an expression—made not entirely voluntarily—of our solidarity.

We only took part directly in the campaign against Yugoslavia after the stipulation on which we had agreed with the Germans had been met, namely, as a consequence of the declaration of independence by the Croat state,

Chapter VII

Yugoslavia ceased to exist. Then and only then, at the general order of the regent, did Hungarian troops occupy part of the formerly Hungarian territories that had been ceded to Yugoslavia. In light of the above, the state of war between the Anglo-Saxon powers and Hungary seems more a matter of technicality, for we have not yet actively taken part de facto in the war between Germany and the Anglo-Saxon powers. The fact that the Anglo-Saxon Air Force has attacked Hungary does not alter the essence of this situation, because the initiative still would not be taken by us and because the Anglo-Saxon Air Force has launched air attacks against territories—France, Belgium, Holland, etc.—which it regards as under foreign occupation.

Were the proposal that was made by the Minister of Defense to be accepted, this would completely upset the existing situation, and it would put a new burden on the Hungarian government, a burden more weighty than any it has shouldered so far, and this at a moment when the outcome of the war is uncertain at best.

Sooner or later, the Anglo Saxon forces will land in the Balkans, so the Hungarian army will efface them in unfamiliar territory. One of the Hungarian government's fundamental principles was that, with the exception of the campaign in Russia, it would not use the Hungarian army outside the borders of the country. Even today we cannot violate this principle, except under the gravest circumstances. Indeed we should make every effort to bring an end to the exception of the campaign in Russia.

Finally, I would be so bold as to note that a few months ago, when the general military situation seemed considerably more favorable from Germany's perspective, we rejected a proposal to send a considerably smaller force to the Balkans. In my modest opinion, we must do this today as well, because the considerations that were valid then today bear even more weight."

On 16 September 1943, after these preparatory measures and debates, the chief of the general staff traveled to Germany, to the general headquarters, to attempt to secure the return to Hungary of the second army, or at the very least to have the seventh and eighth divisions, which were being used as an occupation force, positioned along the Kiev-Lemberg train line and thus brought closer to the Hungarian border, and also to refuse to send Hungarian soldiers to the Balkans.

The situation, which seemed difficult, was resolved fairly smoothly, but also to no real effect. There was hardly any mention of the issue about which the Hungarian government was the most concerned, namely that the Hungarian government send Hungarian troops to secure the German supply lines in the Balkans. Keitel was the only person who mentioned that he had made this request of the Hungarian and the Bulgarian Ministers of Defense. Szombathelyi did not even bring up the question.

With regards to the general situation and future developments, Szombathelyi and Hitler exchanged interesting and important words, as did Keitel and General Zeitzler.

Szombathelyi wrote the following about the conversation he had with Hitler:

"Hitler began the conversation with the events in Italy. He noted that they had created a grave situation… In connection with this, more critical situations would arise. The Anglo-Saxons would continue their military operations in Italy. They might even begin operations in the Balkans. If the Anglo-Saxons were to attack in the Balkans, the German army in Italy would immediately launch a counterattack.

He spoke a great deal about the Italian situation. He looked back on the events, but he said nothing new in connection with them.

In connection with the general situation, he noted that the era of grand military campaigns had come to an end. No decisive campaigns were to be expected on either side.

In connection with reinforcing the Balkans and the Italian front, forces had to be removed from the Russian front. Thus, there were no reserves left there. On the Russian front he would use the tactic of diversion, as he had done until now. In the Balkans, however, he wanted to create central reserves. In connection with the Bosnian partisans, he mentioned that he would settle accounts with them.

There was no talk of the participation of Hungarian forces in the Balkans.

He mentioned that within a few days the submarine war would be launched again, and within a few months the Air Force would launch an offensive. The English should not think that they have nothing to worry about. They would soon get their answer. He was planning a devastating military campaign against the English for the spring.

Chapter VII

In his opinion, the Anglo-American attacks were now coming to their culmination. Hitler asked what the second Hungarian army was doing at the moment. I mentioned," Szombathelyi writes, "that one division was fighting in the first line, while the others had been redeployed towards the back. The command headquarters had been moved to Kremenets, and the material base was in Stanyslaviv. I called Hitler's attention to the fact that at the withdrawal it would be very important to have the eighth army corps join the seventh army corps so that the entire Hungarian army could be positioned along the natural line of communication, the Kiev-Lemberg train line. I informed him that the air attacks against Germany were having a profound effect on Hungary. People were filled with fear, and they wanted to avoid suffering such attacks at all costs.

At this, Hitler interrupted me:

A nation that could not endure the air attacks would suffer the same fate as the Italians. The Germans had behaved exemplarily, and they had made jokes about these horrific events. Even the people of the Rhineland were resolutely withstanding the strikes, even though they were the softest people. Someone who has lost everything becomes hard and ruthless. He demands vengeance, not a separate peace.

And besides, the industrial losses were not nearly as severe as people generally thought. On the basis of the reports, one would have thought on the first occasion that there had been losses of 100 percent, and then 60 percent. In the end, it turned out that the entire loss was 15–20 percent, which we could replace within a few months. The industry in the Rhineland had not suffered major damages, since work was underway almost everywhere, in spite of the damages that had been endured, and industrial production was continuously on the rise, and in his view that was the most important thing."

The conversation with Zeitzler and Keitel had brought nothing new. All signs indicated that the Germans were on the defensive and retreating on all fronts, or as they said, they were "continuing the diversion." They had no reserves left. They were incapable of launching any far-reaching counterattack.

The most striking thing was that now Hitler himself had said that "the era of grand military campaigns has come to an end." In other words, he no longer spoke of a final victory! He sought consolation and hope in mutual exhaustion. He erred in his assessment of the situation and the ability of the German people to resist. Alas, even after all this, our leaders still did not dare take action. They did not see the ominous future! They still believed that they could hold the Russians off at the ridges of the Carpathian Mountains until the Anglo-Saxons arrived either from the west or from the Balkans.

Szombathelyi said that the German retreat and the enemy advances towards the Hungarian borders gave him no respite. He felt that he could not stand by idly and watch as the Germans sacrificed Hungarian troops in the defense of their own interests, without even involving the Hungarian general staff in the planning or oversight of the military operations. The Germans were not even willing to provide any information concerning the situation.

For precisely this reason, in November 1943 Szombathelyi traveled to the German general headquarters, and when he was not given reassuring answers to his questions, he again went to Hitler's general headquarters on 24 January 1944 to get a clear decision concerning the questions and be given some orientation. As he himself said, the chief of the general staff saw that the eastern front had weakened significantly, in particular because he knew that the German military leadership, anticipating an Anglo-Saxon beach landing, had moved a significant share of the fighting force to the western front. Thus, we may have to retreat from an overwhelming Russian attack and pull the frontline back to the Carpathians. In this case, however, it would be necessary to withdraw not only the two Hungarian army corps serving in Russia as an occupation force to the Carpathians to defend the borders of Hungary, but the whole Hungarian military.

Thus, the chief of the general staff still believed, in spite of the grave and alarming situation, that it would be possible to stop the Russians at the Carpathians, even though since Stalingrad the Soviet forces had been continuously pushing back the opposing forces on the eastern front with a momentum that showed no signs of waning. There was no foundation whatsoever, then, for the idea that the Germans, while also preparing for an Anglo-Saxon landing in the west and continuing the military campaign in the east, would be able to stop the Russians along the crest of the Carpathians.

Chapter VII

After November 1943, the situation continued to worsen. The Germans retreated, so in some places the Russians were only 300 kilometers from the Hungarian border. The chief of the general staff considered it necessary to discuss with the German military leadership how the Hungarian army would collaborate to defend the Carpathians. He wanted to regulate the manner in which the Hungarian army would participate and the lines of command. He even wanted to discuss the political and economic advantages that we could expect to enjoy in connection with this, though the general staff would not have been able to make any decisions in these questions anyway.

On 23 January, the regent instructed Szombathelyi to ask Hitler to bring the Hungarian occupation forces further to the south, if possible, to Galicia. The most important demand, however, was that—and on this the regent agreed with Prime Minister Kállay—the defense of the Carpathians be entrusted exclusively to Hungarian soldiers. Kállay justified this wish with the observation that in this case, it would be possible to avoid being attacked by the Russians.

During his conversation with Szombathelyi, Field Marshal Keitel characterized as almost laughable the suggestion that the German line would retreat to the Carpathians. According to him, the Russians were already weakened. They had no fresh reserves. In contrast, in the period between March and May 1944, Germany would put out 42 divisions and three SS divisions. Keitel also doubted that the Anglo-Saxons would actually land in the west. Since he considered it inconceivable that the Russians, having broken through the German line, would advance to the Carpathians, it was superfluous to discuss this question, much as it was superfluous to discuss how the Hungarian military would take part in the defense of the Carpathians.

Hitler received Szombathelyi at 10 o'clock in the evening. In response to Horthy's request, he immediately noted that it would not be possible to regroup the Hungarian forces, because the Germans did not have forces at their disposal with wish they would be able to relieve the Hungarian soldiers. The ability of the military to resist and, indeed, the whole situation on the eastern front depended on ensuring that the supply lines remain undisturbed. He himself considered it completely out of the question that the Russians would be able to push forward to the Carpathians, for "if that happens, then Europe is already lost."

Both Hitler and Keitel thus firmly refused even to consider the idea of using the Hungarian soldiers in Galicia, in the territory near the Hungarian border. When this question had come up in September of the previous year, Keitel had already said at the time that it might be possible to justify bringing the Hungarian second army home, but this might have very serious political consequences, and the enemy might be able to make good use of this.

Since Szombathelyi was unable to arrive at any agreement on the question of the return home of the second army or the defense of the Carpathians, he considered it necessary to familiarize the German military leadership with these questions in writing. On 14 February 1944, he sent a memorandum to Field Marshal Keitel. In this memorandum, he called attention to the importance of the Danube Basin and to the fact that maintaining control over and defending it was in the interests not only of Hungary, but also of the German Reich.

The Germans were now turning their attention to the western front and anticipating an Allied landing. By now, the battles they were fighting with the enemy in the east were intended only to buy time, and it seemed as if, by drawing the enemy out as they pulled back, they were striving to bring them into a disadvantageous position so that then they would be able to deliver a decisive blow. However, the retreat on the eastern front created a situation which put Hungary's territory at risk, because it was now only 250 kilometers from the frontline. And we had to plan for further retreats as well.

"According to the Hungarian records, the Russians have 60 reserve divisions at their disposal, and if they deploy this force in the territory of Rivne-Vinnytsia, they can easily break through the eastern front, which would then be broken into the regions falling to the north and south of the Pripet Marshes.

The mobilization and deployment of the Hungarian military force will take a considerable amount of time, which is why I wanted to be properly informed in January, because if the eastern front retreats further, towards the Carpathians, the chief of the Hungarian general staff must be informed of the possible use of the Hungarian military force. If the theater of war is pushed back to the Carpathians, then the Hungarian forces must take part in

Chapter VII

this as well, since we are determined to defend our borders under any circumstances, and the Hungarian military will show firm resistance there."

After presenting several problems that remained to be clarified, Szombathelyi asked Keitel not to interpret the questions he had raised as pushiness or petulance, "for however pleasant the thought may be that the older sibling, the powerful German Reich, will fight and protect us, it is dangerous for a small nation to be lulled by this thought. Not to mention the fact that the army must be psychologically prepared."

He then requested that the seventh and eighth Hungarian occupation army corps be unified and brought to a territory bordering Hungary.

The memorandum contained one more striking and very interesting sentence.

Szombathelyi was convinced that "at the end of the war, only the Germans and the Hungarians will still be fighting, as happened in the First World War." This prophecy, alas, was fulfilled. Everyone turned their backs on the Germans in time, the Italians, the Finns, the Romanians, the Bulgarians, the Slovaks, the Croats—only we remained in the yoke. We were unwilling to grasp the fundamental directive of national existence! We were the only ones who were blind and deaf when Mussolini fell from power. We endured the occupation of the country on 19 March 1944 without complaint. We followed neither the Romanian nor the Finnish examples. Our politicians and our soldiers helped Szálasi, the apostle of the Arrow Cross madness, assume his place at the head of the country, and thus, together with Germany, we fell!

Chapter VIII

19 March – 15 October, 1944

The Germans grew increasingly suspicious of Kállay, who himself had sensed that he must seek an agreement with the Allies. He tried, taking timid steps and keeping them secret. Some of the members of the Hungarian government, however, were blind supporters of Germany, to such an extent, indeed, that when disbelief and uncertainty were spreading even among the circles of the German military leadership, they continued to believe in a German victory, and they were convinced that we had to hold out and remain at Germany's side. They were opposed to any line of thinking that dared even hint at the possibility of Hungary's withdrawal from the war.

The official propaganda was still piping the old tune. It still praised the might of the Germans, and the reports and other alarming rumors of the devastating attacks launched by the Anglo-Saxon bombers kept the public in a state of continuous terror.

The Germans sensed that only a small portion of the Hungarian people still believed in them. In some of his speeches Kállay had sought to divert suspicion from himself, but in vain. The simple fact that he had not financially completely ruined the Jews in spite of the Jewish laws, and he had not created ghettos or had Jews deported, but at most had dealt a blow to them with the labor units, all this only exacerbated the German government's distrust. Hitler had received reports from his intelligence agents which had convinced him that the Kállay government was trying to reach an agreement with the west. This had persuaded him to remove the Kállay government forcefully and to compel the government to appoint a cabinet which, with its unconditional devotion to Germany, would provide a guarantee that Hungary would not follow the example of Italy and would remain steadfastly on the side of the Reich.

The Hungarian government received reports concerning the impending German move. The first bits of news to arrive were conflicting, but one could nonetheless tell that troops were being concentrated along the western borders of Hungary. The chief of the general staff asked the German military attaché how much of this news was true, and the Minister of Foreign Affairs asked the same question of the German ambassador. Both the attaché and the ambassador gave reassuring answers. As it later turned out, neither was telling the truth. Neither the government nor the chief of the general staff thought it possible that the Germans would occupy Hungary, for they were convinced that the Germans would not want to shoulder the strain of new military and political tension, which could go as far as an open rift or break.

On 17 March 1944, the regent traveled to Klessheim at Hitler's request. He was accompanied by Minister of Foreign Affairs Jenő Ghyczy, Minister of Defense Lajos Csatay, and Chief of the General Staff Szombathelyi. In Klessheim, they met for talks with Hitler and the German leaders on 18 March. Hitler reproached Horthy for the conduct of the Kállay government. He tried to prove that the Hungarian government was playing a two-faced game, for while it strove to convince the Germans that it was remaining faithfully at the side of the Axis powers, it was seeking to establish ties with the western powers. The Hungarian government, in his view, was winking at the left-wing, and preparations were underway for a left-wing putsch in Hungary. In order to prevent this putsch, he had already ordered his troops to occupy Hungary and help the regent ensure that a government would be formed in Hungary that was reliable from the point of view of the Germans.

This was the account given by the regent to Mihály Arnóthy-Jungerth, the permanent deputy to the Minister of Foreign Affairs, of his meeting and confrontation with Hitler. (Mihály Arnóthy-Jungerth told me this himself, when he and I spoke in the camp in Pocking about the events that brought about the country's fall.)

When Horthy entered Hitler's reception room on 18 March, Schmidt, Hitler's translator, was also present. When the regent noticed this, he expressed his disappointment that someone else was going to be present for the conversation. He asked Hitler to confer with him one on one. Hitler sent Schmidt out of the room. Hitler then reproached Horthy, contending that the Hungarian government was in talks with the Anglo-Saxons and wanted to abandon the Germans. The regent protested against this accusation.

Chapter VIII

Hitler, however, stubbornly insisted on the accusations, claiming that he had proof. Horthy was consistent in his insistence that this was not true. He also gave his word that, as long as he was regent, Hungary would not abandon the Germans. Even at this, Hitler was not willing to change his view. He announced that he had already taken the preparatory measures to send German soldiers to Hungary. In the meantime, he placed a document in front of the regent of according to which the German soldiers had marched into Hungary with the consent of the regent.

Horthy pushed this document to the side. He protested against the occupation of his country and also against the fact that Hitler had stuck to his accusations even though he had given his word that the accusations were baseless. He insisted that Hitler had no right to doubt his words. Then he left Hitler's room.

After he had left, he recounted the events to the members of his entourage. It was then announced that they should go to the lunch, to which the regent said that he would not take part in the meal. He wanted to have lunch in his room.

The members of his entourage tried to dissuade him, saying that this would be an insult to their host, Hitler, and they asked the regent to take part in the lunch. They managed to prevail on him to join the others for lunch. The mood was tense and cold. After the meal, Horthy and Hitler conferred again in the room next to the dining hall, but they could not arrive at any mutual understanding, for Hitler stuck to the accusations. Horthy eventually brought the debate to an end by saying that he would withdraw to his quarters and depart immediately.

In the course of the next discussion, which was between Hitler and Szombathelyi, the chief of the general staff strove to make amends and remedy the situation, which threatened to culminate in a complete rift, for Hitler wanted to have the regent arrested. Szombathelyi told him that this would be the biggest mistake he could make. It was cause a scandal so far-reaching that Germany would lose Hungary once and for all. He would give the Allied press a wonderful propaganda opportunity were he to do this. Hitler did not easily give up the idea of having Horthy arrested. (Szombathelyi told me all this himself in the course of one of our walks in Sopronkőhida.)

Horthy gave in to his entourage, and he gave up his resolution not to name a government. Ribbentrop first suggested that Horthy name Szombathelyi prime minister. Szombathelyi, however, recommended Sztójay instead. Later, Szombathelyi also informed me that Hitler had told him that he only sought to acquire a political guarantee, since he was not satisfied with the conduct of the Kállay government. In spite of the warning that he had given the regent in Klessheim in April 1943, no changes had taken place in Hungarian politics. He had no ill-will against Hungary. It was in Germany's interests that a strong, independent Hungary stand at its side. He knew that Hungary had always been an independent kingdom, and not simply a part of the Austrian empire, like the Czech lands. At the moment, it was simply a matter of his troops, which were on the advance, marching into and occupying Hungary. Then, once he had reached his goal, within two or three weeks he would make the country free again.

Thus, the regent and his entourage left Klessheim with this agreement in mind. The first wave of outrage, regrettably, subsided. The regent had given in and accepted the suggestions of his advisor, who counselled restraint, and he had not broken ties with the Germans. Horthy now knew that he could not do anything to prevent the occupation, for in the meantime the armored divisions had crossed into Hungarian territory. In the morning hours, an order was issued from his train instructing the Hungarian authorities not to resist the Germans, because that would have meant bloodshed. However, there was resistance in some places. There could be no talk of direct opposition, however, because according to the chief of the general staff, part of the army and, in particular, part of the officer corps was completely under the influence of right-wing politicians, and there would not have been a show of unified opposition even if an order to oppose the Germans had been given. In his view, the army was completely supportive of the Germans, and it was only waiting for the political leadership finally to end up in the hands of the extreme right-wing parties. It would not have taken up the fight against the Germans, as indeed proved true on 15 October 1944. The regent had lost. He had to confront that, and this was why he had given an order to avoid a show of opposition to the Germans.

If one considers the events that took place in Klessheim and the conduct of the people who were there coldly and objectively, from the perspective of

Chapter VIII

the likely fate of the nation, one must concede that in Klessheim Hungary's fate was sealed, because they failed to take advantage of the moment at which they had every reason to break once and for all with the Germans and withdraw from the war. Kállay's government had failed, and Horthy, as Hitler's captive, could proudly have said that he had saved Hungary's future at the cost of his own liberty and possibly life.

As Szombathelyi said, the reason for the occupation "was to be sought in the politics and personal conduct of Kállay." It had been a mistake, in his view, for Kállay to have avoided all personal contact with the German leaders, since he might have achieved more had he had a personal relationship with them. After the scolding that Horthy had been given by Hitler in 1943, he should have woken up, and he should have realized that the Germans were not guided by the subtle tools of diplomacy, but rather by the brutal use of force without scruple, and it was this force that had to be thwarted. Horthy, alas, did not realize this.

I often got information concerning the events in the world and the fluctuations in politics from Pál Fodor, the editor of *Kis Újság* ["Little Newspaper"]. I knew what was taking place in the political swamps. I learned of all of the government's important plans. This was how I knew that the regent had traveled to Klessheim on 17 March 1944. Fodor informed me that major events were approaching, and the occupation of Hungary by the Germans was imminent. I learned of the news concerning this in a definite form on 18 March. I also learned that the chief of the general staff had instructed Colonel Bajnóczy to interrogate the German military attaché. He had denied, however, that the German divisions that had advanced on Hungary's borders had any kind of aggressive intentions. They were only performing exercises. The idea of an attack against Hungary was a fairytale at most. My informant, however, insisted in spite of this that the Germans were going to attack Hungary. The people in the Ministry of Foreign Affairs had come to this conclusion as well, even if the ambassador in Berlin, Sztójay, had not said a word about it, though he had now been in Vienna for weeks.

In the late morning hours of 18 March, I received a telephone call from the Ministry of Foreign Affairs. I was informed that the German troops had already reached Győr and were on their way to Budapest. I was told to leave Budapest immediately, since as a consequence of the impending German occupation I would no longer be safe. There was good reason to fear that the Germans would arrest me. I did not, however, take this advice. On Sunday 19 March, in the early morning hours I again received reports on the basis of which I could tell that the news was true. The Germans had crossed into the country and indeed were already in Budapest. They took control of the general headquarters, the castle district, and the Hungarian Radio. In other words, they were the rulers of the land.

They said that Minister of Internal Affairs Ferenc Keresztes-Fischer, his younger brother Lajos Keresztes-Fischer (the regent's Adjutant-General), parliamentary representatives Károly Rassay, Károly Peyer, and Géza Malasits, Count György Pallavicini, Count József Somssich, and many other leading politicians had been arrested by the Germans. Endre Bajcsy-Zsilinszky, who had put up armed resistance, had been shot. I later learned that he had not been killed, but rather had only been seriously wounded in the firefight that had broken out when they had tried to apprehend him.

I was enraged by this. This is how our ally treats us? It seems that Germany sees itself as our enemy? We must break all ties with it! We must draw the far-reaching conclusions that this brutal attack entails. We must withdraw from the war! God himself has given us a last chance, served up on a silver platter! The regent must resign, or at the very least he must not appoint a new government. If they occupy Hungary completely and they appoint a new government, it is now clear that as far as we are concerned, the war is over. There are more than enough examples of this. The case of Norway, of Belgium, of Denmark. The Germans occupied these countries. They even appointed governments, but these countries nonetheless had not submitted to them. We would do this as well. No more Hungarian blood would flow for German interests. The world would see that we were not willing to lie down in front of the German boot of our own will. This was how I spoke with the people who asked me what would happen now.

The regent and his entourage had not yet returned from Klessheim. Some people even said that the Germans had arrested them. This, however, was not true. The regent's special train arrived in Budapest in the morning hours. By

Chapter VIII

that time, the city and the administration was already in the hands of the Germans. Kállay had resigned, and he had taken sanctuary in the Turkish embassy. Thus, the Germans were unable to arrest him.

After the regent had returned from Klessheim and appointed the Sztójay government, Mihály Arnóthy-Jungerth had an audience with him. As I have already recounted, the regent brought up the events in Klessheim, and he asked Arnóthy-Jungerth whether he could have done anything other than appoint Sztójay prime minister. To this, Arnóthy-Jungerth replied that he could have done something else. There was the example of the Danish king. By this, he meant that Horthy should not have appointed Sztójay, and he should have resisted the German demands. Perhaps he even should have stepped down. At this, the regent struck the elbow rests of his armchair with both hands and said the following:

"I do not insist on this chair, I will leave, but I cannot watch idly as Archduke Albrecht or Szálasi himself takes my place!"

Nonetheless, it would have been better to have followed the example of the Danish king, for not only did the occupation of the country become permanent, but soon the regent was removed from the seat that was then taken not by Archduke Albrecht, but by the far more dangerous figure: Szálasi.

Sztójay was not eager to accept the mandate concerning the restructuring of the government, because he felt he was both old and sick. The regent, however, essentially compelled him to, justifying his insistence with the contention that Sztójay had the complete trust of the Germans. Under Sztójay's leadership, the country slipped completely to the right, to the edge of the precipice. The German occupying forces put every sign of life in the country under their control. Ministers and politicians who were not faithful adherents of the Germans were arrested or were compelled to flee or go into hiding. The arrest and deportation of Minister of Internal Affairs Ferenc Keresztes-Fischer and his younger brother, the regent's Adjutant-General Lajos Keresztes-Fischer threw open the gates and a series of arrests followed. The arrests of Károly Rassay, Count György Pallavicini, Count György Apponyi, Károly Peyer, Géza Malasits, Dezső Laky, Lipót Baranyay, Károly Huszár, Deputy Minister of Foreign Affairs Andor Szentmiklóssy, and diplomat Aladár Szegedy-Maszák showed clearly that the Germans were conducting themselves as if they were in an enemy country, and the Hungarian government was a craven servant of the German commander.

Now I was earnestly advised to flee Budapest immediately. At this, my wife and I left for Klotildliget to stay with our daughter.

After a week of labor pains, the Sztójay government was formed. The appointment of this government was an enormous mistake. First and foremost, Sztójay was not suitable, as a person, to lead Hungary's government in such difficult and dire times. His outlook, which it was widely known was pro-German, and his political inexperience essentially put him in the hands of the politicians who were under Imrédy's control and who had no aversion whatsoever to having Szálasi take over leadership of the country in Horthy's place. They were the politicians who, not considering the strategic situation and misjudging the abilities of the Germans, not realizing that Germany had reached the limits of its strength and was approaching the bottom of the slope, still believed that they could win this war. They counted on the conflicts that allegedly had arisen between the Anglo-Saxons and the Russians. These conflicts, however, were not so deep that the Anglo-Saxons and the Russians would part ways before achieving victory. These politicians did not consider the actual situation or the tremendous numerical superiority of the allies. They believed that it sufficed to proclaim, as Sztójay said during his first speech to the parliament, that "we will triumph, because we must triumph, and we want to triumph!" Sztójay, however, did not speak about whether or not the preconditions for this desire to win had been met: the strength, the necessary materials, and the psychological endurance. It does not suffice to proclaim the desire to triumph, for if one does not have the necessary strength, this proclamation becomes an empty phrase, and it only fools people who are unfamiliar with the situation. They completely misled the Hungarian public, which was kept unaware of the magnitude of the global war. It did not fathom the strength of the allied great powers or the unflinching determination with which almost every people of the world supported them against Germany, which had been utterly abandoned, and Japan, which was fighting in the Far East and proceeding down its own, separate path.

One of the first acts of the Sztójay government was to issue a decree compelling Jews to wear a yellow star. It closed Jewish businesses and declared

Chapter VIII

that all Jewish property was being taken by the state. It began to steal from and deport Jews on the basis of the German model. For a long time, I had managed to hinder efforts to send the people in the labor units beyond the borders of the country and pull workers out of economic life, but this now came to an end once and for all. The deportations began. Every effort of the people in the government was intended to eradicate the Jewry from the country as quickly as possible. Andor Jaross, László Baky, and László Endre were the loudest voices. The newspapers which had always done little more than incite hostility offered the most fervent support for their policies, and they attacked people—including me—who did not have the heart to be inhumane.

They rounded up the Jews in the areas of the country outside of Budapest. First, they set up ghettos in all of the cities, into which they mercilessly crowded these unfortunate people. Then the deportations out of the country began, in part to Galicia and in part to Germany. The brutality with which the deportations were conducted went beyond anything imaginable. 70-100 people were crowded into a train car designed to transport 40 people, and then the doors were closed. Eye-witnesses told me of how the henchmen who were working under the leadership of László Baky and László Endre carried out their orders with a brutal pitilessness that could not have been more merciless. The doors to the cars were only opened when the trains had reached their destinations, and whoever had survived could get out. The saddest thing was that not a single leading politician or member of the government raised a voice in protest against these atrocities. They washed their hands. The Christian Churches warned Sztójay of the likely international consequences of the deportation of the Jews and, in general, the inhumanity of the treatment to which the Jews were being subjected. The government, however, took care to ensure that news of these steps would not reach the Hungarian public. People spoke only in secret about the protests, which, however, had virtually no effect whatsoever.

When the bombing of Budapest began as the first repercussion of the appointment of the Sztójay government and the measures that had been taken against the Jews, the sound of people crying out for humane compassion became audible. The newspapers spoke out. The enemy bombers were accused of cruelty, of murdering children, women, and the elderly.

The brutal German supreme authority became increasingly visible from behind the Sztójay government. On 17 April, the Gestapo arrested General Staff Colonel Gyula Kádár, leader of the second division of the directorate of the general staff. They had compiled an indictment against him consisting of 26 points. It made clear that the Germans knew the most carefully guarded secrets of the directorate of the general staff. It also made clear that there were people in the immediate surroundings of the chief of the general staff through whom the Germans had acquired knowledge of the most secret affairs.

Later, General Staff Colonel Ottó Hatz was arrested too, the former military attaché in Sofia. However, in the end they were compelled to release him, because they could not prove any of the charges against him.

On 18 April, at the request of the German ambassador, Horthy relieved Szombathelyi of his position. In order to avoid arrest, he too went into hiding. He was brought before the court of the general staff directorate under the accusation of having been one of the people who tried to establish ties with the western powers. The military tribunal acquitted him of this charge, but the proceedings against him were still underway when Szálasi came to power. In any event, the example of Szombathelyi should have served as a warning to all of the pro-German politicians and officers. He had been a faithful adherent of the Germans for some time, but as became clear, even this was not merit enough. The Germans dropped Szombathelyi, and they contrived the most serious accusations against him.

At the request of the Germans, Lieutenant General János Vörös was appointed new chief of the general staff. First, the regent had appointed Colonel General Géza Lakatos chief of the general staff. However, under pressure from the Germans he had been compelled to withdraw this appointment even before it had been announced. The German ambassador had wanted János Vörös to serve as chief of the general staff. At first, the government had not wanted to give in to the German demands, but after five days of wrangling they were compelled to accept the German wish.

The Germans seemed to be satisfied with the internal affairs situation in Hungary, because they had gotten a guarantee that the Hungarians would now be the dutiful servants of German interests. János Vörös even introduced himself at the German headquarters, where they discussed military

Chapter VIII

questions, equipment, and organization, and they also agreed that the first cavalry and seventh light infantry divisions would be sent to the eastern front and Hungary would put one battalion at the disposal of the Germans to be sent to Greece to secure the train line.

After having returned to Hungary, the new chief of the general staff János Vörös wrote a letter to Field Marshal Keitel in which he thanked him for his kind reception. Among the things he wrote was the following: "I would like to express my most sincere thanks to Your Honor for the very kind and friendly reception you gave me, and for acknowledging our particular situation and the financial support you have promised in connection with this. The days I spent at the headquarters of the general staff at the beginning of the beach landing will remain an unforgettable time in my life.

After having returned to Hungary, I immediately reported for an audience with the regent and informed him of my visit to the headquarters. In particular, I enlightened the regent as to the situation and the likely developments on the eastern front, which was presented by the leader with such extensive knowledge of the details."

He then repeated the regent's request that the cavalry division be removed from the frontline to rest once the rainy season had begun. He then continued: "in accordance with Your wishes, I have ordered that we ascertain the superfluous manpower. I hope that, in the interests of sharing the burdens of war, we will be of some assistance in this sphere as well, to the extent that circumstances permit."

Only some of the occupying soldiers left Hungary, Hitler's promise notwithstanding. While internal affairs was dominated by the bloody elimination of the Jews, in the military sphere the Sztójay government put itself completely at the service of the Germans, who gave the Hungarian general staff no say whatsoever in the oversight of military operations. Having promised everything, the Germans kept not a single one of their promises.

Sztójay had no real authority. Everyone did what they wanted. The Minister of Foreign Affairs and his secretaries in particular went their own way.

I lived in complete seclusion in Klotildliget, but I never failed to share my view of the harm that was being done by the Sztójay government with the people who sought me out, and I always emphasized that the Germans were not going to win this war, and we would pay a terrible price for the inhumane measures of this government. Those who survived would pay a high price for the acts of Sztójay, Jaross, Szász, Kunder, Baky, Endre, Imrédy, and their ilk.

They had not yet arrested me, but they were keeping me under observation. A German regimental headquarters was set up not far from our villa in Klotildliget. As the commander of the regiment said once in the course of a dinner at the home of a family. They were watching me. Every day, a car or a motorcycle would pass by our gate. They would stop for a moment, and then continue on. A little while later, they would repeat the game. This lasted for four weeks. Soon, they stationed a German junior officer in my home. The German sergeant behaved perfectly politely, but he asked my servants what was going on and he kept his eye on me. I also learned that two Hungarian detectives were staying with a teacher of German ancestry in the village, and they had also been given the task of keeping me under observation. In the end, I wrote a letter to Deputy Prime Minister Jenő Rátz instructing them not to restrict my freedom of movement and not to write about me in the party newspapers, and to give me permission and the necessary papers to travel to Budapest and Ipolyvisk. In his reply, Rátz denied that I was being kept under observation and indeed that any proceedings were underway against me at all. He promised to put a stop to the press campaign that had been launched against me. He consoled me with the assurance that he knew from experience that people who stood or had stood at the forefront of public life had to resign themselves to the fact that they would be unjustly attacked, much as he had been attacked for five long years.

One day, a gendarmerie sergeant came to Klotildliget who presented himself as a delegate of the third division of the general staff directorate. He produced a document to identify himself that had been signed by Colonel Henkey. He was looking for a friend of mine, József Hartmann. He wanted me to tell him Hartmann's address, and he tried to trick me into revealing it with the feeble claim that they wanted to protect my friend from the Germans and prevent him from being arrested by the Germans by taking him into protective custody.

Naturally, I did not believe a word of this story, and the man left without having accomplished his task. At the train station, however, he instructed the ticket clerk to call him immediately if Hartmann were to show up in Klotildliget. I was very disturbed by all this, and I wrote a letter to János Vörös in which I protested against the steps they had taken. I wrote that if they wanted to ask me something, they should not send a gendarme to harass me.

The following case offers a good example of how suspicious Hitler was of the Hungarians. Colonel General Géza Lakatos submitted a proposal to the German general headquarters to bring the eighth Hungarian army corps, which was fighting in the area around the Pripet Marshes, closer to the seventh Hungarian army corps in Galicia so that the Hungarian soldiers would be at the disposal of the army general headquarters to defend the Carpathian Mountains. Hitler summoned Lakatos for an audience with him, and he fiercely reproached him with the contention that the Hungarians were untrustworthy. He proclaimed that he had evidence proving that the Hungarians wanted to withdraw from their alliance with the Germans. He, however, would take care to ensure that not happen. The Romanians were remaining firmly and faithfully at the side of the Germans. They were a trustworthy ally. To this, Lakatos replied that he had nothing to do with any of this, since he was a colonel general, so he could exert no influence whatsoever on government policy. Having composed himself, Hitler responded that he had received the command's suggestion and he would take it into consideration. However, he also declared that since there could be no talk of the defense of the Carpathians and the battle there, the proposal could already be considered immaterial, since under no circumstances could it be adopted.

This case illustrates clearly how the German general headquarters treated Hungary, and also demonstrates that they sought at all costs to prevent the Hungarian soldiers from uniting near the borders of the country. Hungarians were suspicious in their eyes, and the Germans feared that the Hungarians would follow the example that had been set by Italy. They sensed the dangerous influence of the continuous German retreat, and they also sensed that the Hungarians were continuously losing faith. In contrast, Hitler was unwilling to acknowledge the negotiations that were being pursued by the Romanians—although these negotiations were almost public knowledge—because he would not have been able to continue the war without Romanian oil. He did not want to consider the possibility that the Romanians might turn on him, as indeed they did on 23 August 1944.

My life in Klotildliget did not change much. Old and new adherents of an anti-German political mind frame sought me out. Courageous Hungarians who even at the apex of German triumphs had predicted the coming fall and those who had only recently come to their senses and only now realized that we were racing towards the precipice. Even Szombathelyi no longer believed in a German victory. He sought me out several times in my home in Klotildliget. He said that German defeat was unavoidable and collapse was nigh. Now he openly said that what I had predicted one year earlier was going to come to pass. The German soldiers who had become involved in dealings in the village knew that I lived here, and they spoke about how I was not among their friends. Naturally, they had heard this from their commanding officers. A Gestapo lieutenant in Mosonszentjános sought out mill director István Tóth, a friend of mine, and inquired about his relationship with me. He also told him that I was not a friend of the Germans, but rather of the English. Tóth cleverly replied that Vilmos Nagy was not a friend either of the English or of the Germans, but only of the Hungarians. I could tell from this only that the investigation against me was still underway, even if Jenő Rátz assured me that it was not.

The campaign against me in the press also showed no signs of abating. It was quite natural that Imrédy and his supporters did not rest. Ferenc Rajniss, in particular, seemed to consider it his duty to attack me openly and shamelessly. They attacked me first on 14 April 1944 in *Esti Újság* in connection with the Hungarian Fashion Hall. The article turned into an affair of honor. I had offended László Csávossy Gudenus, who had signed the announcement. This affair had not even been resolved when a new attack was launched on me by *Esti Újság*. They wrote about the reasons for my departure from the ministerial seat. They published the text of the interpolation that my opponents in parliament had not been able to read aloud on 4 May 1943, and which had been expunged from the interpolation record of the House following my resignation. As I have already mentioned, Imrédy's party had circulated an unsigned leaflet among the representatives in parliament, a copy of the memorandum that they had submitted to the prime minister. *Esti Újság* published this, with appropriate embellishments, in the 27 April 1944 issue. I was no longer willing to wait passively, for I felt that I had to defend my hon-

Chapter VIII

or in front of the Hungarian court. *Este Újság* did not print the article that I sent them addressing the mistakes. They cared about scandal, not truth. I initiated a libel suit against them. After the first article, Minister of Defense Csatay intervened, and he was joined after the second by Chief of the General Staff János Vörös, who asked me what I had done after the articles attacking me had been printed and what I intended to do now. I replied in writing that I had initiated a libel suit in response to the article printed on 27 April. To this, the chief of the general staff replied—without waiting for the ruling in the libel case— that he had initiated a preliminary honor inquest against me. Thus, he had joined the politicians who were attacking me. It is possible that his political friends persuaded him to take this strange step, which was completely against regulations.

When the generals' honor committee summoned me for an interrogation, they mentioned in the written summons that, if I wished to do so, I could renounce my rank. This gave me the impression that they were assuming that I would yield, that I did not want to see the fight against my slanderers through to the end and would renounce my rank in order to avoid any further investigation. I was not willing to do this. I appeared before the committee, and when I presented the summons which I had been issued to the head of the committee and protested against the call for my renouncement of my rank, the president lieutenant general apologized and asked for my forgiveness. He declared that the proceedings themselves were flawed, since the goal of a preliminary inquest was to give the commander, in this case the chief of the general staff, a clear overview of the case so that he could decide whether there was reason to pursue the case or not.

So I had ended up on a good path. The Germans were keeping me under observation and collecting information against me, and at the same time the Hungarian chief of the general staff was looking for the right moment to settle accounts with me. I had come to this point. A tragic case, but I had to fight the battle to the end, until the truth had been completely revealed. I had nothing to hide. The events that have taken place in internal and foreign affairs had completely pushed to the side the petty cases and questions. Indeed, I only mention these issues here because they belong to a description of these sad times.

Fateful Years

The petty and unjust accusations were just part of the larger political maneuver at the time, the goal of which was finally to put power in the hands of the alliance between the Party of Hungarian Renewal and the National Socialist Party.

In the interests of providing a complete picture, I cite the following passages from the report I submitted to the honor committee on 10 August 1944:

"As a member of the parliamentary committees, I consistently emphasized that we must not and cannot sacrifice more in this war. We had to replace the materials that had been lost with the destruction of the second army, and we must put together the strongest force of which the country is capable, but we must not sacrifice it fighting on the side of the Germans, for as soon as the situation of the Germans worsens, Romania will withdraw from the axis and turn against us. We must put up opposition to this. On one occasion, I explained this to Sztójay, the Hungarian ambassador in Berlin.

Thus, I did not enjoy the favor of the Germans either, because it was clear that I was not willing to accept haughty German leadership, which primarily took German interests into consideration, and because I said openly and sincerely at a combined sitting of the defense committee of the Lower House and the Upper House that the German military leadership bore the responsibility for the grave blow that had struck the second army because they had not kept the promises that the German leaders had made me personally. They had not provided the heavy weaponry which we had lacked, weaponry without which a battle today became nothing more than a superfluous massacre. Our army, which was equipped according to old ideas of war and only partially equipped with motor vehicles, was at an immeasurable disadvantage against the well-equipped Russians. With the paltry forces at its disposal, the Hungarian second army was not able to defend the expansive stretch along the Don River to which it had been assigned by the German leadership. One of our light divisions had to defend a section of the frontline some 30 kilometers long with 5,000-6,000 guns and very few machines.

The Germans had not given fodder for our horses, and as a consequence, the horses had died in heaps. We did not have enough gas for our cars or cars in general, and the vehicles broke down, leaving the second army essentially incapable of moving. I revealed all this to the people in parliament. I am quite certain

Chapter VIII

that the Germans learned of these reports. Indeed, it was reported to me that in the Hungarian embassy in Berlin people were saying that the Germans would not get Hungary's complete support as long as I was the Minister of Defense.

I must also note that in January 1943, when I was in Berlin with the Hungarian government for the occasion of Göring's birthday, the question of Hungarian-Romanian relations came up in the course of my conversation with Göring. When Göring accused us of wanting to attack the Romanians and explained that this was why he was not making any airplanes available to the army in Hungary, I openly declared that we had no intention of attacking the Romanians, but we are well aware of the support that Germany is providing Romania, and day after day we hear the Romanian leaders rousing their people against us at protest gatherings at which German officers also take part. Violations of the border provoked by the Romanians are an everyday occurrence along our border, and Antonescu has openly declared that they are fighting with the Germans and making such a tremendous sacrifice at Germany's side in order to regain northern Transylvania.

Given all this, I was not beloved of the German leaders or the Hungarian politicians who believed that the Hungarian nation must remain at Germany's side unconditionally, even if the Germans have embarked on a path that is not in our interests. In their eyes, I was not suitable as minister, because I was not willing to put the whole force and strength of the Hungarian nation at Germany's side, but rather was of the view that we must not play the last trump card in our hand.

The accusations that the Party of Hungarian Renewal had contrived against me and that two representatives of the party had wanted to read aloud in parliament as an interpolation were little more than meaningless shows of contempt, as if they had been sticking out their tongues at me. In different times, serious people never would have given them a second thought, but today, if someone were not willing to strike and persecute the Jews, if someone were not willing to bow his head to the ground in front of the Germans, if someone dared say, 'the Hungarian nation must survive, no matter how this war ends,' today these were the greatest sins."

Perhaps this submission of mine contributed to the decision of the authorities on 16 November to order my arrest.

Fateful Years

The situation on the front was continuously worsening. For the moment, only the events on the western front captured the public's attention. Following the initial hard fights, the Anglo-Saxon forces that had landed were continuously pushing the Germans out of France at an ever increasing pace. With its military operations, which had been planned with what was undoubtedly the most thorough attention to detail, the Anglo-Saxon fighting force gave clear proof of its preparedness. In the west, the Germans defended their positions with bitter tenacity, and they sent excellent soldiers into battle. At every turn, the attacking forces had to conquer a host of positions that had been designed with tremendous ingenuity. The Germans thought that the fate of the war would be decided in the west, and so they strove with all their might to drive the Anglo-Saxon forces back towards the sea and annihilate them before the Russians could launch another attack. Every unit that was not considered indispensable in the east was redeployed in the west, and thus the eastern front was drastically weakened. The opposition on the peninsula of Brittany was very stubborn and embittered. For weeks, the attacking forces were only able to push the Germans back slowly. However, when they broke through the German defensive line in Avranches on 25 July and then Anglo-Saxon forces also landed on the beaches of southern France on 15 August, the German general retreat began. Everyone could see that this was the beginning of the end.

The Russians also continuously launched attacks on various stretches of the front. Then, in the middle of August, something unexpected happened. The Russians penetrated deep into Romania, and they dealt a serious blow to the German and Romanian troops.

In response to this, on 23 August 1944, at the order of the Romanian king the Romanian soldiers, which were defending a stretch of the frontline in the area around Iași between two German armies, lay down their weapons and thus left the road to the Romanian interior open to the Russian troops. At this, the fifteen German divisions, which had been stationed, together with Romanian forces in the east, in the territory stretching to the Black Sea, now severed from the other German forces, found themselves encircled, since the lines of retreat leading back towards Transylvania had been cut in several places.

Chapter VIII

The worsening of the military situation had a palpable effect on political life in Hungary. Sztójay resigned, allegedly because of his poor health. The regent asked Colonel General Géza Lakatos, who had served as commander of the first Hungarian army, to form a new government. For the most part, Lakatos appointed politicians who—with the exception of Béla Jurcsek and Lajos Reményi-Schneller—could be characterized as anti-German. The German ambassador only reluctantly accepted the new government. The public also interpreted Sztójay's fall and the formation of the Lakatos government as the first step towards an armistice and peace. Everyone felt that we had arrived at a turning point. The rapid pace of the events spurred János Vörös, the chief of the general staff, to give an overview of the general situation and submit a proposal concerning the steps that would be necessary from a military perspective. This proposal was submitted on 4 September 1944, and it exerted a dire influence on subsequent events.

"In the sixth year of the war," János Vörös wrote, "Germany, which was in a strategically defensive position, was betrayed and abandoned by its European allies, with the exception of Hungary and Finland. (At the time, Finland had not yet broken with the Germans, but soon Finland too would turn its back on the Germans.)

The German military leadership built its military operations against Poland, the Balkans, Norway, France, and Russia (military operations which were based on and executed according to classical principles of the art of war and which were justifiably looked on in wonder by world) on the idea of the Blitzkrieg. Severing its enemies from one another, it defeated them—or sought to defeat them—separately. The German leadership was driven by the idea of annihilating its enemies one by one, before they develop the ability to strike and defeat Germany.

This vision of the German leadership suffered defeat at the hands of the Russian forces, which had unlimited space and had been inaccurately assessed. The Germans had hoped that Russia would fall in 1941, and when it did not, this gave the Allies the time they needed in order to develop the ability to strike and, in doing so, make a total German victory seem doubtful."

After this description of the situation on the individual fronts and the relative size of the forces at the disposal of the Allies, Vörös turned to the eastern front, which touched us more closely.

"The spring and then the summer Russian attacks have lost their momentum in the Baltics and in Poland. At the moment, there are no important battle operations taking place there. However, there are signs of preparations for a Russian attack.

Further Russian attacks can be expected in two primary directions:

From the area around Warsaw towards the west, in the direction of Posen and Berlin;

From the San–Vistula triangle in the direction of Krakow and Breslau[99] against the German industrial region. An attack might be launched at the same time across the Dukla pass in the direction of Budapest and Vienna.

We must count on the launch of one or both of these attacks in the near future, regardless of the battle operations taking place along other parts of the Russian frontline, and they will be launched with the intention of achieving a decisive victory.

According to the information currently available, the proportion of the Russian and German forces currently facing each other in the Baltics and Poland may be 4 to 1.

As a consequence of Romania's withdrawal from the war, the attack launched by Russian forces on the Romanian front—from the old Tripoint border to the Black Sea—has gained significant momentum, and according to the most recent reports, the Russian forces have reached the Ploiești-Bucharest-Giurgiu line. According to the Bucharest military attaché, they are advancing primarily towards the west.

The Romanian forces either have laid down their weapons or, together with the Russians, they have turned against the German forces deployed here. They have wiped out some of them, and others they have forced to retreat to the borders. There is no resistance to the advancing Russian troops here. In consequence, at the moment this section of the frontline is the most endangered part of the eastern front, and this makes the situation of the entire eastern front critical, and it may end up determining the outcome of the war.

The Russians have 75 infantry divisions and 15 armored brigades along the Romanian frontline. (In the terms we would use for our forces.)

---

99 Today Wrocław, Poland.

Chapter VIII

The Russian forces that have burst onto the Romanian plains have three choices:

They can advance, in part through the passes in the southern Carpathian Mountains and in part along the banks of the Danube River, towards the Great Hungarian Plain;

Advance towards Bulgaria;

Forge ahead in the direction of Albania, towards the Adriatic Sea.

If the Russians are guided purely by questions of military strategy, then we should expect the bulk of their forces to advance towards the Great Hungarian Plain very soon. From Hungary's perspective and the perspective of the entire eastern front, this is the most dangerous possibility. However, since recently there have been more and more signs indicating that, instead of questions of pure military strategy, conflicts of interest between the Russians and the Anglo-Saxons concerning the Dardanelles and the Balkans may come into consideration, it is possible that a kind of race will begin, and the Russians will turn first and foremost towards the Mediterranean or Adriatic Sea. Bulgaria's endeavor to declare itself neutral or, ultimately, to switch to the other side may have significant weight in an assessment of the fate of the Balkans and the Danubian Basin. Furthermore, there has been very strong partisan activity in the territory of Greece and the former Yugoslavia, which would constitute a significant additional force if the Russians were to push forward. The internal situation in Croatia is also such that, with the Russian advances, one has to count on a possible volte-face at any moment. Finally, there have even been signs of efforts to change sides in Slovakia. Although an advance of Russian troops into the Balkans would undoubtedly be unpleasant for the Anglo-Saxons, there is no reason to anticipate any military measures to counterbalance it in the near future, since there have been no serious signs so far of any approaching launch of a beach landing in Greece or the Istrian peninsula. The German forces in the Balkans are numerically inferior to the Russian forces that have arrived there.

A summary of the overall situation:

Even if the Russians achieved their greatest successes along the Romanian section of the frontline and the Hungarian-German forces that can be assembled against them do not appear to be adequate, considering the size of the Russian forces deployed on the eastern front, the most likely direction of the main Russian attack nonetheless is from Warsaw towards Berlin or, even more probably, from the San-Vistula triangle towards Breslau or the Dukla pass, accompanied naturally by a parallel attack on the Balkans.

The Scandinavian front:

... The German divisions in Finland will only be able to retreat through Norway and, as far as can be foreseen, only at the cost of considerable difficulties, so these forces cannot be counted on in the near future.

Hungary:

These changes in the situation on the frontlines have vital consequences for the military and political situation in Hungary. If the war is decided on the western front, this will constitute the least unfavorable situation for Hungary, since in this case, the victorious Anglo-Saxon powers will be able to assert their wills advantageously over the Russians. If the fall begins with the collapse of the eastern front, there will be nothing to stop the Russians from asserting their will without any inhibitions whatsoever. If the Germans assess the situation purely from the perspective of military strategy, the burning idea will inevitably come up of pulling back the fronts to the shortest possible line, the eastern borders and the eastern line of the Alps, as a consequence of which, following a transitional campaign to defend Hungary's territory, the surrender of this territory, even if only part of it, would be inevitable.

As the sketch of the situation makes clear, at the beginning of its sixth year, the European war has reached its culminating point, and in the present state of this grave crisis, the decisive moment could come at any time. Considering the events completely objectively, I would not rule out the possibility that, as a consequence of the gradually increasing numerical superiority of the enemy, the German Reich, which was leading the European battle, will be forced to abandon any thought of continuing the battle and will ask for an armistice. Indeed, it is not at all impossible that German resistance will collapse overnight.

The Hungarian leadership should prepare for any and all eventualities, including the worst, since this is the only way to ensure the country's survival. The primary element of our efforts to prepare must be the striving to ensure that, no matter what turn the events take, even if it be the direst, domestic order remain unshakeable and firm and our armed forces be and remain in a state of complete strength, ready to strike. We must be clearly aware that if the decisive moment of this war finds the country and its armed forces again in the state in which they were in 1918, the complete destruction of our homeland and people is inevitable and will come to pass with fatal certainty. Only order and the uncompromised strength of the army offer any guarantee that we will be able to bridle the ambitions of the neighboring small peoples (the Romanians, the Slovaks, the Croats, and the Serbs), for we must confront the fact that if we find ourselves at their mercy, it will mean the complete eradication of our people.

But the maintenance of our armed forces intact and of domestic order would also constitute the only factor that we could use to our advantage in the case of an armistice or peace negotiations. The example of 1918 or the events of the recent past that took place in Italy and Romania also clearly show the future that awaits a country that surrenders unconditionally. We would suffer unavoidable complete destruction on the personal and material level.

Thus, in the case of Germany's collapse, as the worst possible case, our only possible way out is armed negotiations supported with domestic order and military force. We cannot allow things to go so far that our enemies knock the weapons from our hands. Rather, we must enter negotiations when we can still do so with weapons in hand."

The chief of the general staff speaks in these lines with tremendous determination and resolution, as if the second Hungarian army had not suffered the terrible defeat and the many losses that it endured along the Don River in January 1943 and as if Hungary had since had the opportunity and the ability to replace the enormous losses and assemble a strong, powerful military. One can only say of this thinking that it is naïve and bombastic. The small Hungarian military force hardly could have been considered a factor that would have made the enemy feel willing or compelled to negotiate with Hungarians who stood "with weapons in hand." The history of war in the modern era offers not a single example in support of this notion. Roman history has shown how true the old dictum is: Vae victis, or woe to the vanquished. And we were the vanquished. But the agreement reached by the Allies at the Tehran Conference also showed that the Allies were only willing to enter negotiations with their enemies, whether concerning an armistice or peace, if they enemies had laid down their weapons unconditionally.

And yet what did the chief of the general staff have to say?

"The first and most important precondition of our efforts to maintain the strength of our army and its ability to strike is that we continue the battle on the side of the German Reich with the trustworthiness of an ally and loyalty to our brotherhood of arms, as long as the Germans remain committed to defending our borders with the trustworthiness of an ally and are capable of doing so. When that is no longer the case, then we must seek an honorable but not traitorous compromise, for we cannot cast aside the nation in the name of German interests. Unquestionably, given the state of our industry, the capacity of which has been drastically cut by air attacks, we can only maintain the current strength of our army if we replace what has been lost or used up with war supplies given by the Germans. Naturally, we can only count on this if we support them in their fight—a battle waged for Europe (!)—with all of our might. In this case, however, we must count not simply on maintaining the fighting force we have at the moment, but also on increasing this force to some extent by arming the manpower at our disposal which at the moment remains unused, reinforcing our existing divisions, and assembling new divisions. But unquestionably another consideration that demands that we remain at Germany's side as long as is reasonable is that only as Germany's ally will we be able to hold on to the current Hungarian territories until the war comes to an end. In other words, only thus will we be able to stop the enemy at our borders. For without German assistance, it would be completely impossible to defend the long borders with the forces we have at the moment. Our military is not adequate for this. And yet we must remain clearly aware that if the country falls into enemy hands, the very roots of the Hungarian people—out of which a future Hungary might someday spring, however this war might end—will be destroyed.

The defense of Hungarian territories and the maintenance of firm control over these territories until the end of the war are thus the other fundamental condition of Hungarian survival. Studying the current strategic situation in southeastern Europe, which is the sphere of the war that touches us the most

Chapter VIII

closely, and considering the military options, it is clear that, as a consequence of the ambitious Russian attack in the Balkans and in Galicia and the resulting gain of territory, a general and political situation would arise or indeed is arising on the southern wing of the eastern front which, from the perspective of the further oversight and direction of the military operations in this territory, would compel the supreme German military leadership, which is leading a battle in defense of Europe, to make decisive resolutions."

And so now I ask, why did they not station us there? For the fights that had been fought thus far in retreat showed clearly that the Germans were no longer up to this great task, so any further fighting on our part would mean only futile and superfluous casualties. We had to abandon the Germans! We had to lay down our arms, for there was no other way out for us! Every other path would only lead the nation to destruction! Perhaps this was even clear, if in misty obscurity, to the Hungarian leaders. They too knew that the war was lost, but they continued to hope in some kind of miracle. They were still unable to draw the final conclusion. They continued to hope that perhaps Germany knew of some path that led out of this devastation!

"So it is likely," János Vörös wrote, "that the German military leadership will support the defense of the line of the Carpathians, the Danube River, and the Sava River, i.e. the territory of Hungary, with all possible force and with sincere determination. Indeed, they are all the more likely to do so, given that, if lose the Danube Basin, they will need significantly more forces to defend the Carpathians and, thus, the southeastern border of Germany. If the Germans fail to do this, either because of a lack of will or because of a lack of strength, then we must unconditionally begin negotiations while we are still in control of our armed forces and can negotiate with their support, i.e. can engage in armed negotiations. (?)

The defense of the Carpathian Mountains compels the German leadership to make a two-pronged exertion, much as it also compels the Hungarian leadership to do so because of a particular Hungarian interest. Taking control of the southern Carpathians and firmly defending the Dukla pass, the most sensitive part of the Carpathian line, are preconditions of holding on to the Carpathians. Only the high, impassable range of the southern Carpathians provides the necessary support for defense against the foreseeable attack coming from the Balkans. If we do not take control of the mountain passes in the southern Carpathians and the Russians cross into southern Transylvania and launch an attack from there, even forces several times larger than those currently at our disposal would not be capable of holding the current line of demarcation (Nagyvárad-Kolozsvár). And clearly, if we had to give up the defense of the eastern Carpathians, we would have to retreat to the line of the Danube and Drava Rivers as the border of the last core of Hungary. So our troops had set out to occupy the southern Carpathians and, with the help of the Germans, establish the defensive line that offered the most advantageous position from which to defend Hungary.

The danger that threatens us from the direction of the Dukla pass could mean the outflanking of the line of the Carpathians, or in other words, the surrender of Hungary. In order to prevent this, it is my goal, after having completed the occupation of southern Transylvania and taken control of the passes in the eastern Carpathians, to create a strong central reserve force by drawing on the forces that can be withdrawn from here and breaking up the first army, stationed in the eastern Carpathians. This reserve force will be entrusted with the task of securing the western wing of the first army against an attack coming from the Dukla pass or, in a case of extreme necessity, providing support for the forced recapture of the eastern front. This central reserve force would also be called on to extend our defensive line in the south if the Russians were to go around the Carpathians to the south and attempt to overrun Hungary by crossing the line of the Danube and Sava Rivers. I am going to make the newly established army corps, which will soon be armed using Romanian and Slovak war supplies put at our disposal by the Germans, part of this central reserve. The army corps currently returning home from the territory of the Polish General Government (the second reserve army corps) would also be made part of this central reserve force, after having been reinforced and brought up to strength.

In addition to all this, my intention is to bring the defense of all of Hungary's borders under unified Hungarian leadership, in other words, to put all of the Hungarian and German forces called on to defend the line of the Carpathians and the line of the Danube and Sava Rivers under Hungarian military leadership.

Chapter VIII

In order to achieve the goals outlined above and support the efforts of the military leadership to attain these goals, I ask the political leadership to maintain friendly relations with the German Reich whatever the circumstances, as long as Germany vigorously supports Hungary in the defense of its borders and does not unclasp the Carpathians and the line of the Danube and Drava Rivers from its defensive system. By doing this, the political leadership will both support our military efforts intended to further the rapid delivery of the necessary war supplies with which to equip the Hungarian army corps and create a favorable political climate in which we will be able to secure a large German force to defend the Hungarian borders and give political emphasis to our wish concerning unified Hungarian military leadership in the territory within the Carpathians.

This seems desirable if for no other reason simply because we may find ourselves facing unexpected political surprises. For instance, there was recently news of preparatory measures for a Russian-Japanese-German alliance.

Finally, I wish again to emphasize that in its efforts to save the country, the Hungarian army will only be able to fulfill the hopes with which it has been entrusted if the political leadership of the country ensures the firm maintenance of domestic order and discipline and uninterrupted production. Furthermore, the battles, struggles, and heavy Hungarian casualties will all be in vain if the military leadership cannot be sure that the politicians have realistically assessed the situation and are listening neither to the tempting promises nor to the threats of the enemy or the Allies, but rather, remaining on the honorable path, are striving exclusively to ensure the survival of the Hungarian nation and, if we should find ourselves compelled to make an offer of peace, will turn to the Anglo-Saxons in search of a political resolution.

The question of determining when this moment has arrived is the most difficult task of the politicians. Haste as much as hesitancy could lead to the annihilation of the nation. Even if we assume that Germany has lost the war, we still must defend our borders to the very end, lest we fall prey to Bolshevism, for in the worst case, the case of a national tragedy, we can only ensure the survival of our nation if we keep the Russians at bay and win time for the Anglo-Saxons to launch a tragic occupation of the country."

With my own hand, Vitéz Colonel General Vörös

This characteristic memorandum, which comes to an end with these words, sheds harsh and revealing light on the ideas and plans of the Hungarian military leadership, even in the absence of other corroborating documents.

Vörös was very vague and cautious in his comments concerning a German defeat when he wrote that Germany's attempt "to annihilate its enemies one by one suffered defeat... and a German victory has become doubtful."

In his depiction of the military situation at the time, he offers an accurate picture of the German situation. What he says about the eastern front, however, is unsettlingly accurate. The Romanian forces have laid down their arms, the chief of the general staff writes in his memorandum, or, together with the Russians, they turned against the German forces. They wiped out some of them, and others they forced to retreat to the borders. There was no resistance to the advancing Russian troops. In consequence, at the time that section of the frontline was the most endangered part of the eastern front, and that made the situation of the entire eastern front clear and might well have ended up determining the outcome of the war.

And then comes the wondrous optimism! He claims that on the eastern front, although the forces that could mount opposition to the Russians do not seem to be adequate, the main Russian attack in all likelihood would not come here, but rather from Warsaw in the direction of Berlin or from the San-Vistula triangle in the direction of Breslau or the Dukla pass, and this attack would be accompanied by a parallel attack in the Balkans.

When he puts Hungary against this dark background, his faith and hope in a German victory reemerge. He nonetheless takes into consideration the possibility that, "as a consequence of the gradually increasing numerical superiority of the enemy, the German Reich will be forced to abandon any thought of continuing the battle and will ask for an armistice. Indeed, it is not at all impossible that German resistance will collapse overnight."

One would then expect the author of the memorandum to draw, coldly and objectively, the only possible conclusion, having ascertained that it would be quite impossible to defend Hungary against the foreseeable overwhelming Russian attack, that any continuation of the struggle would mean only a pointless and unforgiveable waste of life, and one would expect him to pro-

Chapter VIII

pose to the Supreme Council of National Defense to follow the Romanian example without delay and surrender! Instead, with completely incomprehensible blindness, he claims that Hungary must "continue the battle on the side of the German Reich with the trustworthiness of an ally and loyalty to our brotherhood of arms, as long as the Germans remain committed to defending our borders with the trustworthiness of an ally and are capable of doing so."

And he considers this necessary in order to ensure that the Germans will provide material support for a non-existent military force the mere creation of which at the time was little more than a plan, a military force the inadequacy and weakness of which the chief of the general staff himself acknowledges. For according to him, we could only count on this German support if we supported them with all our might. But unquestionably another consideration that demanded that we remain at Germany's side was that only as Germany's ally would we be able to hold on to the Hungarian territories until the war came to an end, and only thus would we be able to stop the enemy at our borders.

The Hungarian chief of the general staff made these declarations on 4 September 1944, at a time when the German divisions on the Romanian front were being pulverized as a consequence of the Romanians' volte-face on 23 August. They no longer represented a force on which the defense and maintenance of the eastern and southern borders of Hungary could be based. The conclusions Vörös had drawn had been reached without complete examination or consideration of the power relations or the distances. There is no discussion whatsoever in the memorandum of whether we had adequate forces to mount resistance to a foreseeable Russian and Romanian attack, or what the Germans might be able to provide in order for us to be able to defend our borders from the enemy forces, which had already reached the Ploiești-Bucharest line. There is no reference to the relative sizes of the forces at the disposal of the various participants in the struggle, for the mere mention of 75 Russian infantry divisions and 15-20 Russian tank brigades advancing on Hungary does not suffice as an overview of the imbalance of power. Had the chief of the general staff actually considered the imbalances of power and the possibilities that lay open to us, he never for a moment would have thought of sending the weak Hungarian forces in Transylvania on an offensive to take control of the ridges of the southern Carpathians, nor would he have thought that the Hungarian forces could reach and capture the peaks of the Fogaras mountains[100] before the Russians did. Had he conscientiously considered the situation, he immediately would have realized that we still had to advance some 100 kilometers, while doing battle, to reach these lines, while the Russian troops could advance by motor vehicle unimpeded towards the Brassó and Nagyszeben[101] basins, and they would cross the line that had been selected as a defensive front long before we would even reach it. Meanwhile, the Romanian soldiers in Transylvania could set out, and departing from Brassó, they could immediately cross the current Hungarian border. There could be no talk of defending the Székely Land, holding the line on the eastern Carpathians, or assembling a central reserve force when the Russian and Romanian forces were already advancing on the Ploiești-Bucharest line.

He then adds to this incomprehensible plan the notion of holding the Carpathians against the overwhelming enemy force attacking from the south until the Anglo-Saxons, who at the time had not even reached the Rhine, were at our backs.

He even writes of an alliance between Russia, Japan, and Germany. This was little more than one of the hoaxes which blurred any clear discernment of the situation with the notion of a possible fight among the Allies.

The notion of having the political leadership turn to the Anglo-Saxons in the hope of reaching some resolution failed to take into consideration the fact that the Allies would only negotiate a peace collectively. It failed to recognize that we were at war with the Russians, not the Anglo-Saxons.

As accurate as the assessment of the situation given by the chief of the general staff was, the conclusions he drew on the basis of this assessment were every bit as vague, questionable, and dangerous. His suggestions and desires concerning Hungary's further conduct in the war were quite simply incomprehensible. The time had come to begin negotiations with the Russians, for it was quite clear that the Germans would not be able to provide the support that would have been necessary in order to stop the Russian advance.

---

100 Fogaras was the name of a city and also a county in Transylvania with some of the highest peaks in the southern Carpathians. The Romanian name of the city is Făgăraș.
101 Today Sibiu, Romania.

Chapter VIII

The regent must have sensed that it was no longer possible to postpone taking action. At the Crown Council held on 7 September, he announced that he was going to request a ceasefire. At this council, the chief of the general staff supported this decision. Even János Vörös realized that we had no other choice, and he no longer gave any consideration to the ideas to which he had given voice in the 4 September memorandum.

The visit of Colonel General Guderian, the German chief of the general staff, to Hungary at the end of August had significantly strengthened the regent's resolve. Guderian was unable to provide any news that would have offered the regent reassurance concerning the successful continuance of the war. Guderian openly declared that the rumors that had spread concerning miracle weapons were completely baseless. He said quite sincerely that yes, the weapons industry in Germany was working on first-rate inventions, but it was not producing any weapons that would decide the outcome of the war. Thus, the legend of the miracle weapon unraveled. But even more important than this revelation was the fact that, with the withdrawal of the Romanians, the section of the front that had collapsed was precisely the stretch across which the enemy threatened to overrun Hungary. The regent came to the decision to request an armistice and to lay down our arms. This was our last chance to extend our hand to the Russians before the Russian military marched across the territory of Hungary as an enemy army and at the cost of serious battles. The regent, Prime Minster Lakatos, Minister of Defense Csatay, Minister of Foreign Affairs Hennyey, Colonel General and Chief of the General Staff János Vörös, head of the cabinet Gyula Ambróczy, and Adjutant-General Antal Vattay took part in the crown council held on 7 September 1944. The regent announced that he was going to ask the allies for a ceasefire because Germany had not provided the assistance it had promised, and according to reliable sources some five Russian armored corps were advancing across the Carpathians from Romania, armored corps against which Hungary was defenseless.

Following a brief discussion, those present offered their unanimous support for the regent's decision, and Horthy decided to present the question of a ceasefire to the crown council that very evening, the evening of 7 September.

The Crown Council was also unanimous in its support for the regent's plan. The Council declared that Hungary must ask for an armistice. The prime minister and the chief of the general staff were instructed to inform the German ambassador Veesenmayer and Colonel General Greiffenberg, the German military delegate, of this resolution that evening, the evening of 7 September. The Ministry of Foreign Affairs would also take the necessary preparatory steps to deliver a written request for an armistice to the Allies through the mediation of the Swedish and the Turkish ambassadors. This Crown Council resolution, however, was never implemented. Although at the Council held on 7 September not a single minister had spoken out in opposition to the regent's plan or his decision, at the Council of Ministers held on 11 September the unanimous decision of the Crown Council met with strong opposition. Several people spoke out against the resolution, and indeed some of the people who had accepted the regent's proposal at the Crown Council now opposed it in the most vehemently terms. This was a tragic turn. The only discerning, astute decision thus came to nothing. It was also tragic, furthermore, than now the German ambassador could clearly see that Hungary in all likelihood would not remain at Germany's side, and the Germans had to take into account the possibility that we would soon follow the examples that had been set by Italy, Finland, and Romania. No longer could there be any talk of a surprise. The Germans had won time in order to adopt countermeasures and take the necessary preparatory steps in order to put Szálasi in power.

On 8 September, the German ambassador had an audience with the regent. László Bárdossy also requested and was given an audience with Horthy that same day. Bárdossy had learned a few days after the Crown Council that we wanted to request an armistice. Veesenmayer and Bárdossy managed to persuade the regent to change his original plan. He agreed to postpone the request for an armistice. The German ambassador held out the prospect of bringing five German armored divisions to Hungary within a week, and indeed he claimed that some of them were already on their way. He also said that within 10-14 days four or five of the German divisions in the Balkans would be stationed in the territory between Belgrade and Orșova. He reassured Horthy that the Germans would not abandon him, and they would not give up Hungary. After the Council of Ministers was informed of the German promises on 11 September, trusting that the Germans would keep their

Chapter VIII

word, it changed the decision to request and armistice and resolved instead to wait for the Germans to keep their promises.

Since the regent was of the opinion that the signing of an armistice belonged to his sphere of authority and thus it was not necessary to announce this ahead of time to the parliament, the preparatory steps continued in spite of the postponement. He had already informed the prime minister and Minister of Foreign Affairs separately and in strict confidence of the negotiations he was conducting. But he had entrusted neither of them with the management of these negotiations. Rather, the negotiations were being arranged by Gyula Ambróczy, the head of the cabinet, and Horthy's other confidents. Thus, apart from the regent himself, there was no "managing editor" overseeing the whole affair.

The Minister of Foreign Affairs established contacts with the Anglo-Saxon powers through the Swiss embassy. He openly revealed the dire circumstances in Hungary, and he explained, in accordance with Horthy's wishes, that he sought at all costs to prevail on the Anglo-Saxon powers to use paratroopers to occupy Hungary. In his view, the public in Hungary, which was under the influence of the one-sided propaganda campaign that had been underway for years, would not accept the idea of a Russian occupation. They wanted at all costs to persuade the Anglo-Saxons to send paratrooper divisions to Hungary and, by doing so, to enable the Hungarian government to ask them for an armistice instead of the Russians. This was their intended method of explaining why we wanted to negotiate with the Anglo-Saxons, who were still several hundred kilometers away, in spite of the fact that we were in battle with the Russians. To all of our inquiries, the Anglo-Saxons replied that they would accept only an unconditional surrender, and we could only reach an armistice with all of the allied powers collectively.

When this became clear, the regent sent István Náday, a retired Colonel General, by plane to Rome to begin negotiations. Lieutenant General Gábor Faragho, the former military attaché in Moscow, flew to Moscow to begin negotiations with the Soviet government. He was accompanied by university professor Géza Teleki and special envoy and minister plenipotentiary Domokos Szentiványi. Thus, the regent remained distant from these negotiations, which were held in secret. Although Prime Minister Lakatos and Minister of Foreign Affairs Hennyey were aware of the talks, they could not officially acknowledge them. When the Germans and the right-wing parties began to suspect what was going on behind the curtains, however, they called the prime minister to account. Lakatos was compelled to claim that he had no knowledge of the negotiations. During an audience with the regent, András Tasnády-Nagy, the president of the House of Representatives, warned Horthy that without the consent of the parliament he did not have the right to initiate armistice negotiations.

Even prominent leaders (who opposed Szálasi) felt that we had to support remaining in the war because no one had yet tried to convince the public that we first had to arrive at an agreement with the Soviet Union. Each government had laid emphasis on the struggle against the Soviet Union and the impossibility of reaching an agreement with it. There was widespread fear of Bolshevism. If no preparatory steps were taken, the Hungarian public would not be easily persuaded that we should surrender ourselves to the Russians. According to the official propaganda and the views of the pro-Germans and even some of the members of the government, we had obligations to Germany that demanded that we continue to fight at its side. They thought that if we were to pull out of the war, the country would become a battlefield, because the German military would not be willing to withdraw from Hungary as it had done in the case of Finland. There were several hundred thousand German soldiers in Hungary, while the Hungarian supreme command had only peacetime divisions and supplementary corps. Thus, any opposition to the Germans would have been hopeless from the outset.

It was on the basis of this kind of thinking that the idea emerged according to which, if Germany were to support Hungary by providing the necessary forces, we must continue the war, and with the capture of southern Transylvania, the front must be pushed to the crests of the Carpathians, because this constituted a realistic line of defense. However, this all depended on whether or not the German support arrived quickly. If Germany were to collapse in the middle of military operations, however, or the government were to decide to negotiate an armistice after all, then we must choose the path of negotiations, for otherwise the country would become a battlefield, and it would be destroyed.

Chapter VIII

It is easy to raise arguments, in addition to the considerations I have already mentioned, against this view and, most importantly, against the reasoning in support of continuing the war. With regards to the public, the contention that it was completely unprepared for negotiations with the Russians was entirely true. But in my view, if we were to insist, on the grounds of 1920 statute I, that the preparatory measures for an armistice were not under the jurisdiction of the parliament if, as part of the sphere of authority of the regent, they could be implemented without the parliament, then there was no need whatsoever for any propaganda effort to prepare the public. The launch of any such propaganda campaign was unthinkable anyway, given the occupation of the country by the Germans. But it didn't even matter, for the war was hardly popular, except among the small number of Arrow Cross members and politicians who were completely German in their orientation. The majority of the Hungarian nation was well aware of the fact that this was not our war. No one understood why we were at war with Russia when we had no territorial claims against Russia and Russia had no territorial claims against us, as indeed Molotov himself had declared to Kristóffy, the Hungarian delegate to Moscow, at the beginning of the war. The fear of Bolshevism cannot have been serious either. After all, Hitler himself had signed a non-aggression pact with Soviet Russia. And we had accepted the return of the 1848 flags of the Hungarian revolutionary army, and we had saluted the Comintern in the Buda castle when the Russian delegation had presented the flags.

I know of no obligations and there were no written agreements ordering us to continue to fight at Germany's side when this was in no way in the interests of the Hungarian people. It was no longer possible to hope realistically to protect the territory of the country from temporarily becoming a battlefield, but this would be all the more likely if we were to continue the fight. Every leading figure should have known, simply on the basis of the information provided by the chief of the general staff, that we would not be able, neither with our forces nor with the support of the Germans, to hold off the advancing Romanian and Russian forces, which were far stronger. Only a layman in military affairs could still have nurtured this hope. And yet the regent, the prime minister, the Minister of Foreign Affairs, the Minister of Defense, and the chief of the general staff, each of whom had to take a position on this question, were all soldiers.

The fact that the government had almost no Hungarian forces to use against the 500,000 German soldiers in the country should also not have been an obstacle to the request for an armistice. Had the first and second armies, which were stationed along the line stretching from the Dukla Pass to Nagyvárad, laid down their weapons, as of that moment the Germans stationed in Hungary would not have been able to continue the fight. The whole German front in this territory would have collapsed just as it had in Romania.

On 9 September, Colonel General Vörös sent a memorandum to Colonel General Guderian, the chief of the German general staff. In this memorandum, he sought to explain that it was in the interests of the Germans to defend the line of the Carpathians, the Danube River, and the Sava River and, thus, Hungary. He tried to convince Guderian that, were Germany to retreat to its eastern border, it would need a stronger force than were it to remain on the aforementioned defensive line. He then wrote the following:

"In the situation at the moment, the most immediate necessity is to take control of the mountain passes in the southern Carpathians and pacify southern Transylvania.
In order to achieve this goal, the Hungarian leadership brought together all of the forces at its disposal, with no regard for any other consideration, and launched an attack to capture the southern Carpathians on 5 September. However, given that we have only supplementary divisions and training squads with very little artillery, in the interests of success it is absolutely necessary that we receive appropriate tank and air support from the Germans in order to increase ability of the Hungarian soldiers to strike effectively. Without this assistance, we will be unable to capture and use the strategical advantage that presents itself. Indeed, on the contrary, we expose ourselves to a counterstrike that would make the entire attack against southern Transylvania little more than a superfluous sacrifice, and indeed once we have abandoned the eastern Carpathians we would have to adopt an improvised—ad hoc—defensive position, since there is no other defensive position in Hungary!

Chapter VIII

In the German assistance described above, we Hungarians will take part with complete determination and by deploying all of our forces, if the highest echelons of German leadership assure us that they will support Hungary with complete confidence until the very end, will not sacrifice Hungarian territory to other interests or in order to gain time, and finally, will not use the Hungarian army to cover a possible retreat. If the German leadership is not able to guarantee that we will hold the line of the Carpathian Mountains and the Drava River under any circumstances, we will be compelled to consider gradually pulling back the Hungarian eastern front in order to avert the danger of being surrounded on two sides. The eastern Carpathian front can only be held if we resolutely defend the southern Carpathians, stretching all the way to the territory of the Dukla Pass. This is only possible, however, with vigorous German support."

The most striking thing about this letter is that it requests German assistance in writing on 9 September for an attack that was launched on 5 September to capture the passes in the Fogaras Mountains. There is no mention in the letter of any previous negotiations or agreements concerning German cooperation or the precise nature of any German forces to be put at the disposal of the Hungarians. Thus, it already seemed out of the question that any support that might be sent by the Germans would arrive in time. In the letter, the Hungarian chief of the general staff also says that the Hungarian attack force is not adequate for the task that has been set. On 5 September, supplementary divisions were sent to attack, not soldiers equipped with up-to-date weaponry. He himself sensed that with these forces he was incapable of achieving the task he had undertaken. He should have prepared this attack well in advance, back when the news first arrived of the Romanian intentions to withdraw from the war. I spoke with intelligence agents according to whom the Hungarian general staff had already heard reports of the Romanians' plans in April 1944. They had shared these reports with the Germans. The Germans, however, had not wanted to give them any credence. They had said that the Hungarians wanted to turn their backs on the Axis.

After having sent the letter on 9 September, the chief of the general staff felt it necessary to take steps to ensure prompt German support. On 11 September, he flew to the general German headquarters to meet with Hitler.

Hitler not only promised to deliver the five divisions he had mentioned, he also assured Colonel General Vörös that he would soon launch operations that would go beyond the Carpathians, into Romania.

The Hungarian leaders who sensed that the war could not be won still hoped, after these magniloquent promises and reassurances, that the Anglo-Saxons might perhaps drop their plans to destroy Germany and arrive at an agreement, not with Hitler, but perhaps with a more moderate, non-Nazi government. They thought it permissible to wait for the promised German support and the results of the attack that had been launched to capture the line of the southern Carpathians, and then to decide whether or not to continue the inquiries that had been made in the interests of initiating armistice negotiations.

Events, however, did not unfold as the pro-Germans and the military leaders who still nurtured hope had expected. The assistance that had been promised by the Germans never came. What Vörös had mentioned in his letter to Guderian came to pass. With the weakened Hungarian soldiers, they were able to achieve only worthless partial successes. In Transylvania, the Hungarian troops advancing from Kolozsvár towards the south made it to the Maros River [the Mureș River in Romanian]. There, however, they collided with the Russians, and their advance was brought to a halt. The Hungarian troops attacking in the direction of Arad also suffered defeat. It proved impossible to achieve certain and lasting successes with an attack that had been so haphazardly planned, improvised, and hurried. It also became clear that, however alluring a plan may seem, if the forces entrusted with its implementation are not adequate and the necessary material foundations have not been laid, even the most heroic soldiers cannot work miracles!

The request that was made to the Germans came late. The attack should not have been launched until the divisions promised by the Germans had arrived. If their arrival remained uncertain because of the Russian advantages in time and space, the attack should have been dropped, however clever the military strategy on which it was based may have seemed, and we should have realized that the situation that had been created on the eastern front by the Romanian withdrawal could not be salvaged.

The Russians advanced into Transylvania. In the Romanian territory, nothing and no one hindered them. Thus, the Soviet military force, which

Chapter VIII

was vastly superior in number, made it through the narrow passes and out onto the Hungarian plain, and the path to Budapest lay open before it.

The president of the Hungarian government, the Minister of Foreign Affairs, and the chief of the general staff asked the German ambassador and Guderian to put the forces that were stationed in the country at their disposal, but in vain. They repeatedly affirmed that the Hungarian soldiers were bleeding to death while more than half a million Germans were in Hungary, of whom at most 100,000 soldiers were engaged in the fighting, but in vain. They observed that three tank divisions were idle in the area around Budapest, and they could immediately be deployed against the approaching Russians, but in vain. Horthy again turned to Hitler, but in vain, for none of these efforts yielded any results. On one occasion, on 18 September, a tank division in Örkény was loaded up and then unloaded the very same day. Of the five tank divisions, in September only one arrived in Kolozsvár, at a time when the enemy forces approaching from the south were already threatening Nagyvárad. The division was then sent to Nagyvárad. An SS cavalry regiment was deployed near Arad. The other divisions arrived for the Battle of Debrecen, but they were unable to change its outcome.

And thus we arrived at the anniversary of the Tripartite Pact, 29 September. The German government wanted the Hungarian Minister of Foreign Affairs to hold a speech on the radio in which he would speak of the pact. When the German ambassador informed the Minister of Foreign Affairs of this wish, Hennyey declined, and he noted that the country had ended up in a disastrous situation as a consequence of Germany's failure to keep its promises. The German ambassador may have gotten the impression, in the course of this conversation, that the anxieties that had given rise to the idea of seeking a ceasefire at the beginning of September had not have faded, and indeed they might well have been exacerbated by the defeats which had been suffered in the meantime. On 28 September, he flew to the German general headquarters to make a report, and he returned to Hungary with authorization to put Szálasi in power at any time, with force if necessary.

This did not happen at the time, however, because Veesenmayer, the ambassador, and Winckelmann, the SS general, differed in their assessments of the prime minister. While Veesenmayer supported Szálasi because he felt

Szálasi was the leader of the most effectively organized party in Hungary, Winckelmann would have preferred to have retired Lieutenant General Jenő Ruszkay serve as prime minister, since he regarded him as a forceful soldier. He also supported László Baky, the former state secretary of internal affairs. The prime minister and the Minister of Foreign Affairs learned of these plans. When Lakatos reproached the German ambassador, Veesenmayer denied having maintained any ties or having hatched any plans. Lakatos attempted to take measures using the Ministry of Internal Affairs to have Szálasi and his immediate circle arrested, but ultimately he was unable to do this.

At the beginning of October, the situation was getting continuously worse. The troops that the Germans had promised to send either did not come at all or arrived only with considerable delays. The Germans were constantly waiting for the Hungarian government to take steps to negotiate an armistice, so they wanted to keep their troops near Budapest. They feared that they might not have sufficient forces to help Szálasi come to power. Politics was more important to them than the situation on the battlefield. With every passing day, the Russians were closer to the capital. Not a single one of the divisions which were supposed to have been sent from the Weichs army in the Balkans to the banks of the Danube and Sava Rivers actually arrived. This was entirely natural. The transportation lines in the Balkans had become very unreliable because of the unusually strong opposition of the partisans. The regrouping and redeployment of the scattered German divisions along the Danube-Sava line was very difficult. Thus, the Soviet troops advanced unimpeded towards Yugoslavia. They occupied Belgrade, and they crossed the Danube River, joined the troops advancing through Transylvania, and took control of the Bánát. They were able to cross the line of the Tisza River without a shot being fired, as it were. They also captured Szeged and Bácska.

In the meantime, the troops advancing from the valley of the Maros River made it to the territory to the south of Debrecen, and on 9 October the battle began for control of the city. Of the tank divisions that the Germans had promised would arrive on 14 September, only two divisions arrived, and only on 7 October, and they were unable to change the outcome of the battle. The momentary hope that flickered when the German tanks arrived proved delusive and vain. They failed to turn back the Russians. The longer the protract-

Chapter VIII

ed battles lasted, the more the city of Debrecen was left in ruins. Even Colonel General Frießner, the German Commander-in-Chief, had no faith in success. At the very beginning of the battle, he asked the regent what stance he would adopt if the Germans were to pull the defensive line back to Balassagyarmat-Budapest-Balaton-Nagykanizsa.

In the early days of the Battle of Debrecen, it seemed as if the advancing Russian wedge had been cut off from the bulk of the Russian forces. The first reports were very encouraging. According to these reports, the Russians had been unable to force the Germans to retreat, and indeed on the contrary, the Germans were going to annihilate the enemy forces, which they had encircled. However, after a few days of fighting, the balance of the battle tipped in favor of the Russians, and soon they had occupied the entire Transtisza region. Indeed, Soviet units had even been seen in the region between the Tisza and the Danube Rivers.

Sztójay dissolved the political parties, and political life began to wane. At the initiative of András Tasnády Nagy, the president of the House of Representatives, the "National Alliance of Legislators" was formed, consisting of right-wing representatives of the parliamentary parties. As the prime minister was unwilling to allow the president of the House of Representatives to serve as the head of a political formation the work of which essentially was directed against the government itself, András Tasnády Nagy stepped down and was replaced by Lajos Szász, the former Minister of Public Welfare. It was quite typical that Minister of Finance Lajos Reményi-Schneller and Minister of Public Welfare Béla Jurcsek were both in this anti-government alliance. On 5 October, Lajos Szász asked the prime minister to meet with the executive committee of the alliance. Prime Minister Géza Lakatos met with the committee, and he was joined by Minister of Defense Lajos Csatay and Minister of Foreign Affairs Gusztáv Hennyey. With the exceptions of Bárdossy and Imrédy, all fourteen members of the committee were present, including representatives Lajos Szász, Jenő Szöllösy, Andor Jaross, Ferenc Rajniss, Jenő Rátz, Gábor Vajna, Iván Nagy, György Oláh, and Mihály Kolosváry-Borcsa. Lajos Szász presented the alliance's platform, the essence of which was that Hungary would remain at Germany's side until the very end. Then Jaross spoke. He explained his party's platform. Then Rajniss rebuked the government in biting terms. Iván Nagy, Mihály Kolosváry Borcsa, and György Oláh also spoke up. Essentially, they all contended that the government was unconstitutional. They also raised the question of the negotiations begun by Lieutenant General Gábor Faragho in Moscow. They complained that the Hungarian people were not doing their share in the war, and so Germany was suspicious of Hungary. They also objected to the fact that the Brothers-in-Arms Alliance of the Eastern Front [Keleti Arcvonal Bajtársi Szövetség] had been dissolved.

Prime Minister Lakatos responded to most of the questions and criticisms, and Minister of Foreign Affairs Gusztáv Hennyey answered the questions concerning foreign affairs. Lakatos painted a sincere picture of Hungarian-German relations, the essence of which was that Germany had abandoned us. It had not kept any of its promises. The military forces that had been promised had never arrived, and Hungary, in consequence, now found itself in a critical situation. Some 200,000 trained soldiers could not be sent into battle because Germany had not sent the arms and equipment it had promised, even while, furthermore, it had taken the bulk of our horse stock. We were losing one section of the country after another, but the country was full of German soldiers, and the two Hungarian battalions in Budapest were under the watch of three German divisions. When the most devastating air attacks had been launched against Hungary, the German high command had withdrawn all of its fighter planes, leaving Hungary defenseless. The replies given by the prime minister and the Minister of Foreign Affairs appeared to have a profound impact on the representatives present, and they left the room downcast. It is revealing that Ferenc Rajniss, who had been the most strident and forceful, sent a cable to the prime minister the next day thanking him for the information and insights, while Vajna acknowledged that they had not achieved their aim at the talks.

Thus, the National Alliance of Legislators was given a detailed and sincere overview of the critical situation in which Hungary found itself because of the conduct of the Germans, and they had all heard from the most authoritative and informed position how desperate the military situation was. This meeting constitutes the most devastating indictment of those who, even after all this had been made clear, still did not hesitate to help Szálasi seize power with the help of the Germans. Every participant in this discussion could clearly see the chasm into which we were plunging.

The period between 1 September and 13 October was a time of growing mistrust for Germany. Romania's unexpected withdrawal from the war had had disastrous consequences for Germany, and the Lakatos government did not provide an adequate guarantee that Hungary would remain at Germany's side.

On 12 September, Hitler informed Colonel General Vörös that he did not trust the Hungarian government. Vörös insisted that he was determined to continue the battle. The prime minister and the Minister of Foreign Affairs soon were convinced that the Germans had grouped the bulk of their forces around the capital in order to prevent Hungary from switching sides in the war. The Minister of Foreign Affairs received telegrams almost every day from Hungarian delegates abroad urging an armistice.

In connection with the prospect of switching sides, the idea was raised that the regent would go, together with a few ministers, to the Carpathians, where the first army was engaged in battle. This would have been a momentous step, since on 15 October the bulk of the Hungarian armed forces probably would have fallen in line behind the regent. Not only the army, but even the civilian population felt that the country urgently needed peace. However, the prime minister and the Minister of Foreign Affairs called the regent's attention to the fact that the army did not stand entirely behind him, and he should take into consideration the effects of anti-Soviet propaganda, as well as German influence. The regent, however, gave these claims little credence, and on 15 October, following the decisive Crown Council, he continued to believe that the army supported him. In my view, it would only have been possible to switch sides had the regent remained committed to the plan outlined above. This would have been particularly justified after the German and Arrow Cross plans for a putsch had been discovered. The regent, however, decided that neither he nor his family would leave Budapest. If his enemies were going to use force against him, he would resist "with revolver in hand." He explained his decision to remain in Budapest with the contention that, were he to leave, the Germans would form a rival government and a civil war would break out. This had to be averted in the interests of the capital and the country. This was the situation of the country on 15 October, when the decisive step was taken.

Chapter IX

What happened after 15 October 1944?

On Saturday 15 October, Gyula Ambrózy, the head of the cabinet bureau, presented Prime Minister Géza Lakatos the text of the proclamation which was to be made the next day. Lakatos made changes to the text. That afternoon, the Prime Minister summoned the ministers to join him for a confidential discussion. All of the ministers attended with the exception of Minister of Finance Lajos Reményi-Sándor and Minister of Public Welfare Béla Jurcsek. Reményi-Sándor and Jurcsek had close ties to the German plenipotentiary, so the other ministers did not want to discuss affairs that were confidential in nature in their company. During the discussion, Prime Minister Lakatos informed us that on 15 October at 11 o'clock Horthy had called a meeting of the Crown Council to talk about the question of a ceasefire. The Crown Council had to decide what stance the ministers would take with regards to the regent's request for a ceasefire. After they had discussed the military situation, they spoke about the question of the ceasefire to be concluded. They all agreed that a ceasefire was necessary, since the situation was completely hopeless and the decision could no longer be postponed. They had to agree upon what measures to adopt with regards to the parliament and the Germans. For when he had first taken office, Prime Minister Lakatos had promised not to ask for a ceasefire without the knowledge and consent of the parliament.

With regards to dealing with the parliament, an opinion was formed according to which, if the regent were to adhere to his belief and resolution that there was no need to inform the parliament ahead of time or seek its approval, the government would resign. If, however, the regent were then to call on Lakatos to form a government again, all of the ministers would remain in place and take a new oath of office. Thus, a new government would be formed which, though it would consist of exactly the same people, would not be bound by the promise the first Lakatos government had made with regards to the parliament. In this new government, however, in all likelihood neither Lajos Reményi-Schneller nor Béla Jurcsek would accept a portfolio. The regent himself would inform the German plenipotentiary. He did not have to bother informing him, however, because Veesenmayer himself asked for an audience with the regent. The regent received the plenipotentiary on the 15 at 12 o'clock. The German plenipotentiary had no inkling that in the course of the audience the regent would inform him that Hungary was going to ask the Allies for a ceasefire.

Antal Vattay informed the Council of Ministers of the measures that had been taken in the interests of ensuring the personal safety of the regent. He indicated that they were working from the assumption that extreme right-wing elements would use violent means to prevent the ceasefire, and the Germans would definitely provide support for them in this effort with arms. According to Lieutenant General Vattay, Lieutenant General Károly Lázár, commander of the gendarmerie, was in charge of ensuring the safety of the royal castle. He would use the guards, reinforced with the 9/II battalion. But in all likelihood, he would also "soon" have the cavalry corps fighting to the southeast of Budapest and, within "a few days," the 10th army corps, which would be sent to Budapest, at his disposal.

In addition to these two battalions, there was also a river force division the size of a battalion in Budapest which could be used for special forces purposes.

They agreed that request for a ceasefire would be made in person by the Minister of Foreign affairs, who would communicate it in person to the Swedish and Turkish envoys. The written instructions would be given to the Hungarian envoys in Stockholm and Ankara so that, on the basis of these instructions, they would be able to ask the two governments to pass on the request. The Hungarian envoys would also present the condition, as part of the request, that the German troops withdraw from Hungary as they had from Finland and the armies of the Allied powers occupy the country collectively; the organs of the Hungarian police would cooperate in the maintenance of order, and Budapest would be occupied by the Allies working in concert.

When the ministers were rushing to the meeting of the Crown Council on the morning of 15 October, they knew that the Germans had set a trap for Miklós Horthy II, the regent's son. Miklós Horthy had been confronted by members of the German Gestapo in the apartment of Félix Bornemissza, a retired naval officer. In the firefight that had ensued, he had shot one of aggressors, but he had also been wounded. The Germans had disarmed him and dragged him off. At the time, no one could determine where. At the beginning of the Crown Council, the regent knew nothing of what had taken place.

Many contradictory rumors spread concerning what the proceedings at the Crown Council. Since the fate of the country would depend on what had taken place there, and the conduct of the people who had taken part was not irrelevant from the perspective of further developments, it is worth knowing the details of the proceedings.

The regent opened the Crown Council on Sunday, 15 October, at 11 o'clock. In addition to the ministers, Chief of the General Staff János Vörös was present, as was Head of the Cabinet Bureau Gyula Ambrózy and Lieutenant General and Adjutant General Antal Vattay, the head of the office of the military. István Bárczy, State Secretary of the Prime Minister's Office, kept the minutes.

In his introductory speech, the regent began the council by saying that he had called together the members of the government in the gravest hours of Hungary's history. Our military situation was dire indeed. There was no doubt anymore concerning the military collapse of Germany. If this were to happen, and the Allied powers were to find us along at Germany's side, Hungary might very well cease to exist as a state. With regards to a ceasefire, we had reports indicating that we would be given acceptable conditions. Our situation today, with neither relatives nor friends, was extremely difficult. Budapest still stood. Every life sacrificed in this hopeless fight was a life wasted. We must prepare ourselves to be exposed to the brutality of the Germans. They can scatter our troops, but whatever trial we may face, if we continue the battle, the hopeless fight, then we imperil our homeland and our people and cast both into annihilation.

Prime Minister Géza Lakatos then suggested that before we begin the Council the chief of the general staff inform the members of the government of the military situation.

Fateful Years

János Vörös began by saying that the military situation at the moment raised two grave questions. One was that we had been compelled to withdraw our troops on the Debrecen front. The other was that the area between the Danube and the Tisza rivers was completely without protection. The advancing enemy would find only weak units that had been thrown together in haste.

Our cavalry division, which had been brought back from Russia, had been immediately deployed almost as soon as it had arrived. It had suffered grave losses. The remaining parts were gathered at the moment in Kecskemét. The Russians had turned northward at Debrecen. As a consequence of this, they might cut off our first and second armies. Of the five German armored divisions that had been promised, two had come. If they were to be deployed, it might be possible to hold the front for a little while. We could not go into Slovak territory. The territory between Debrecen and the Slovak border was very narrow, so if the Russians were to attack here with larger forces we would be able to take back even less. Given this, he had written a long telegram informing the German general staff of our situation, and he had also suggested that we withdraw our two armies to the line of the Tisza-Bodrog[102] and the Meszes. He also indicated that Budapest would be guarded as a bridgehead by the cavalry division, one armored division, and one Hungarian infantry division. If the Russians were to exert stronger pressure from the south, then we would retreat to the line of the Danube. He also indicated that the tenth Hungarian division, which was in reserve behind the first army, could also be brought to defend Budapest. The Germans had not agreed to any of this. He nonetheless had given orders that these measures be taken and that the first and second armies withdraw to the Tisza-Bodrog line. The Germans had rejected the transfer of the tenth Hungarian division, saying that they would defend Budapest themselves.

At 10:15, Guderian, the German chief of the general staff, had demanded an ultimatum concerning the retraction of the order that had been issued to withdraw. He had given twelve hours for a reply.

The Crown Council decided that the measures that had been ordered by the chief of the general staff would remain in effect.

---

102 He was referring to the line stretching from the confluence of the Tisza and the Bodrog Rivers to the Meszes Mountains in Transylvania, or in Romanian the Meseş Mountains.

Chapter IX

All further debate on this weighty question was set aside, and the issue of the ceasefire became the subject of discussion.

Prime Minister Lakatos said that he had revealed our military situation at a sitting of the Supreme Council of National Defense. Already then he had emphasized that the Battle of Debrecen would only end in success if the Germans did not simply halt the Russians, but actually defeated them. The other dangerous territory was the area between the Danube and Tisza Rivers, where the Germans had already occupied Szeged and Szabadka. There was also reason to fear that Szentes and Csongrád would soon be in their hands. Even if defeat in the Battle of Debrecen did not constitute a great danger, as the Russian pincer closed it could bring our armies into an increasingly dangerous situation. If the Russian army were to arrive on the outskirts of Budapest, all further fighting would be hopeless.

The chief of the general staff noted that, during the military operation, the Russians would be able to avoid our units, because you cannot deploy a cavalry division against armored units and use it to bring them to a halt.

Lakatos said that the regent feared for the future of the country if we were to continue to support remaining in the fight, which seemed hopeless. The stance of the government was that if we were to resist we could win time. (The prime minister was probably thinking of winning the time that would be necessary for the Anglo-Saxon parachute divisions to arrive before the Russians.)

Lakatos called everyone's attention to the distrust of the Germans, which had become apparent with the kidnapping of Szilárd Bakay, the commander of the Budapest first army. We were giving the Germans preliminary notice and requesting a ceasefire from the Allies. According to Lakatos, we could not wait until the moment came when the Russians were already lords of the situation. However, he had accepted an obligation with regards to the House of Representatives. In his view, he had to ask the national assembly, even if perhaps in a closed sitting. In the meantime, the Alliance of National Legislators had formed in the parliament, and he had already informed the delegation of the Alliance that the moment would come when we would no longer be able to adhere to our resolution to continue the fight. So he would ask for the regent's consent to present the fact of our request for a ceasefire first, in order to get consent, to both of the houses of parliament.

A debate began concerning the necessary of parliament's consent. The regent's stance was that the law applied to a peace treaty and not a ceasefire. The House of Representatives today, given its composition, did not represent Hungarian public opinion. The National Alliance of Legislators had formed out of elements that were too extreme. The very composition of the leadership, according to which, in opposition to the Party of Hungarian Life (which constituted the majority), much smaller parties were guaranteed two seats each in the leadership, made clear that we were dealing with a union of extreme right-wing tendencies. And furthermore, many representatives and members of the Upper House had been dragged off by the Germans, so the parliament was not complete. Many legislators were prevented from coming by the military situation. As a consequence of the fear of the Gestapo terror, the representatives did not really dare state their opinions openly. We were an occupied country.

Then Minister of Justice Gábor Vladár and Minister of Religion and Education Iván Rakovszky offered their remarks on the question.

Prime Minister Lakatos raised new arguments in support of the necessary of a ceasefire. He explained that our dire military situation, and, furthermore, other considerations, such as the case of Bakay or the almost unsolvable question of the provision of food and lodging for refugees had put us in such a terrible situation that we must now resign ourselves to making a serious decision. We were compelled to admit that, faced with each of these questions, we were virtually powerless. We wanted to save the population of the nation, but we could not relocate one half of the country to the other. In his view, the question of a ceasefire had to be presented to the parliament. However, before we did this, we had to determine what the stances of the ministers were, who would oppose the conditions of the ceasefire and who would accept them.

The regent interrupted: "I have already decided."

After the Minister of Internal Affairs, Baron Péter Schell, János Vörös, and Lakatos had spoken, the regent spoke up again. He insisted that we could not expect any help. Victory was out of the question. So now, before the last minute was upon us, with weapons in hand we must ask the Allies for a ceasefire. We were surrounded by our hostile neighbors. If they were to move, Hungary would cease to exist. Guderian's raw ultimatum, which

Chapter IX

had arrived that very day, had convinced him even more of his view. The ultimatum made it easier to reach a decision. The Germans had not kept a single one of their promises. When they had lured him to Germany on 19 March, Hitler had proclaimed that he had heard reports according to which we wanted to switch sides and join the enemy, and so he had to occupy Hungary militarily. For hours, he had pleaded with Hitler not to take this step, but in vain. He had been told that the question of the military occupation had already been settled, and as long as the Hungarian military did not put up any resistance, the administration would remain entirely in Hungarian hands. And yet, along with the occupation forces, the Gestapo had also come to Hungary. In response to his pleas, which he made several times, they promised to withdraw the Gestapo in time. To this day they had failed to do this. They had promised that Hungary would retain complete sovereignty as long as it appointed a government that enjoyed Germany's trust. He had accepted this as well. And nonetheless, the Gestapo remained was still in the country, and it had arrested an array of parliamentary representatives and men prominent in public life and deported them to Germany. He then asked the ministers at the Crown Council who wished to comment on this resolution. Did they accept responsibility for the resolution, and who did not accept responsibility for it?

Minister Béla Jurcsek was the first person to speak up. He gave a long-winded rebuttal of the regent's arguments, and he tried to convince him that the request for a ceasefire was premature.

Minister of Foreign Affairs Gusztáv Hennyey then spoke up, announcing that we faced a weighty decision. We had to decide whether to request a ceasefire or continue fighting. Hungary's situation was dire. He emphasized that he had heard reports concerning the grave internal situation in Germany. There were circles within Germany who felt that the Reich would not be able to hold out beyond February 1945. Hennyey also felt that we should request the conditions of a ceasefire while we still had arms in hand. If we were to do it any later, we would be in a much more disadvantageous position.

After ministers Tibor Gyulay and Lajos Reményi-Schneller had spoken up, Prime Minister Lakatos saw that the regent was firm in his decision, and so he made a declaration announcing the resignation of the government. He again explained that in his introductory speech to the parliament, which he had held in both houses, he had made a pledge that, were the government to present him with such a fateful, pivotal decision, he would first submit it to the parliament. Now that he had seen that the regent had already reached a decision on the question of a ceasefire, he was offering his resignation and the resignation of the government which had been formed on 29 August 1944.

The regent gave the following reply to this proclamation of resignation: "I immediately accept the government's resignation, and since I observe that none of the representatives of the government have spoken up in opposition to my decision to ask the enemy to inform us of the conditions of a ceasefire I also immediately reappoint the members of the government. I ask those ministers who, after having heard my decision, are not willing to remain in the government please to stand up."

None of the members of the government moved, indicating that they accepted their appointment by the regent and they accepted responsibility for the head-of-state's decision.

Lakatos, who had just been reappointed prime minister, then proclaimed that, having seen that all of the members of the government were willing, after having heard the question raised by the regent, to remain in the new government which would be formed under the his leadership, he thanked the regent for his trust both in his own name and in the name of his ministers.

The regent then interrupted the Crown Council and asked the members of the government to remain where they were. He announced that he had to leave the Council, because he had summoned the German plenipotentiary Veesenmayer to meet with him at 12:00 noon. He was going to inform Veesenmayer of his decision in the presence of the prime minister and the minister of foreign affairs. After the German plenipotentiary had left, he would return to the Crown Council chamber to have the prime minister and the members of the government that had formed under him take their oaths of office. Until then, the sitting of the Crown Council was suspended.

With this, the question of a ceasefire was resolved. Now, there was no turning back. The dramatic events had begun to unfold. The debate concerning the prerogative to request a ceasefire was interesting at most from the perspective

Chapter IX

of whether or not the step that was taken by the regent was in harmony with the text of the 1920 Law I, and whether or not his interpretation of this law was right. At the moment, this was a negligible question, for even if the law had obliged Horthy to submit the request for a ceasefire to the parliament, the measure he took still would have been the proper was to proceed, since a literal interpretation of the law would only have resulted in delay, postponement, and failure. One can imagine the consequences of a debate in parliament. The Germans would have been completely informed. And the pro-Germans in parliament would have found ample opportunity to prolong the deliberations to no end or stifle the whole issue with scandal. There was no time for legal niceties. It was quite clear that we had to request a ceasefire at all cost!

In the meantime, news began to come in about Miklós Horthy II's abduction. The Gestapo considered the regent's son to be his father's undoing, which is why they had wanted to get a hold of him at all costs. Two Gestapo men, having presented themselves as delegates sent by Tito, had lured him to the apartment of Felix Bornemissza, the managing director of the free port. There they had revealed their true identities, and they had wanted to arrest Horthy like a criminal caught in the act. Horthy had put up armed resistance. He had shot one of the captains, the Gestapo deputy. The man later died of his wound. At the same time, one of the bodyguards in the entourage was also killed. The Germans took Horthy to an unknown location.

At 12:00 o'clock, the regent, in the company of the prime minister, the foreign minister, and the adjutant general, received the German plenipotentiary. At the beginning of the audience, Horthy rebuked the German plenipotentiary in a sharp tone, asserting that the German troops and the Gestapo were committing serial acts of violence all over the country. He said reliable reports had come in according to which the Germans were treating the country like an enemy territory. The Germans had made resolute promises to support the Hungarian military forces, none of which, however, they had kept. As a consequence, the Hungarian military had already suffered a fateful defeat on the bank of the Don River and then in Transylvania, in Arad, and in Debrecen. Most of the country was in the hands of the enemy. And in spite of this, the German government was supporting and providing money for extreme right-wing parties. Lieutenant General Szilárd

Bakay, the commander of the Budapest army corps, had been arrested and dragged off by the Gestapo. "Having taken all of this into consideration," Horthy said, "I have decided not to continue the fight any longer and to request a ceasefire."

The regent also reproved the German plenipotentiary for having underhandedly lured his son into a trap. Leaping up from his chair, he slammed a German magazine missing rounds onto the table in front of the plenipotentiary: "Here is proof that you have also stolen from fourth child from me!"

The German plenipotentiary pretended to be surprised. He claimed to have no knowledge of the attack against Miklós Horthy II. SS General Winckelmann had been responsible for it. Having thus denied all responsibility, he then tried to cajole the regent again. After all of his attempt to prevail upon Horthy had failed, he asked the regent to receive Ambassador Rahn, who was bringing a message as Hitler's special envoy, and who would arrive in Budapest on the afternoon of the 15th.

After his audience of roughly an hour and a half with the regent, the German plenipotentiary left the castle palace in order to bring Ambassador Rahn from the German embassy himself.

Following the report by Zsigmond Perényi, the regent, accompanied by Perényi, again went to the chamber of the Crown Council, where the members of the newly appointed government took their oaths of office. After they had been sworn in, the regent delivered a short speech to the government. He thanked the members of the government, and in particular the prime minister, for having accepted their positions in this difficult situation. He deeply regretted that, finding himself compelled to make such a crucial decision, he had burned all bridges behind him. This would have dire consequences and mean grave ordeals for the members of the government.

The regent then left the council chamber and withdrew to his study.

The door to the aide-de-camp's room between the regent's study and the Crown Council chamber was left open, and one could hear the regent's proclamation, which was broadcast on the radio. The ministers, who were waiting together for the regent to return, heard the appeal with surprise. None of the ministers had known Horthy would take this step, only the prime minister. The proclamation was as follows:

Chapter IX

"Ever since the will of the nation put me at the helm of the country, the most important aim of Hungarian foreign policy was, through peaceful revision, to repair, at least partly, the injustices of the Treaty of Trianon. Our hopes in the League of Nations in this regard remained unfulfilled.
At the time of the beginning of a new world crisis, Hungary was not led by a desire to acquire new territories. We had no aggressive intention against the Republic of Czechoslovakia, and Hungary did not wish to regain territories taken from her by war. We entered Bácska only after the collapse of Yugoslavia and at that time in order to defend our blood brethren. We accepted a peaceful decision of the Axis powers regarding the eastern territories taken from us in 1918 by Romania.
Hungary was forced into war against the Allies by German pressure, which weighed upon us owing to our geographical situation. But even so we were not guided by any ambition to increase our own power and had no intention to snatch as much as a square meter of territory from anybody.
Today it is obvious to any sober-minded person that the German Reich has lost the war. All governments responsible for the destiny of their countries must draw pertinent conclusions from this fact, for, as a great German statesman, Bismarck, once said: 'No nation ought to sacrifice itself on the altar of an alliance.' Conscious of my historic responsibility, I have the obligation to undertake every step directed to avoiding further unnecessary bloodshed. A nation that would allow the soil inherited from its forefathers to be turned into a theater of rearguard actions in an already lost war, defending alien interests out of a serf-like spirit, would lose the esteem of public opinion throughout the world.
With grief I am forced to state that the German Reich on its part broke the loyalty of an ally toward our country a long time ago. For a considerable time it has launched ever- new formations of Hungarian armed forces into the fight outside the frontiers of the country against my wish and will. In March of this year, however, the Fuehrer of the German Reich invited me to negotiation in consequence of my urgent demand for the repatriation of Hungary's armed forces. There he informed me that Hungary would be occupied by German forces and he ordered this to be carried out in spite of my protests, even while I was retained abroad. Simultaneously German po-

litical police invaded the country and arrested numerous Hungarian citizens, among them several members of the legislative assembly as well as the minister of the interior of my government then in office. The Premier himself evaded detention only by taking refuge in a neutral embassy.

After having received a firm promise from the Fuehrer of the German Reich that he would cancel acts that violated and restricted Hungary's sovereignty, in case I appointed a government enjoying the confidence of the Germans, I appointed the Sztójay government. Yet the Germans did not keep their promise. In the shelter of German occupation the Gestapo tackled the Jewish question in a manner incompatible with the demands of humanity, applying methods it had already employed elsewhere. When war drew near the frontiers, and even passed them, the Germans repeatedly promised assistance, yet again they failed to honor their promise. During their retreat, they turned the country's sovereign territory into a theater of looting and destruction.

Those actions, contrary to an ally's loyalty, were crowned by an act of open provocation when in the course of measures for the maintenance of order in the interior of Budapest, Corps Commander Field Marshal Lieutenant Szilárd Bakay was treacherously attacked and abducted by Gestapo agents who exploited the bad visibility of a foggy October morning when he was getting out of his car in front of his house. Subsequently German aircraft dropped leaflets against the government in office. I received reliable information that troops of pro- German tendency intended to raise their own men to power by using force to effect a political upheaval and the overthrowing of the legal Hungarian government which I had appointed in the meantime (Premier Lakatos) and that they intended to turn their country's territory into a theater of rearguard actions for the German Reich.

I decided to safeguard Hungary's honor even in relation to her former ally, although this ally, instead of supplying the military help he had promised, meant to rob the Hungarian nation finally of its greatest treasure—its freedom and independence. I informed a representative of the German Reich that we were about to conclude a military armistice with our previous enemies and to cease all hostilities against them. Trusting your love of truth, I hope to secure in accord with you the continuity of our nation's life in the

Chapter IX

future and the realization of our peaceful aims. Commanders of the Hungarian army have received corresponding orders from me. Accordingly, the troops, loyal to their oath and following an order of the day issued simultaneously, must obey the commanders appointed by me.

I appeal to every honest Hungarian to follow me on the path beset by sacrifices that will lead to Hungary's salvation.

This was followed by the regent's general order:

"Hungarian soldiers!
In the devastating fight flowing into the heart of our faithfully beloved homeland, considering the forces doing battle, I do not await a turn that would be now decisive and favorable to our country. I have therefore resolved to request a ceasefire. As the supreme commander of the armed forces, I call on you to remain faithful to your oath as Hungarian soldiers and fulfill my orders, passed on to your commanders, loyally and with unconditional allegiance. Our very existence depends on every member of the Hungarian army showing dutiful and unflagging discipline in this dire situation."

The regent's proclamation had been broadcast by the time Veesenmayer, the German plenipotentiary, had made it back to the castle with Ambassador Rahn, Hitler's special envoy. Veesenmayer introduced the regent to Ambassador Rahn. The prime minister and the minister of foreign affairs were both present for the audience. When Rahn expressed his desire to speak with the regent one on one, Lakatos and Hennyey left the regent's study.

Before the German ambassador had arrived, in one of the separate chambers of the castle Minister of Foreign Affairs Hennyey had already informed the Swedish and Turkish envoys that Hungary was requesting a ceasefire. In a telegram he had also informed the Hungarian envoys and ambassadors active abroad of the step taken by the regent.

The prime minister, the minister of foreign affairs, and Gyula Ambrózy then returned to the chamber of the Crown Council. Since some of the members of the government had had no preliminary knowledge of the regent's proclamation and had only learned of it a few moments earlier from what they had heard on the radio, and even then they had only heard some of the details, they asked Ambrózy when the proclamation had not been read aloud earlier, at the Crown Council. They reproached Ambrózy, who replied that since the Crown Council, which had been called on to convene at 10:30, had only begun at 11:00 and the regent had had to receive the German ambassador at 12:00 there had not been time for the Crown Council to deal with the text of the proclamation. At the request of the members of the government, Ambrózy then read aloud the entire text of the proclamation, after which János Vörös read the text of the document that he had written to Guderian, the German chief of staff.

The prime minister then informed the other ministers of what had taken place during the audience with the German ambassador.

The regent returned to the chamber of the Crown Council at 2:30. After the sitting had been opened again, he informed the ministers that he had spoken with Rahn for almost an hour, who was in fact Germany's ambassador to Rome. Rahn had been entrusted by Hitler with the task of restoring trust between Hungary and Germany. The regent had presented to Rahn the reasons that had prompted him to seek a ceasefire. He reproached Rahn for the ultimatum with which the German chief of staff had presented Hungary.

Rahn had used an array of arguments to try to sway the regent in his resolve and prevail on him to change his decision. Rahn had told the regent that the Germans could take over the press, and if the regent were to announce that he knew nothing of the proclamation and it had been issued by the clique in his immediate surroundings then nothing would come to the knowledge of the world outside and he would still be considered a loyal ally. The regent had rejected this offer, saying "what do you think? Who do you think you are dealing with?"

Rahn had also told the regent that he wished to meet with him again that afternoon for further negotiation. To this, however, Horthy had replied that he should only negotiate with the prime minister.

With this, the Crown Council came to an end. After Horthy had departed, Prime Minister Lakatos took his leave of the ministers with the remark that the government would strive to maintain order as long as it could, though he was convinced that the Germans were going to take immediate action in response to the proclamation and the request for a ceasefire. There

Chapter IX

could be no doubt that they would demand the formation of a new government, and they would do so that very day.

I must say a few words concerning an interesting episode in connection with the broadcast of the regent's proclamation on the radio. When in the course of their audience at noon Horthy had informed Veesenmayer that the conduct of the Germans until now and their foreseeable defeat in the war compelled him to ask the Western powers for a ceasefire, the widowed Mrs. István Horthy had been standing in the door to the study and observing the conversation. When the regent had said the word "ceasefire," she had given a sign to Ambrózy, at which the Ambrózy had called the radio on the telephone and instructed them to read the proclamation.

Archduke Joseph[103] had learned of the decision of the Crown Council to request a ceasefire. He immediately contacted Lakatos and Hennyey. He asked both of them to go back and find the regent and prevail upon him to change his resolution and persuade him to rescind his decision concerning a ceasefire without delay. Neither of the two ministers agreed, however.

Events were becoming increasingly confused. The Germans had taken control of the radio. They had gotten help in doing this from the Hungarian anti-aircraft artillerymen. Not long after the German raid an anti-aircraft artillery detachment had shown on in Sándor Street under the leadership of an artillery lieutenant colonel. The Germans had thought that the detachment was going to take a stand against them, and, fearing an attack, they had prepared themselves for battle. The lieutenant colonel, however, had informed the German commanders that he wanted to help them gain control of the radio. The regent is no longer giving orders, he had said, indeed, he is no longer regent.

This is how in the late-afternoon hours of the day, at the very spot where, just a bit earlier, the regent's proclamation had been read aloud, the Arrow Cross men expounded the views of their leader. In a summons address to the "armed nation," Szálasi called the regent's step a betrayal, and he insisted that the nation would not acquiesce, and it would continue the fight until the last drop of blood had been shed.

---

103 Archduke Joseph August of Austria (1872–1962), Prince of Hungary and Bohemia.

The moment Szálasi spoke into the microphone, it became clear that the regent had lost the battle once and for all, and it also became clear that the Germans would use any and all means to ensure that the Arrow Cross come to power. The negotiations in which the prime minister and the minister of foreign affairs took part with the German envoy and Ambassador Rahn in the late afternoon hours served no other purpose than to prevent Lakatos and Hennyey from taking any countermeasures, while in the meantime, with the support of the German troops and the Gestapo, the Arrow Cross seized Budapest and took control. Veesenmayer had not been willing to hold the negotiations at the office of the prime minister. Rather, he had summoned Lakatos and Hennyey to his offices. He had objected on this occasion, saying that he was unable to leave the castle because the Hungarian government limited his freedom of motion. What had taken place was this: the guards, on the order of their commander, had closed off the streets leading up to the castle with mines, and indeed the entrance to the palace was blocked by several wagons loaded down with bricks. When the German plenipotentiary had taken his leave of the regent, the guards had opened the road. The ministers had known nothing of the mine barrage. The German embassy had spoken with the commander of the guards and Lieutenant General Vattay and instructed them to remove the mines. But the mines also had to be removed because in the meantime the commander of the 24th German armored division had issued an ultimatum demanding of Csatay that he immediately remove the mines. If this were not done within 23 hours, he would have the castle shelled.

Time passed with negotiations. Prime Minister Lakatos and Minister of Foreign Affairs Hennyey were kept at the German embassy, and during this time all of the measures were implemented to put power completely in the hands of Szálasi and his adherents. The two ministers held what were ostensibly negotiations concerning the interpretation of the ceasefire and the release of the regent's son. The discussion came to an end at roughly 8:30, and they agreed that on this matter they would deliver a written memorandum to the German envoy. It was typical that Ambassador Rahn tried to convince the Hungarian ministers that the request for a ceasefire had been premature, because the Germans were definitely going to win the war. In Germany, one-million people had been called up for service, and they were going

Chapter IX

to use these people to set up new divisions by February. By then, the miracle weapons would be ready too. They included, for instance, an artillery shell that would kill every living creature in a three square-kilometer area. But there were unusual airplanes too. With the newly formed forces, they Germans would launch an attack in the east and the west, and the final battle would end with a German victory.

The negotiations yielded no results whatsoever. Upon returning to the office of the prime minister, Lakatos and Hennyey wrote the memorandum for the Germans, and at 22:30 they took it to the regent for his approval. Minister of Culture Iván Rakovszky accompanied them. The regent received the ministers in the company of Adjutant-General Vattay and head of the Cabinet Bureau Ambrózy. The prime minister had only barely begun recounting the negotiations that had taken place at the German embassy when Ambrózy announced that Lieutenant General Faragho's negotiations in Moscow had been successful. The Russians were expecting a reply on the 16th at 8 o'clock. As a precondition to the launch of ceasefire negotiations the Russians demanded the following:

The Hungarian soldiers had to retreat to the Trianon borders. They had to break every tie to Germany immediately, and they had to attack the Germans.

The ceasefire negotiations would begin in ten days.

If we were not to accept these preconditions, they would break the negotiations once and for all. We had to give our reply by 8:00 o'clock on 16 October.

Ambrózy then wanted to give a bundle of documents to the minister of foreign affairs so that he would be able to give the Russians our response now. However, Hennyey refused, saying that he did not know the details of the Russian-Hungarian negotiations, and thus he could not agree to present the reply. Ambrózy would have to do this. But there was no need for any separate answer anyway, since officially at 14:00 o'clock the minister of foreign affairs had already informed the Allied powers of the question of a ceasefire through the Swedish and Turkish envoys. Thus, the planned reply never made it to Szeged, to Field Marshall Malinovsky.[104] Events in the meantime continued to unfold at lightning speed.

---

[104] Rodion Yakovlevich Malinovsky (1898–1967), a Soviet commander who played important roles in the German defeats at the Battle of Stalingrad and the Battle of Budapest.

Having returned to the prime minister's office, Lakatos and ministers Hennyey, Rakovszky, and Péter Schnell gathered to deliberate. They concluded that the Germans would probably attack the castle in the morning. If they could not reach some kind of peaceful solution by then, they could count on the Germans to ignite a civil war the outcome of which was beyond any doubt. The ministers wanted at all costs to prevent the flow of blood on the streets of Budapest and the destruction of the city. In the end, they reached the following resolution: the government would resign and the regent would authorize the German plenipotentiary to appoint the Hungarian government. They chose this solution because they were certain that the regent would not be willing to allow Szálasi to form a government, although forceful intervention could come at any time.

At 23:00 o'clock, Lieutenant General and Adjutant-General Vattay arrived at the office of the prime minister. They shared their idea with him, and after he had considered their suggestion they discussed the situation of the regent as well. They decided, as a result of their deliberation, that the regent should withdraw from any active role in governing, but he should not resign. The adjutant-general agreed to address the question with the regent. He soon had succeeded in doing this. The regent accepted the suggestion. He insisted only that no harm come to Adjutant-General Vattay, Chief of Bureau Ambrózy, Lieutenant General Lázár, and Lieutenant Colonel and Aide-de-Camp Tost.

In the meantime, the prime minister had informed the German plenipotentiary by telephone that he would soon send a communiqué of decisive importance. Until then, he should not take any forceful steps and he should prevent any attack. Lakatos wanted to inform the German plenipotentiary of the agreements which had been reached and the decision of the regent.

When the regent's decision came, the prime minister summoned the German plenipotentiary to his office. Veesenmayer did not come, however. Rather, he sent Dr. Feine, an embassy councilor, to meet with Lakatos. The prime minister briefly discussed the fate of the regent and the government with Feine. Lakatos essentially dictated the following to Feine: "The Hungarian government has come into possession of information of which it had no knowledge until now and for which it cannot accept any responsibility. As a consequence of this, the government was resigning immediately. The regent was turning over power."

Chapter IX

Feine asked Lakatos to prevent and bring an end to any use of firearms. In response, Lakatos called the castle and issued the relevant instructions to Lieutenant General Vattay. At Feine's request, he got into a car with Feine was driven to the German embassy. At the German embassy, Veesenmayer also got in the car and together they hurried back to the castle to get the regent to safety. The other members of the regent's family had already been taken to the palace of the apostolic nuncio. The regent had to be taken over by 6:00 in the morning, because that was when the German armored divisions would begin attacking the castle. In the meantime, the German plenipotentiary and the prime minister strove to prevent armed clashes.

The regent was waiting for them in the stair house of the palace in mantle and cap. Veesenmayer immediately informed Horthy that they would be taking him to a baronial mansion. and there he would be considered a guest.

I must have been roughly 5:45 when the regent, the prime minister, and the German plenipotentiary departed for the Hatvany mansion in Verbőczy Street, the building of the Gestapo.

At 6:00 o'clock the assault on the castle began. By that time, however, neither the regent nor his family was in the palace. When the firefight had died down, the palace was soon in the hands of the Germans and the Arrow Cross.

In the early morning hours of 16 October, the German plenipotentiary and the regent returned to the palace. The regent's quarters had been ransacked. The Germans and the Arrow Cross had turned everything upside down so the regent conferred with the prime minister and Veesenmayer in the bathroom. The German plenipotentiary prevailed on him to resign and turn over power to Szálasi. The regent had been completely broken by the grave events of the 15th; his son's disappearance, staying awake through the night, and the fruitless deliberations. In the end, he let himself be persuaded, but he insisted that they give him back his son. With this stipulation, he accepted the German demand, and he signed the document proclaiming his resignation. Veesenmayer promised that his son would join him in Vienna or, at the latest, Linz. This promise, however, was not honored.

In the meantime, the German soldiers had turned over power completely to the Arrow Cross. The castle was occupied by paratroopers under the command of Otto Skorzeny. At roughly 6:30, the German plenipotentiary showed up at the office of the prime minister. In Lakatos' absence, he was received by Minister of Foreign Affairs Hennyey. The plenipotentiary politely asked about the safety of the ministers and the people who were in the prime minister's office, and he assured Hennyey that the occupation of the palace was only temporary; soon, they would all be free to leave. The Council of Ministers, which Prime Minister Lakatos had planned in order to inform the other ministers of events, would be held. Of course, this was a lie too. A Gestapo officer and Vajna, the Arrow Cross Minister of Internal Affairs, arrested the ministers. Hennyey, Rakovszky, Péter Schell, and other high-ranking civil servants in the prime minister's office were taken to the jail in Fő Street that afternoon.

The German embassy handled the takeover of power of the head of state and the appointment of a new government.

Before interrupting the story of this tragedy, I must mention one episode that took place in the Hatvany mansion, when the regent and Prime Minister Lakatos were waiting in one of the rooms of the mansion to learn of further developments. Horthy was lying, exhausted, on a sofa when a German soldier came into the room, turned to the regent, and said, "Hören Sie mal, der Ministerpräsident will mit Ihnen sprechen!"[105]

Lakatos interrupted, saying that was not possible, since he was the prime minister.

To this, the German soldier replied, "nicht Sie, der neue."[106]

Horthy went into the neighboring room. There, he found Szálasi standing in front of him.

The head of the Arrow Cross assured the regent that neither he nor his family would come to any harm. Szálasi wanted to get Horthy to sign his appointment as prime minister. Horthy, however, turned around immediately and left Szálasi standing there.

In addition to Prime Minister Géza Lakatos, the Germans had also taken Lieutenant General and Adjutant-General Vattay and Lieutenant Colonel and Aide-de-Camp Tost with Horthy to the Hatvany mansion. Vattay and

---

105 "Listen, the Prime Minister wishes to speak with you!"
106 "Not you, the new one."

Chapter IX

Tost left the regent and Lakatos to themselves and went into the neighboring room, where the Arrow Cross proclamation was being broadcast on the radio. At 12:00 o'clock, lunch was brought for the people being held in custody. When they had finished lunch, Tost stood up and went over to the desk. Vattay thought he was looking for an ashtray and wanted to light a cigarette. At that moment, however, the aide-de-camp pulled out a pistol and shot himself. He was immediately taken to the sanatorium on Sváb Hill, but they were unable to help him.

At 1:00 o'clock in the afternoon, the regent was left entirely on his own, while the others were taken to another room. At roughly 2:00 o'clock, Lakatos, and only Lakatos, was taken to the German embassy.

From this moment on, at the German embassy Lakatos played only the role of mediator between Horthy and Veesenmayer. Veesenmayer demanded the rescission of the proclamation and the withdrawal of the general order issued to the army.

The German embassy handled the takeover of power of the head of state and the appointment of a new government.

With this, the tragedy came to an end. Horthy, the regent, became a captive of the Germans. Limited in his freedom of will, distressed over the fate of his son, and fearing an uncertain future, he was master of neither his will nor his ability to make decisions. At the beginning of Miklós Horthy's twenty-sixth year of rule, politicians who not long ago had competed with one another in their efforts to be in his good graces now turned away from him. It was thus that Ferenc Szálasi came to be at the head of the country. The people who, with the help of the Germans, had seized power knew only one law: hatred, aggression, unlawfulness, and murder!

At 20:30 on 16 October 1944, the Hungarian Telegraph Office issued the following announcement:

"The Regent has withdrawn from management of the affairs of state, and he has acknowledged the resignation of Prime Minister Lakatos and his government. Upon consideration of the unusual situation and circumstances, he has agreed to allow me to form, in order to address the question of the head of state, a three-member regent's council and to exercise the authority of regent temporarily in the capacity of royal Hungarian prime minister until the submittal and ratification within legal frameworks of the proposal concerning the exercise of the power of the head of state, lest any delay cause our nation and our homeland serious harm or peril.

Budapest, 16 October 1944
Ferenc Szálasi
(Prime Minister)

The text of the regent's new proclamation, which was broadcast on 16 October 1944 and which declared the proclamation of the 15th null and void, was the following:

"I hereby declare the proclamation issued by me on 15 October to the Hungarian nation null and void, and I repeat the command of the Hungarian chief of the general staff to the troops, which ordered the continuation of the battle. The grave military situation demands of the Hungarian army that, as befits its glorious reputation, it defend its homeland. May the good Lord guide the army and Hungary to the path that leads to a better future.

16 October 1944
Miklós Horthy"

On 16 October, Horthy informed the Hungarian national assembly of his resignation from the office of regent with the following declaration:

"To the Right Honorable President of the two Houses of the Hungarian legislature! My greetings as regent to the Hungarian national assembly!

In this grave and weighty hour of Hungarian history, I hereby proclaim my decision, in the interests of the successful continuance of the conduct of war and the internal unity and cohesion of the nation, to resign from the office of regent and to surrender all of my legal rights in connection with the power of the position of regent. Simultaneously, I entrust Ferenc Szálasi with the task of forming a government of national cohesion.

16 October 1944
Horthy"

Chapter IX

These announcements aroused consternation in every true Hungarian soul.

Why were these announcements issued? What did they mean? Was it really true that the regent had turned power over the Szálasi? Horthy, the regent, who had said to Ambassador Rahn, when Rahn had tried to prevail on him to deny having made the proclamation to the nation on the 15th and the general order issued to the army, "what do you think? Who do you think you are dealing with," now rejected the proclamation after all, declaring it null and void and calling on the army to continue the battle? He had resigned from his position as regent?

What kind of psychological collapse would come in the wake of this?

If we examine the consequences of the proclamations and commands he issued, it becomes clear that they sealed the tragic fate of the country. Control of the fate of the Hungarian state was now in the hands of Szálasi and the extreme right wing. With the collaboration of shortsighted politicians, we continued down the path with the Germans towards utter defeat!

Chapter X

The role of the army in the events of October 1944

At noon on 15 October 1944, Horthy issued on the radio the proclamation in which he announced that the Germans had lost the war and he was therefore asking the Allied powers for a ceasefire. He had also ordered an end to all hostilities.

The regent had absolute trust in the army, and he was convinced that most of the army would help him lead the country out of the abyss. The prime minister and the minister of foreign affairs saw the situation much more clearly. They cautioned the regent that the army was far less trustworthy than he thought. They quite rightly noted that for years the most extreme propaganda had been underway preaching the mental, ethical, and military superiority on the one hand and the swaying opinion against the Soviet Union on the other. The same propaganda campaign which proclaimed the ascendancy of the German race, and thus condemned the Hungarian nation to a second-class or, one could even say with only slight exaggeration, a servant role. This had infected a significant segment of the officer corps of the Hungarian army, and it had won many converts to Nazi thinking and anti-Russian sentiment.

Most of the company officers were devoted to the regent, and it quite certainly never would have occurred to them to do anything that would have gone against the oath that they had taken to the regent. The regent was convinced that the officer corps would keep its oath and line up behind him if he were to take a historical step the importance of which it was unable to grasp at first. Horthy could not imagine that there were people in the officer corps who were weaving a conspiracy in the interests of a foreign power and were betraying their own people, and were more concerned about the interests of the German Reich than they were about the interests of their own homeland.

One must ask the following question: in October 1944, why did the army help bring about Horthy's fall? What role did it play in the fiasco involving the head of state, and why did the army not obey the appeal made by Horthy on 15 October?

There were profound reasons for this tragic historical fact. The police had already been reporting for years that some of the army officers in Budapest had close ties to the extreme right-wing parties. They took part in Arrow Cross gatherings, in particular in the "Kakaskapu"[107] restaurant in Buda but also in a number of other places. When I had been commander of the Budapest army corps, I myself had been compelled to deal with these kinds of reports on several occasions. The documents pertaining to several inquests passed through my hands, but for the most part the inquiries did not yield irrefutable facts. The men in question were far too cautious to have made appearances in the company of Arrow Cross groups at gatherings, cafés, or restaurants. It was true, however, that I had had to punish one officer, for he had been caught in the act of posting Arrow Cross placard. The following case was also typical:

At the funeral for an air force officer, the Arrow Cross placed a wreath on the coffin. The text on the ribbon on the wreath revealed that the deceased had been a member of the party for years. Similarly, the funeral oration held at the burial of Infantry General Tamássy revealed that he too had been a party member.

Although it was impossible to establish the precise facts and only in exceptional cases did it turn out to be possible to prove that a given officer had connections with extreme right-wing parties or was a member of one of the Arrow Cross groups, nonetheless it was evident that part of the active officer corps had sympathy for the operations and efforts of the right-wing parties. One of the reasons for this was the failed media policy of the army supreme command. In the officers' dining halls, one found only right-wing newspapers, and reading a so-called left-wing newspaper was considered an offence. The officers leafed through *Magyarság*, *Új Magyarság*, *Függetlenség*, *Virradat*, *Esti Újság*, *Magyar Futár*,[108] and the other right-wing newspapers. Anyone

---

107 "Rooster's Gate."
108 The titles of the first two periodicals are perhaps the most difficult to translate "Magyarság" could be translated literally as "Hungarian-ness." The word has been used and continues to be used in a variety of different contexts with often diverging connotations, ranging from nationalistic on the one side of the spectrum to a mere interest in Hungarian culture and history on the other. "Új Magyarság" is simply "New Hungarian-ness." The other titles are "Independence," "Daybreak," "Evening Newspaper," and "Hungarian Courier."

Chapter X

who was nonetheless bold enough or curious enough to pay attention to the organs of the press of the other side and read "left-wing" newspapers could count on being called to task for it by his commander.

Once, when traveling home by train, I myself purchased an issue of *Az Est* in the station and read it. I was a general at the time. A lieutenant colonel was traveling with me in the train compartment. I fell asleep while reading. When I woke up, I barely had time to fold up the paper and hurriedly get off the train. Having arrived home, when I opened the paper I noticed that on the first page someone had written "A Hungarian doesn't read this kind of newspaper!"

I was enraged by the temerity and, most of all, by the approach the lieutenant colonel had chosen, who, instead of having told me of his opinion face to face, had furtively scribbled it on my newspaper. The next day, when I encountered him on the train again, I called him to task. Frightened, he made excuses for what he had done, and he asked my forgiveness. I explained to him that every open-minded person needed to know the opinions and mentality of the other side. Even if the left-wing or bourgeois parties did not enjoy his sympathies, he should nonetheless be reasonable and read their papers from time to time to inform himself. I also explained that the officer corps should not engage in politics, but it was also wrong to interpret this political disengagement to mean reading exclusively the right-wing press. He should not deliberately blind himself. He should know of the events taking place in the world and the powerful forces at work behind these events. He would never have a broad horizon if he listened only to the continuous, one-sided reports of the mouthpiece of a single party. Even if he shared the view of this party, he still had an obligation to know the opposing opinion.

The sentence scribbled by the lieutenant colonel on my newspaper cast a bring light on a perception that was increasingly widespread in the officer corps. In general, the company officers did not engage in politics. When they did, however, many of them came under the influence of right-wing politics. The civilian government also did everything to allow this one-sided orientation to gain ground.

The officer corps was not satisfied with the Treaty of Trianon. They regarded the borders which had been drawn as unjust, much as they regarded as unjust the fact that such large chunks of the Hungarian people had come under the rule of the Czechoslovaks, the Romanians, and the Yugoslavs, and these Hungarian had had a very difficult lot. As a consequence of this, every officer dreamt of a victorious war, with which the country would retrieve the territories which had been taken. They had no faith in the possibility of peaceful revision of the borders. For this reason, they wanted the supreme command to begin the organization and the work of equipping a new, modern and strong Hungarian military immediately, as soon as the Entente's monitoring came to an end.

In the eyes of the people in the know and, in particular, the members of the general staff, the work undertaken by the Ministry of Defense and, working together with the ministry, the government was not adequate. In their view, the organizational work was not proceeding quickly enough.

When I had been serving as the chief of the general staff, I too had not considered our potentials for mobilization adequate, and I was very clearly aware of the fact that we were at a disadvantage in comparison with the military forces of the neighboring countries.

The officer corps—proceeding from this essentially military assessment—soon began to consider purely political questions too. More and more of the officers began to concern themselves with land reform, social problems, and the Jewish Question. Thus, our officers came under the influence of political parties which promised a radical and, in their view, national solution to land reform, social issues, and the Jewish Question. And they presented all this to the soldiers as if the successfully solved problems included the solution to the question of state-of-the-art armament.

Most of the officer corps was anti-Semitic. Jews had served in the old army. The officer corps did not deal with questions of religious or racial belonging. The harmful impact of the Jewish Question began to become palpable in the army when they almost demanded an anti-Semitic cast of mind from the soldiers, and the sway it exerted became complete when the Jewish laws were passed in 1939 and the subsequent period, and these laws were applied to the army. With the passage of these laws, a mentality began to dominate within the officer corps which almost made heroes of people who harmed or tormented Jews.

Chapter X

Some of the officers in the Ministry of Defense competed in devising measures with which the Jewish Laws would be implemented.

It is common knowledge that the older officers never supported these severe measures, which were harmful to the spirit of the army. Anyone who did not take his place alongside the people who persecuted the Jews was considered offensive by a segment of the officer corps, in particular by those who were tied to the Germans by blood.

This was also one of the factors that steered officers who did not wish to think and who had fallen under German influence towards the extreme parties. One of the primary platforms of these parties was the marginalization, isolation, and, eventually, extermination of the Jewry. The Arrow Cross party and the Hungarist Movement, which were under the leadership of Ferenc Szálasi, pushed for the most ruthless pace. Thus, the political line was as straight as an arrow: the point of departure should be sought in the revisionist movement brought to life by the Treaty of Trianon. The idea of the moral, economic, and social restructuring the nation was a mere step from here, a restructuring which the pro-German political camp believed possible if they economic tools taken from the Jewry were put in the service of armament or at least the promise were made that the officer corps would win the largest share of this spoil.

Blood ties to the German people were also an element of this political shift to the right that should not be underestimated. Given Hungary's position in Europe, Hungarian and German families intermarried, and many people from the families that came into being through these marriages had careers as army officers. Thus, a high percentage of the people in the officer corps had a German background. While Germany was still struggling with the manacles of the Treaty of Versailles, the Germans did not come into conflict with the Hungarians. The sense of German identity, which over the course of the decades had withered, was not palpable in their work. They had assimilated to such an extent that they had even taken Hungarian forms of their German names. The Order of Vitéz even required members to take Hungarian family names. Thus, behind the Hungarian names hid many officers who were of German descent. Their real attitudes only became clear when, following the initial German victories, a view began to spread in the officer corps according to which the German military was undefeatable. As they marveled at the Blitzkrieg, naturally their sense of German identity was roused, and a process of re-Germanization began among the officers. Some of the officers reassumed their German names. A few months proved adequate for them to forget that they had been raised on Hungarian bread, and that they had become Hungarian officers and leaders, who made decisions concerning the fates of hundreds or thousands, sometimes even whole armies or even the entire nation. Thus, the purely Hungarian segment of the officer corps, which was not entirely willing to sacrifice itself on the altar of the German people's quest for world dominance, gradually was pushed into the background. In this disadvantageous position, it strove to help by defending against the ever stronger German pressure.

Thus, the general staff and the company officer corps were almost split in two. Loyalty to the government was firmer among the officers who were Hungarian by blood than it was among the officers of German descent. I do not wish to fall into the trap of making generalizations, and I acknowledge that even among the purely Hungarian officers one found a few clamorous propagators of extreme right-wing ideas. I must note, however, that in the course of the war, the Hungarians saw and understood the situation increasingly clearly. They realized ever more clearly that the Germans sought to give us a subordinate role, and we were just a tool in the hands of the German military leadership. The officers of German descent, however, even after having realized the war was lost, wanted to continue fighting on the side of the German Reich as it was swept towards defeat.

People of German descent began to gain ground in the officer corps of the Hungarian army as early as 1919. After 21 March 1919, most of the officers of the old Hungarian army took part in the battles fought by the Hungarian Red Army, since the army had turned against the advancing soldiers of the neighboring powers, which were eager to acquire Hungarian territories. As a consequence of this, following the victory of the counterrevolution, proceedings were launched against many of them. The officers who had taken part were put in the bench for the accused. Officers who had been in the common army, who had cautiously kept their distance from the battles launched by the Soviet Republic in defense of the country, acted as prosecutors. This was when the process began which nurtured a sense of separation in the officer corps. During the time of the Monarchy, there had already been an antagonism between the officers of the Hungarian army and the officers of the common army. The so-called regiment days and the gatherings which were held in order to nurture the frame of mind of the old army also served to prevent these two tendencies from unifying. Officers of the common army continued to maintain their German relationships and their faith in the organizational power of the Germans, which was seen as superior. The effects of the mentality of the common army found manifestation even in small, insignificant things: retired officers would speak German with each other, and sometimes a wife of German descent represented German influence in the family of an officer.

When the Hungarian army was reestablished in the 1920s, several of the divisions of the Ministry of Defense were led by officers who had served in the common army, and they oversaw the army personnel issues. I know of one instance when one of the ministers of defense, who himself had served in the common army, asked one of his heads of division why he did not like the people who had been in the common army. Clearly, he was pushing them into the background, since his division was full of officers from what had been the Hungarian army. In the training division, however, former officers of the common army were in the majority. As a consequence of this, the children of families with German backgrounds were admitted in larger numbers not only to the lower level military schools, but even to Ludovika. Students of German descent predominated among the students at the general staff college. On one occasion, as head of department in the Ministry of Foreign Affairs, I read the list of names of the students in one year at the general staff college, and I noticed that, of the 15 students, only 5 were purely Hungarian.

As a consequence of these circumstances, in particular the general staff but also a segment of the company officer corps adored the Germans, and since they were unfamiliar with the military establishments of the Western powers and the Soviet Union and did not speak their languages, like the old common army the followed the German model.

Some legendary recollections of the First World War also survived. From the vista of the years which had passed in the meantime, which beautified the past, German-Hungarian cooperation seemed exemplary. They forgot that in the joint military campaigns there had been more than one example of infamy, like during the battles on the Don River and the collapse of the Voronezh front, and in particular during the retreats.

But one should also not fail to mention the fact that high-ranking soldiers in the Hungarian army who were in leading positions had been reared in the old monarchy, and they could not free themselves from the idea that Hungary had never lived an independent life, neither culturally nor economically, but rather had always proceeded on German railway tracks. But our Western enemies were also at fault in the fact that we could not be independent, because they neither knew us nor concerned themselves much with us.

Gyula Gömbös had a strong influence on the officer corps and, in particular, the general staff. First as the president of the Hungarian National Defense Association (Magyar Országos Véderő Egylet or MOVE) and then as the state secretary of the defense, the minister of defense, and then prime minister, he surrounded himself with the young general staff and staff officers who, in his opinion, were the most suitable to organize the Hungarian army of the future.

Gömbös career exerted a strong influence on the young officers, in particular on the officers who worked in his immediate circles or in other ministries as his observers and became the leaders of the preparations for war in the so-called national mobilization efforts. Thus, Gömbös' men assumed places in the ministries of industrial affairs and trade and transportation.

The officers who had been active in the leadership of MOVE when Gömbös had served as president were not willing to return to path that was required by the military sphere of activity of the army. This rigid framework did not permit anyone who had not demonstrated his merits as a soldier to wield any outstanding military sway. For precisely this reason, Gömbös' acolytes threw themselves more and more into politics. They were continuously "saving the homeland," either from the Jews or from statesmen who, in their assessment, were under the influence of the Jews. Gömbös' acolytes were dissatisfied with everything.

The officers of the general staff unquestionably played a major role in shaping the mentality of the country and, in particular, the army and also in nur-

Chapter X

turing the idea of remaining steadfastly at Germany's side. Károly Beregfy himself said at one of the "Szálasi" Crown Councils (but also on many other occasions) that in his view the Arrow Cross takeover of power—i.e. the volte-face in October—would not have gone as smoothly as it did had a segment of the officer corps and the general staff not supported the Arrow Cross Party and the Hungarist Movement with its expertise and its power.

When examining the role of the Hungarian army in the October catastrophe, we should not ignore the question of military instruction. The spirit of the staff college was not appropriate in this regard. I do not wish to praise the spirit of the Vienna military college where I was a student for three years: but it was more fitting than the military higher education in Hungary in the 1920s and 1930s. One of my instructors at the time, General Staff Colonel Pfeiffer, once said that he did not need brilliant general staff officers, but rather honest, hard-working officers, who aspired not to be commanders, but faithful and steadfast pillars for their commanders. Clearly, he wanted to impress upon us that the desire to create a sensation at all costs and the Napoleonic pose were more harmful to the general staff of an army than thorough knowledge of the occupation.

In our time, we were concerned with military questions and the problems of organization and leadership. We were only familiarized with the questions of constitutional law and political science to the extent that any educated soldier would need to be. These lectures did not awaken in us the idea of seeking, alongside our vocation as soldiers, to be influential in politics.

In the Hungarian general staff college, they departed from this line of thought completely. The Gömbös effort to ensure that observant officers of the general staff had seats in every ministry eventually convinced the young general staff officers that they had to understand every branch of state life. The modesty which had been characteristic of the old general staff vanished. The young general staff officers knew everything better than the old, and they preferred to offer answer to all kinds of questions other than questions concerning the military. They began to think like the members of the general staff of a great power can think. We know that one of the commanders in the general staff college held a war gam involving state leadership in which the object was not army leadership, but rather the political and economic setup of a reconquered country.

As an inevitable consequence of this, the general staff officers who were raised in this spirit were not content with the narrow frameworks that the army offered them. They yearned for broader political fields, and they wanted to assert their influence there. Ferenc Szálasi was one of these general staff officers, as did the people who had been in the same graduating class as Szálasi. They were the people who wanted to save the homeland at all costs, and only because they wanted to attain positions of sway, and they wanted to change the structure of the entire Hungarian state according to their ideas.

When Szálasi began to be active in politics like the misunderstood man of greatness (or at least so he thought of himself), the officers of the general staff who had been in the same class with him at the general staff college maintained their ties to him. Some of them were open about their desire for him to take over leadership of the country, and far more wished this in secret, because then not only would the army prosper, but the whole country would proceed in the right direction. They wanted the military development which had come to a halt following Gömbös' death, to gather momentum again.

This is why there were so many followers of Szálasi among the general staff and the young officers who could be swayed by propaganda. The people of German descent saw in Szálasi and in the Arrow Cross the political tendency that, like German National Socialism, could link German and Hungarian interests, and that could have advantages not only for the great German Reich, but also, "in the shadow of the Reich," for little Hungary too. The general notion according to which the October volte-face had been carried out by the Hungarian general staff, and thus the general staff was responsible for the destruction of the country is not accurate. If we take into consideration everything I have said about the Hungarian general staff so far, and we examine the composition of the general staff more closely, we see that the people who had a harmful influence were German in their cast of mind. Many such people worked in the central offices of the general staff, so they had leading roles in determining the direction of events.

In connection with this, it is worth familiarizing ourselves with the names of the officers with Arrow Cross sympathies, who more or less openly maintained ties to Szálasi. In January 1943, the regent sent me a memorandum written in his hand with a list of the names of the officers who "had paved the way for one another." The regent drew my attention to the following individuals:

> "*Ferenc Bardóczy*, General Staff Colonel; unusually cautious, in his divisions one finds almost exclusively Arrow Cross men;
> *Jenő Tömöry*, General Staff Colonel; almost all of his references have Arrow Cross sympathies.
> Sándor Makray, General Staff Colonel;
> *Dr. Mihály Bán*, General Staff Colonel; in 1938–39, he was compromised because of his Arrow Cross sentiments, there was even an inquiry against him;
> *Dr. Gyula Hankovszky*, General Staff Colonel;
> *Mihály Nagyőszi*, General Staff Colonel; he is considered dangerous;
> *Vitéz Mihály Kudriczy*, General Staff Colonel; a big Arrow Cross man, at one point, Baky's man;
> Elemér Sáskal; proceedings currently underway against him;
> *Vitéz Ferenc Deák*, General Staff Colonel;
> Dénes Dobák, spread Arrow Cross propaganda at the command headquarters of the first army corps along the Imrédy-Rácz line (!), had officers who were loyal to the regent – they say – sent to the front;
> Vitéz Elemér Somfay, shows extreme Arrow Cross sympathies;'
> József Nováky, Major; Bardóczy's orderly officer, received officers who entered his chamber with his arm raised and the salutation "Heil Hitler".
> According to intelligence:
> János Vörös, General;
> Ferenc Horváth, General Staff Colonel;
> József Vasváry, General Staff Colonel;
> Zoltán Zsedényi, General Staff Colonel;
> Ferenc Szász, General Staff Colonel;
> József Grassy, general;
> Lajos Vince, General Staff Colonel;
> Sándor Szávay, General Staff Colonel; his wife openly wore the Arrow

Cross emblem at Ludovika;
János Henkey-Hering, General Staff Colonel; no one is willing to shake hands with him; he was expelled from the general staff college because of serious suspicions;
Valér Stefán."

For the sake of completeness, let us also consider who the soldiers were who played leading roles in October 1944 according to their original names.

Nádas, General Staff Colonel: Nadler;
Sándor Szávay, Major General: Szlávits;
Mihály Bán, General Staff Colonel: Friebert;
Jenő Németh, General Staff Colonel: Popovics;
Emil Szörényi, General Staff Captain: Reischl;
Valér Porzezsinszky, General Staff Lieutentant Colonel:
Pál Darnóy, General Staff Captain: Danzinger;
Jenő Dénes, General Staff Captain: Dotzauer;
Dienes, General Staff Major: Turcsin;
Antal Radnóczy: General Staff Captain: Riedl;
József Ijjas, General Staff Captain: Freiler;
Albin Kapitánfy, General Staff Major: Kratzner;
Lajos Hajdú, General Staff Captain: Rösler;
Artúr Rády-Péntek, General Staff Captain: Freitag.

This is a smattering of the general staff officers who played active and important roles in the October events and who staunchly supported remaining in the war until the end. This list shows that it was not the Hungarian general staff as a whole that stood in the service of the Arrow Cross idea, But the people whose names appear on this list collaborated as a foreign block, as officers of the general staff, in the Arrow Cross takeover of power.

On the basis of the reports that were coming in, the regent was constantly wary, and on several occasions, he ordered the higher-ranking commanders to exert their influence and remove officers from the officer corps and in particular from the general staff who had ties to political parties or who themselves had given voice to political opinions. In the course of one of the audiences with these higher-ranking commanders in the castle in the presence of the commander-in-chief of the army, the chief of the general staff, and the minister of defense, he spoke on these questions to the army corps commanders who had assembled. He spoke out against any involvement in politics by the officers corps.

When Lajos Keresztes-Fischer took over the position of chief of the general staff from Jenő Rátz, the first step he took was to remove the officers from the general staff who were suspected of harboring Arrow Cross sympathies from the general staff or transferring them to positions in a town or city other than Budapest. By doing this, he sought to bring an end to any involvement in politics and daunt the officers who had a penchant for politicizing. The main obstacle to a thorough resolution to the underlying problem lay in the fact that so-called "right-wing" thinking had gained ground in the corps of generals as well. These commanders did not consider the conduct of the officer corps politicization, and they attributed the whole thing to the dissatisfaction which dominated the officer corps in general as a consequence of the crippling influence of the Treaty of Trianon. For they themselves were not content with the situation. They too wanted the shackles which prevented the development of the army to fall to the ground as soon as possible. In their assessment of the situation, the officer corps may well have spoken a great deal, but the basic reason for this was their patriotic sentiments, not some desire to play the part of a political opposition. Yes, the officer corps was given numerous admonitions by the higher-ranking commanders, but it was more protected than it was punished.

There were also some members of the officer corps who quite seriously entertained the notion that the ruling political party had to be brought down and the extreme right-wing parties had to be put into power. These officers saw the only chance for any improvement in the situation in a right-wing dictatorship, and so they were admirers and adherents of Hitler's ideas.

I have already mentioned the memorandum given to me by the regent when I was serving as minister. I shared this list of names with the chief of the general staff. He first summoned them to speak with him, then dressed them down, and then took them for an audience with the regent so that they could hear directly from him the opinion of the supreme commander-in-chief's opinion of their conduct. This quieted them down a little bit.

There were some officers who, in violation of their oaths, maintained close ties with Szálasi's party or were even members of the party.

Now that I have considered these questions in greater detail, cases come to mind which, at the time, I did not consider particularly significant. I am compelled to note that there were members of the officer corps who wholeheartedly supported Szálasi's ambitions for power, and they envisioned measures the goal of which would have been to remove the regent forcefully and put Szálasi in power.

In 1938, I was commander of the first Budapest army corps. On one occasion, one of my former general staff officers came to my office to find me, a man who, when I had served as the chief of staff for this command, had been responsible for financial matters. At the time when he came to see me, he was serving in the Ministry of Defense. In the course of our conversation, the situation of the army came up. All of a sudden, he asked me, "Why does your Honor not stand at our head, why do you not take the leadership into your own hands? We should dismiss these talentless leaders and do what the army and the country needs done!" One can imagine how much this talk surprised me. I did not interpret his words as any kind of resolute plan, but rather merely as an unguarded outburst by a former subordinate of mine who had been prompted by overzealousness and pure good intention, someone who wanted to see me at the head of the army at all costs in the hopes that then the questions of equipping and organizing the military would be addressed sooner and would go more smoothly. In an appropriate manner, I explained to him that if I were to do this, it would be tantamount to an uprising, and I was held back from taking this step both by my oath and by the consideration that as soldiers, we were not to interfere in the political leadership of the country. We should focus on the tasks that we understood. We should address military question, but we should not seek to lead the country. With this, I brought the question to a close, and the issue was never presented to me again. Only much later did I learn that serious organizational work was underway in the officer corps in 1939 the goal of which was the takeover of power. Today I see the connection. I know that the request that was made of me was not a passing thought, but rather a carefully

Chapter X

thought-out appeal. The officer in question was a good friend and confidant of Szálasi, who suffered aggravations for having sought me out.

Since Szálasi's party was able to maintain ties with company and general staff officers in Budapest without any great stir, naturally the Arrow Cross leadership had followers among the officers, including among the officers in Budapest. One saw this, for instance, on 16 October 1944, when these officers appeared on the streets wearing the Arrow Cross armband, though only party members could wear these armbands. Thus, it was clear that the people who demonstrated their attachment to the Arrow Cross in this manner had already been secret members of the party.

The officer corps learned of the regent's proclamation from the radio broadcast. The broadcast was met with the same surprise and joy among most of the officer corps as it was among most of the Hungarian nation. There were a few people knew of the events that had preceded it and, knowing the situation on the front, considered the proclamation natural and approved of it. In general, the troops awaited further developments with a sense of ease and hopeful expectation. The only thing they found strange was the fact that they had been given no information concerning this important step from their command headquarters. No one knew what the next tasks to be done were. The did not consider the radio broadcast alone enough, especially because the opposition radio had been continuously insisting that the Hungarians should not continue the fight, but rather should give themselves up and turn against the Germans. They were not certain as to whether or not the regent really wanted a ceasefire and the radio broadcast was not part of some intrigue.

In general, the mood was calm. The second field artillery division, which was a unit in the 25th army division, heard the news on the radio of the cessation of hostilities at Zilah,[109] while retreating. The news was met with great joy among the soldiers. A few hours later, however, they heard the command given by the chief of the general staff, according to which it was not certain that we were going to sign a ceasefire, and so we had to resist the Russian attack with all our might. Later, the rumor spread among the sol-

---

[109] Today Zalău, Romania.

diers that the whole proclamation and the news of a ceasefire was a mistake. The regent's second proclamation, which retracted the proclamation of 15 October, confirmed this.

The fifth army division in Poland also heard the news of the proclamation with surprise. They were unable to take any action, however, because the Germans had disarmed the division and stationed an SS army division behind their positions. The news of the ceasefire was soon denied, and so the excitement soon subsided. When Szálasi's proclamation was broadcast on the radio in the evening and the incitement against the regent began, the segment of the officer corps which had always sympathized with the right wing immediately turned sharply against the regent.

The explanatory command which had been issued by the chief of the general staff confused the soldiers, because the regent's proclamation had ordered the continuation of the fight in a resolute tone and in contradiction with the general order. Thus, the soldiers did not know which to obey. This widespread uncertainty and hesitation would have been brought to an end with a single stroke had the command headquarters of the army, the army corps, and the army divisions received the telegram from the chief of the general staff which should have been sent to the troops. For when, on the afternoon of 15 October, the minister of foreign affairs had given the Swedish and Turkish ambassadors the regent's memorandum requesting a ceasefire and the radio had broadcast the regent's proclamation and general order, the minister of foreign affairs had asked the chief of the general staff to ensure that the proclamation declaring a ceasefire and the general order be forwarded by telegraph to the army command headquarters. This had never been done, however. The army commands had never gotten the order, because the first division of the general staff directorate had deliberately not forwarded it. At first, they had tried to justify this act of sabotage with the contention that they had been unable to forward the command because the Hughes line hadn't been working! (?) Later, when Adjutant General Vattay had urged them to send it, General Staff Major Albin Kapitánfy had reported to Vattay that he had already passed on the command. This was not true, however, for he had not forwarded the command, but rather had tucked it away in the drawer of his writing table. Later, Vattay again asked Kapitánfy if the telegram had been passed on to everyone. He again claimed that he had, though yet again he had not submitted the telegram to be forwarded. It appears that, like Kapitánfy, no other subordinate of the chief of the general staff had urged that the telegram, which would have convinced the army of the authenticity of the proclamation, be sent either. And yet not only Vattay but also János Vörös should have verified that such an important order had indeed been forwarded. On 16 October, Kapitánfy boasted of several things, including having never sent the telegrams and thus of having been the person who had prevented the ceasefire.

The regent's proclamation announcing the request for a ceasefire and the general order issued to the military did not reach their goal. The unfettered extreme right-wing propaganda, which was no longer hindered, now took revenge. The army did not follow its regent and commander-in-chief. Along with the pro-German spirit that had come to dominate within the military, the blunders that had been made in the preparations for the announcement also played a significant part in the failure. The most effective solution would have been for the regent not to have informed the armies and the country of the proclamation and the general order from Budapest and exclusively in a radio broadcast. He should have done as he had been advised to do, i.e. gone to where the first army was stationed and given the command for the cessation of hostilities there. And, if circumstances required, he should have gone over, together with Béla Miklós, to the Russian forces. Had the regent done this, the bulk of the army probably would have obeyed him immediately.

People had been whispering about the idea of requesting a ceasefire since early September. The Germans had certainly been counting on it, since the German plenipotentiary had been informed of the resolution of the Crown Council on 7 September. Thus, Veesenmayer had had plenty of time, during the long delay, to reach a pact with Szálasi and make all the necessary preparations for the takeover of power. The idea that the regent would remain in the castle and mount some kind of defense there until he was liberated was a hopeless and inexecutable plan and intention from the outset. There were not sufficient forces to put up resistance.

At Lavocsne on the Hungarian border, partisan recruitment was allegedly already underway among the Hungarian soldiers, who were ready to leave their units and form partisan groups behind the German formations. They sought, by doing so, to prevent or at least hinder any German resistance in Hungarian territory. The army command headquarters was counting on Hungary following the example of Romania, and they assumed that the time would soon come when, having brought an end to the fighting, the Hungarians would begin ceasefire negotiations with the Russians. This would only be possible, however, if the German units which had been stationed among the Hungarian forces by the German leadership were to be removed from the frontline of the army. By 15 October, the Germans had been removed. Thanks to General Staff Colonel Kálmán Kéri, the chief of the general staff of the first army (and my aide-de-camp when I had served as minister), the German units had been almost completely removed from the army. First, he had assembled the German units which had been in the zone of the first Hungarian army and sent them to German territories. Then, when the Germans had asked for troops to be sent from the Hungarian front, he had put first and foremost the German divisions which had been wedged in among the Hungarian divisions at the disposal of the German army group.

On 11 October, Commander General Béla Miklós came by car to Budapest to learn about the situation there and to be given instructions concerning the role the army was to play in subsequent events. Regrettably, he was not clearly told that the regent would take the final step on 15 October. Béla Miklós was also able to speak directly by phone with Lajos Veress, the commander of the second Hungarian army. Both commanders had been instructed that "order 1921.III.1 is to be carried out." This meant that 1. fighting was to be brought to an end; 2. contact had to be established with the opposing Soviet forces; 3. we had to fight against the Germans; 4. particular emphasis had to be placed on order and discipline. Vattay himself informed Miklós, and Veress had the instruction taken to him by Lieutenant Colonel László Geréb, who revealed it to the Germans.

In the meantime, as a consequence of the attack launched by the Russians, who, advancing from Transylvania, were outflanking our forces, the strategic situation had changed. Soon it would be necessary to pull the first lines further back, lest the Russians threaten the rear of the first and second Hungarian armies and make it impossible to retreat to the west. Béla Miklós decid-

Chapter X

ed to move the army command headquarters from Huszt[110] to Beregszász.[111] The commander of the army and Colonel Kéri were themselves in Huszt on 15 October, when the regent's proclamation had been broadcast on the radio, and they had heard it there. The staff of the army command had learned of the proclamation from the radio broadcast. General Staff Colonel László Székely, the head of the operational staff, called together all of the high-ranking commanders and divisional officers of the staff. He informed them of the situation. He called on all of them to remain composed and continue their work. He explicitly declared that he agreed entirely with the proclamation, as it was the only path in the current situation and the only rational solution.

In the meantime, General Staff Colonel Kéri had arrived at the command headquarters in Huszt. He called an assembly of the high-ranking commanders and general staff officers and called on them to take a clear stance. All of them unambiguously declared that they would act in accordance with their oaths of loyalty to the regent. Then, in the precautionary measures issued to the troops, he stipulated that none of the solders should lay down their arms. If the Russians were to attack, they should be resisted and the attack should be repulsed. We would not launch any attacks anywhere. General Staff Colonel Kéri then called Lieutenant General Vattay on the phone, and Vattay informed him that for the moment things were calm in Budapest, and he clarified that the regent's proclamation had been authentic and was in force.

In the evening, General and Army Commander Béla Miklós arrived back from Beregszász. Since we had to assume that the Germans were going to implement countermeasures against the army, he ordered that the city of Huszt be secured from the west as well. He too spent the night in the office.

In the late evening hours, General Staff Colonel Kéri had a frigid conversation with the chief of staff of the command headquarters of the German Heinrici army group.[112]

The army command learned from radio broadcasts that Szálasi had assumed power. The assault against Horthy met with very mixed feelings among the staff officers. Those who weighed matters carefully spoken openly

---

110 Today Khust, Ukraine.
111 Today Berehove, Ukraine.
112 The Army Group Vistula, which was under the command of General Gotthard Heinrici.

about how Szálasi's rise to power could be catastrophic from the perspective of the Hungarian people.

Originally, they had planned to have the command set out from Huszt for Beregszász on the morning of 16 October. The departure, however, was continuously delayed. Army Commander Béla Miklós was still in Huszt at the time, as was General Staff Commander Kálmán Kéri, General Staff Colonel László Székely, and division commanders Major General Kudriczy and Major General Vasváry. The staff left for Beregszász roughly one hour late.

After they had arrived in Beregszász, they immediately called Huszt, and they were informed by General Staff Colonel Kéri that the Huszt segment was also departing for Beregszász. Béla Miklós and he were setting out immediately. They were going not to Beregszász, however, but rather to joining the sixteenth army division and would go from there to the Russian side. They wanted to speak with the Russians about the conditions of the ceasefire.

In Beregszász, General Staff Colonel László Székely requested that Lieutenant General Hollósy-Kuthy, the senior division commander, temporarily assume command of the army. The mood among the staff was very tense.

According to Captain Eszenyi, the dismissal of the commander, who was beloved by all, and the army chief of staff strengthened the belief that we could not expect the Arrow Cross government to take any reasonable action.

Károly Beregfy, the new Minister of Defense, had dismissed Béla Miklós and replaced him with Colonel Dezső László. After his arrival, the new army commander delivered a lecture to an assembly of the staff officers. He labelled the ceasefire negotiations announced in the regent's proclamation treason, and he made false claims concerning the alleged demands of the Russians that roused sympathy for the Arrow Cross among many of those present. Very few of them doubted Colonel László's assertions.

On 17 and 18 October, captive Hungarian officers brought the command headquarters of every army group a written command from Béla Miklós bearing the signature "Colonel Miklós." According to this order, the individual army groups were to open the path to the Russian forces and gather in the designated places until they received orders from the Russian liaison officers. The commanders of the army groups, who had already been given news of the dismissal of the army commander (according to Dezső László, his "de-

Chapter X

sertion"), submitted the order which had come in from Béla Miklós to the army command headquarters.

Considering the events which have been recounted here, I must pause to note that never has the fate of a country been imperiled in this manner.

The strategic situation of the country justified the request for a ceasefire from every perspective. It could not be postponed any longer. This decisive step was necessary, but the manner in which it was taken should have been planned attentively, resolutely, and with determination.

It is not possible to implement a measure of such tremendous importance—the army switching sides, the cessation of hostilities, an uprising against an ally suddenly declared an enemy—without a clear plan. One can imagine the sentiments and thoughts that are roused in a soldier who for years has been a passive party to a bloody war and who sees that, as a consequence of the continuous retreats, much of the territory of the country has already fallen under enemy occupation and his modest family home and the members of his family are perhaps already in the hands of the enemy. Peace, an end to the fighting is their most ardent wish. It is not hard to speak to their souls, one must simply find the right way and then the most difficult obstacles can be overcome.

The regent's proclamation was meant to set the direction which the two armies were to follow.

The proclamation, however, did not give a complete overview. Horthy failed to mention that his delegates were already in Moscow, and on 11 October they had already signed the ceasefire.

On the evening of 14 October, the Crown Council already knew what had taken place in Moscow. When he arrived from Szeged, Colonel Utassy reported to the regent's office to announce that the ceasefire had been signed. The proclamation, however, only made mention of Horthy's intention to ask the allies to inform him of the conditions of a ceasefire, although Horthy should have said that Faragho had already participated in negotiations in Moscow on his instructions. If the proclamation had made clear mention of this and had expanded on what the armies should do, the army commanders concerned could have acted independently.

Even János Vörös, the head of the general staff, did not act independently, because, it seems, he was not seriously seeking any accord with the Russians. In his earlier cited memorandum of 4 September, he had referred to negotiations with the Western powers, and he had entertained hopes for an Anglo-Saxon occupation of the country. The situation on the battlefield, however, reduced these hopes to ashes. The Soviet troops had already occupied Szeged, and they were coming ever close to the capital. Even under these circumstances, János Vörös still did not dare declare that all was lost. We had to lay down our arms!

On 7 September, when he knew that the regent was seeking a ceasefire at all costs, the chief of the general staff should have begun preparing to switch sides. But he did nothing. He was afraid of the Germans and the Arrow Cross. And thus he contributed to the failure of the attempt to switch sides and the rise to power of Szálasi.

I am constantly struck by the thought of how different the situation might have been had the regent not issued the proclamation from Budapest, but rather from the command headquarters of the first army, under military protection, and had issued the general order there.

The proclamation of 16 October, which retracted the proclamation of 15 October and declared the request for a ceasefire null and void, followed by the news of the regent's resignation and Szálasi's assumption of power confounded the officer corps.

A few days later, Moscow radio broadcast the surprising news that János Vörös and deserted and joined the Soviet soldiers. People learned of Béla Miklós' and János Vörös' appeal to the Hungarian troops to abandon the battle and go over to the Russian side. There were some soldiers who did this, but most, in their fear, continued the battle and gradually retreated further west.

With this, the fate of Hungary and the Hungarian army was fulfilled. Shaken by the dizzying maelstrom of events, I watched the destruction of our army uncomprehendingly. Now, weighing the events with a soberer mind, I too see that this was inevitable. An army which began its operations with the reign of terror of the various detachments, an officer corps which proudly proclaimed that, outpacing the Germans and the Italians, it had created the rule of fascism and the white terror, officers who vented their sadistic tendencies on unarmed and defenseless tens of thousands, and an army which, thanks to twenty years of ceaseless propaganda, had learned only to belittle and disparage the enemy, but never to weigh the prevailing power relations, an army tan-

Chapter X

gled in the web woven with Satanic brilliance by German spies, paid hirelings, and traitorous followers of Hitler, this army had to fall, for it never actually fought for the country, but rather had become self-serving, and it swelled to become an independent country to the detriment of the real country.

I was in Klotildliget when I learned of the October events. I listened to the regent's proclamation with overjoyed surprise. At roughly 5:00 in the afternoon, a new announcement was made on the radio, in which János Vörös explained the regent's command, saying that we must continue the battle, since it was not yet certain what the outcome of our request for a ceasefire would be. On the basis of this, I concluded that János Vörös did not agree with the regent's proclamation.

Another broadcast came from the radio, an announcement that Szálasi was going to speak to the "armed nation." This swept away all my hope and faith. I knew that the game was lost. The Arrow Cross had taken power into their hands. Horthy's attempt to seek peace had failed. The Arrow Cross had risen to power with the help of the Germans, and now the terror would begin. Later, the radio broadcast a summons, calling on Colonel Beregfy to report to Budapest immediately.

On 16 October, I got the first pieces of news from Budapest. The people in the service of the Arrow Cross had arrested the officers, checked their identities and disarmed them, taken their cars, and called on them to take an oath of loyalty to Szálasi. The proclamation issued by Szálasi explained everything. Horthy's request for a ceasefire was branded treason. The nation was called on to continue the battle and remain at Germany's side. Szálasi announced that he was assuming the authority of the head of state and as prime minister and head of state he would lead and address the affairs of the country.

The most surprising thing was that most of the politicians did not sense the terrible consequences of this step. They did not see that a man had taken power who was capable of driving the country to destruction for no other reason than to realize his deranged phantasmagoria of leading a state.

The National Alliance of Legislators supported the Arrow Cross, and some of the members of the Upper House also joined them, with Archduke Joseph in the lead. On 4 November, the Szálasi soldiers of fortune gained legal legitimacy when the House of Representative and the Upper House elected Szálasi "national leader" and allowed him to take an oath on the Holy Crown in the marble room of the castle palace in the presence of Archduke Joseph.

This turn of events embittered me, first and foremost the news that the regent had withdrawn the proclamation and himself had turned power over to Szálasi. The parliamentary vote and the taking of the oath cannot be treated as if they had never taken place. As national leader, Szálasi took the affairs of what was left of the country into his hands with unrestricted power. The persecution and harassment of the Jews began again. Minister of Internal Affairs Gábor Vajna saw to this with sadistic delight.

Four weeks passed with continuous anxiety and sad conjectures. Refugees arrived from Transylvania and the Hungarian lowlands, so in our home we had to find room for 24 people. My nephew, a second-lieutenant artilleryman, came to us. He did not want to return to his unit. And the Soviet army was getting closer and closer to Budapest. I did not think that they would try to defend Budapest. I knew that the bridges across the Danube had been mined, but I still had faith that common sense would prevail and they would abandon the idea of blowing up the bridges, since from a strategic point of view they were irrelevant.

By then, I did not go into the city with any regularity, because I felt that I had no business there. I went into the city on two or three occasions only to save some of my belongings out of my apartment in Pest from the larger bomb attacks. And thus came the saddest day of my life: 16 November 1944.

On 13 November, a friend of mine informed me that my older brother Béla had been arrested Saturday evening, and the authorities were looking for me too. He advised me to flee, because the Arrow Cross wanted to arrest me and my wife. I did not want to leave Klotildliget, we did not want to abandon the house, which was full of refugees. We decided that we would spend the nights at the home of one of our good friends. During the day, however, we always returned to our home, because our experiences suggested that the arrests were usually made in the evening. We spent three nights out of our house. We also could have gone to Ipolyvisk, because there happened to be a car which had to return to Ipolyvisk from Klotildliget. We dropped this idea, however. On 16 November, we decided not to leave our home, since no one had come looking for us yet.

Chapter X

On 16 November, the gendarmerie showed up at the villa and arrested us. They took us to the Arrow Cross prison in the Lomnic Hotel on Sváb Hill. I was held there until 18 November. I met my brother Béla there, and many other political prisoners, with whom I was taken on the 18th to the state prison in Sopronkőhida. As the Russians approached, I was taken on a bitter trip with the other political prisoners, 54 of us in total, first through Kismarton[113] and Ebenfurth to Passau and then from Passau to Pfarrkirchen in Bavaria under the leadership of Gendarmeries Lieutenant Colonel Árpád Barcsay. When they finally decided that the Arrow Cross would maintain its own internment camps in Germany, we were made to march on foot from Pfarrkirchen to Gschaid, where they had us set up the internment camp in a school building. We remained here, guarded by twenty gendarmes, until the American military crossed the Danube and the Arrow Cross were forced to retreat. They wanted to move us to the area around Salzburg in the hopes that they would be able to stand their ground in the Austrian mountains.

Here our fates took a new turn. The Ministry of Defense interceded and approached Minister of Internal Affairs Gábor Vajna. The ministry requested that the minister of internal affairs turn over the prisoners who were or had been officers, since it could not allow high-ranking soldiers who had been in positions of leadership to be dragged all over the country. General Staff Captain Dezső Thold, whose father-in-law, Colonel Gusztáv Hennyey (who had served as Minister of Foreign Affairs under Lakatos), was also among us, spent time in Gmunden with the minister of domestic affairs dealing with the issue of our transfer. Our group of prisoners had to wait for the decision in Simbach. Until then, they could not continue the march. Gendarme Lieutenant Colonel Barcsay was not at all pleased to have the Ministry of Foreign Affairs intervene, and he wanted to prevent us from being set free at all costs. He made preparations to turn us over the Gestapo, which in his view would have been the best way for them to be free of us as a superfluous burden. General Staff Captain Thold persuaded the Minister of Internal Affairs that there was no sense in continuing to maintain a separate Hungarist internment camp, since the Arrow Cross had fallen. Thus, Vajna released not only the soldiers, but also

---

113 Eisenstadt, Austria.

the civilian prisoners. Barcsay, however, did not want to acknowledge the order issued by the Ministry of Domestic Affairs, saying that the minister of domestic affairs had no right to take measures affecting him. He therefore traveled to meet with state secretary Láday to speak with him about further developments.

On the morning of the 28th, however, five of the general staff officers of Ministry of Defense arrived in Simbach and by force of arms they compelled the gendarmes to release us. We were put on trucks and taken to Tann, where the Ministry of Defense was stationed.

With this, my sufferings came to an end, and we were free people again. We were abroad, far from home, and completely at a loss as to what to do. We could not even consider immediately setting out for home. We had very little money. Only a few pengős, which were useless to us in Bavaria.

Help was given to us, in our perplexity, by General Staff Captain János Balikó, who offered us his parents' home and support. His father was Lajos Balikó, a Lutheran army archdeacon. I joyfully accepted this offer, because thus at a single stroke we were freed of many problems. Aladár Miklós, the older brother of Prime Minister Béla Miklós, came with us to Zimmern.

On Sunday, 28 April, we went from Tann to Zimmern, where, together with my brother Béla, we were given lodging on the farmstead of a Bavarian farmer. On 1 May, the Americans began to arrive in Zimmern. The Americans allowed us, as former political prisoners, to move freely within a specified territory. In Hiltraching, the neighboring commune, Gusztáv Hennyey was living with his son-in-law. Some of the general staff officers of the Ministry of Defense were also in Hiltraching. I often went to their place to listen to the news, because they had a radio and so were connected to the world. Documents came into my hands here which had been which had been taken from Szálasi's military office. After having read them, I saw more clearly what had taken place following the German occupation of the country on 19 March 1944. I spoke with the general staff officers and politicians who had been active at the time, and on the basis of these conversations and documents I wrote down and pieced together the events the history of which I have recounted, something like a mosaic, here.

Piliscsaba, 25 June 1964

Name Index

Ambróczy, Gyula 199, 201
Ambrózy, Gyula 213, 215, 225
Anfuso, Filippo 121
Antonescu, Ion Victor 68, 69, 70, 73, 100, 185
Apponyi, György 175
Archduke Joseph August of Austria 227, 259, 260
Arnóthy-Jungerth, Mihály 170, 175

Bajcsy-Zsilinszky, Endre 130, 131, 134, 138, 139, 140, 158, 174
Bajnóczy, József 21
Bakay, Szilárd 81, 82, 107, 217, 218, 22, 224
Baky, László 112, 117, 177, 180, 208, 242
Balikó, János 262
Balikó, Lajos 262
Bán, Mihály 247–248
Baranyay, Lipót 175
Barcsay, Árpád 261, 262
Bárczy, István 51, 215
Bárdóczy, Ferenc 247
Bárdossy, László 41, 415, 200
Bartha, Karoly 17–18, 26, 36–37, 40–42, 45–46
Batthyány, Lajos 35
Béldy, Alajos 33
Beneš, Edvard 14
Bengyel, Sándor 36, 55
Beregfy, Károly 19, 35, 245, 256, 259

Bethlen, István 158
Bonnet, George 11
Bornemissza, Félix 215
Brockdorff-Ahlefeldt, Walter 73

Chamberlain, Neville 11–12
Csatay, Lajos 85, 126, 135, 145, 147–149, 159, 170, 183, 199, 209, 228
Cvetković, Dragiša 42

Daladier, Édouard 11
Darnóy, Pál 248
Deák, Ferenc 247
Deák, László 59
Decleva, Zoltán 18, 21
Dénes, Jenő 248
Dobák, Dénes 257

Endre, László 187
Eszenyi, László 256

Faragho, Gábor 201, 210
Feine 230–31
Feketehalmy-Czeydner, Ferenc 59–61
Fodor, Pál 173
Fütterer, Herbert Kuno 95

Gaál, Iván 67
Geréb, László 254
Ghyczy, Jenő 160, 170
Gömbös, Gyula 130, 245
Göring, Hermann 42

Grassy, József 58–59, 247
Greiffenberg, Hans 200
Groza, Petru 29
Gudenus, László Csávossy 182
Guderian, Heinz 199, 204, 206–207, 216, 218, 226
Gyímessy, Ernő 85
Gyulay, Tibor 219

Haase, Curt 96
Hajdú, Lajos 248
Hankovszky, Gyula 247
Hartmann, József 55–56, 180
Hatvani-Perlusz, Gyula 142
Hatz, Ottó 178
Heinrici, Gotthard 255
Hellebronth, Antal 95
Henkey-Hering, János 180
Hennyey, Gusztáv 209–10, 229, 261–262
Hirsch, Hugó 31
Hitler, Adolf 8, 9, 11–13, 18, 30, 40–47, 50, 53, 67, 69, 71, 73–80, 84, 87, 93, 100, 102–105, 107, 122, 125, 139–140, 145–147, 150, 152–153, 156, 158, 162–166, 170–173, 179, 181, 203, 205–207, 211, 219, 222, 225–227, 249, 259
Homlok, Sándor 96
Horthy II, Miklós 215–16, 222
Horthy, Miklós 4, 18, 41, 43–44, 46, 51, 62, 107, 112, 120–122, 150, 165, 170–173, 175, 178, 199, 200–201, 207, 213, 215–216, 222, 226, 227, 231–235, 237–238, 255, 257, 259
Horváth, Ferenc 247
Horváth, László 21
Huszár, Károly 175

Imrédy, Béla 22–24, 37, 55, 63, 94, 113–117, 119–121, 132, 176, 180, 182, 209, 247

Incze, Antal 114–115

Jány, Gusztáv 24–25, 36, 53–54, 83, 97–98, 102, 103, 131
Jaross, Andor 177, 209
Jaross, Béla 29
Jaross, János 30
Jékely, Ferenc 23
Jurcsek, Béla 35, 187, 209, 213–214, 219

Kádár, Gyula 178
Kállay, Miklós 41, 58, 62, 64, 67–68, 69, 70–71, 73, 92, 100, 107, 110, 114–115, 120–124, 131–132, 135, 140, 159–160, 165, 169–170, 172–173, 175
Kánya, Kálmán 14
Kapitánfy, Albin 248, 252–53
Kárpáthy, Kamilló 20
Kassay-Farkas, László 109
Keitel, Wilhelm 53, 69, 74–75, 79, 97–98, 105, 147, 162–163, 165–167, 179
Keresztes-Fischer, Ferenc 62, 116, 121, 174–175
Keresztes-Fischer, Lajos 6, 15, 36, 62, 64, 110, 174–175, 249
Kéri, Kálmán 67, 95, 123, 254, 256
Kiss, János 128, 140
Kolozsváry-Borcsa, Mihály 210
Koszorús, Ferenc 36
Kristóffy, József 50, 51, 203
Krofta, Kamil 12
Krúdy, Ádám 50
Kudriczy, Mihály 247, 256
Kunder, Antal 23–24, 256

Lakatos, Géza 178, 181, 187, 199, 201–202, 208
Laky, Dezső 175

Names Index

László, Dezső 256
Lázár, Károly 214
Lejtényi, Gedeon 56–57, 95
Littay, András 20, 36
Lukács, Béla 90

Major, Jenő 110, 117
Makray, Sándor 247
Malasits, Géza 174
Malinovsky, Rodion Yakovlevich 229
Máróthy, Károly 117
Mészáros, Lázár 35
Miklós, Aladár 262
Miklós, Béla 20, 21, 34, 86, 110, 112, 115, 138, 253–258, 262
Milch, Erhard 98
Mokcsay, Dezső 111–112
Molotov, Vyacheslav Mikhailovich 50
Mussolini, Benito 9, 12–13, 121–122, 126, 147, 150, 151, 167

Náday, István 20, 55, 93, 201
Nagy, Elek 32
Nagy, Iván 210
Nagy, Jenő 140
Nagyőszi, Mihály 247
Németh, Jenő 248
Novák, Elemér 36
Nováky, József 247

Oláh, György 209–210

Paduschitzky, Alfréd 6
Pallavicini, György 174–175
Pappenheim 70–71, 73
Pataky, Ferenc 32
Paulus, Friedrich 105
Pavelić, Ante 48
Perényi, Zsigmond 222
Petőfi, Sándor 35

Peyer, Károly 174–174
Piukovics, József 120
Poincaré, Henri 87
Porzezsinszky, Valér 248

Radnóczy, Antal 248
Radvánszky, Albert 92
Rády-Péntek, Artúr 248
Rahn, Rudolf 222, 225–226, 228, 235
Rajniss, Ferenc 113–115, 120, 182, 209–210
Rakovszky, Iván 218, 229–230, 232
Rassay, Károly 138, 174–175
Rátz, Benő 85
Rátz, Jenő 8, 15, 17, 22, 24, 113, 117, 180, 182, 209, 248–249
Reményi-Schneller, Lajos 35, 95, 187, 209, 213–214, 219
Ribbentrop, Joachim 17
Röder, Jenő 95
Runciman, Walter 11
Ruszkiczay-Rüdiger, Imre 92, 128

Sáskal, Elemér 247
Schell, Péter 218, 232
Schlachta, Margit 111
Schmidt, Paul 170
Schweitzer, István 21, 37
Skorzeny, Otto 231
Somfay, Elemér 247
Somssich, József 174
Sónyi, Hugó 7, 15, 19
Stefán, Valér 248
Stomm, Marcell 101
Szabó, Géza 28
Szálasi, Ferenc 1, 35, 41, 140, 167, 175, 176, 178, 200, 202, 207, 208, 210, 227–228, 230–235, 241, 245–247, 250–253, 255–256, 258–260, 262.
Szász, Ferenc 209, 247

Szász, Lajos 209, 247
Szávay, Sándor 247–248
Székely, László 255–256
Szentiványi, Domonkos 201
Szentmiklóssy, Andor 160, 175
Szöllösy, Jenő 209
Szombathelyi, Ferenc 52, 61, 63, 66, 93 107–109, 114, 149, 154, 156–157, 159, 162–167, 170–173, 182
Szörényi, Emil 248
Sztójay, Döme 8, 22, 41, 43, 96

Tamássy, Árpád 111
Tarcsay, Vilmos 141
Tasnády-Nagy, András 202, 209
Teleki, Géza 201
Teleki, Pál 17, 26, 39, 41, 43, 45
Tildy, Zoltán 20, 24, 138
Tiso, Jozef 14
Toldalaghy, Mihály 30
Tombor, Jenő 138
Tost, Gyula 230
Tóth, István 182

Uray, István 110
Utassy, Géza 257

Vajna, Gábor 117, 209–210, 232, 260–261
Vákár, Artúr 142
Vasváry, József 247
Vattay, Antal 199, 214–215, 228–233, 252, 254–255
Veesenmayer, Edmund 200, 207–208, 214, 220, 225, 227–228, 230–231, 233, 253
Veress, Lajos 86, 254
Vince, Lajos 247
Vladár, Gábor 218
Vörös, Géza 138
Vörös, János 178, 181, 183, 187, 193, 199, 215–216, 218, 226, 247, 253

Weichs, Maximilian 84, 87-88, 102, 208
Weizsäcker, Ernst 96–97
Werth, Henrik 15, 18–20, 26–27, 31, 34–35, 37, 52, 56–57, 93

Zeitzler, Kurt 79, 147, 162–163
Zilahy, Lajos 138
Zöldi, Sándor 60
Zsedényi, Zoltán 247

Photo Gallery

Vilmos Nagybaczoni Nagy with his brother Army Lieutenant Béla Nagybaczoni Nagy
• Museum of Military History: Budapest

Vilmos Nagybaczoni Nagy in Gyimesbukk 1917
• Nagybaczoni Nagy Family Archive

Vilmos Nagybaczoni Nagy in Budapest 1919
• Nagybaczoni Nagy Family Archive

Hungarian Army entering Komárom at the time of the First Vienna Award November.4. 1938
• Nagybaczoni Nagy Family Archive

Major General Vilmos Nagybaczoni Nagy commander of First Hungarian Army Entering Marosvásárhely (Tárgu Mureş) Transylvania after the Second Vienna Award: September 10, 1940
• Museum of Military History: Budapest

Major General Vilmos Nagybaczoni Nagy enters Marosvásárhely, Transylvania
September 10, 1940 • www.fortepan.hu

Lieutenant General Vilmos Nagybaczoni Nagy
• Museum of Military History: Budapest

Kalmán Kéri Colonel of the General Staff. Colonel General Vilmos Nagybaczoni Nagy
• Museum of Military History: Budapest

**Vilmos Nagybaczoni Nagy
with his son, Béla a cadet
at the Kőszeg Military School**
• Museum of Military History: Budapest

Vilmos Nagybaczoni Nagy with his wife at their home in Klotildliget (Piliscsaba)
• Nagybaczoni Nagy Family Archive

Portrait of Vilmos Nagybaczoni Nagy
• Nagybaczoni Nagy Family Archive

General of the Infantry Vilmos Nagybaczoni Nagy, Commander of the 1st Hungarian Army (10th from left) with his fellow officers. (3rd from left) Chief of the General Staff -General Ferenc Feketehalmy-Czeydner, (4th from left), Lt. Colonel Gedeon Lejtényi , (5th from left) Lt. General Elemér Gorondy-Novák, (6th from left) Lt. Colonel András Zákó,, (8th from left), Former minister, Captain Antal Kunder, (11th from the left) Former Prime Minister, Reserve Captain of the Hussars, Dr.vitéz Béla Imrédy. 1940 • Nagybaczoni Nagy Family Archive

Minister of Defense General Nagybaczoni Nagy inspecting the conditions of a labor unit, 1942
• Nagybaczoni Nagy Family Archive

Minister of Defense General Nagybaczoni Nagy on an inspection tour in Soviet Territory
• Nagybaczoni Nagy Family Archive

Prime Minister Miklós Kállay and General Vilmos Nagybaczoni Nagy Minister of Defense • Nagybaczoni Nagy Family Archives

January 12, 1943 Berlin. Left to right Döme Sztojay, Vilmos Nagybaczoni Nagy, Kálmán Kéri, Hermann Göring – Vice Chancellor of Germany, Vilmos Hellebronth • Nagybaczoni NagyFamily Archive

Vilmos Nagybaczoni Nagy with his wife at their home in Klotildliget (Piliscsaba)
• Museum of Military History: Budapest

Nagybaczoni Nagy Klotildliget Family Home • Nagybaczoni Nagy Family Archive

Regent Miklós Horthy letter naming Nazi sympathizers in the military.
• Images taken by permission from András Kisfaludy's documentary film: *The Fateful Years* (Munkart Budapest 1994)

Vilmos Nagybaczoni Nagy being awarded "Righteous among the Nations" December 14, 1965 Budapest • Collection YAD VASHEM
http://db.yadvashem.org/righteous/righteousName.html?language=en&itemId=4016567

Vilmos Nagybaczoni Nagy being awarded "Righteous among the Nations" December 14, 1965 Budapest • Collection YAD VASHEM
http://db.yadvashem.org/righteous/righteousName.html?language=en&itemId=4016567

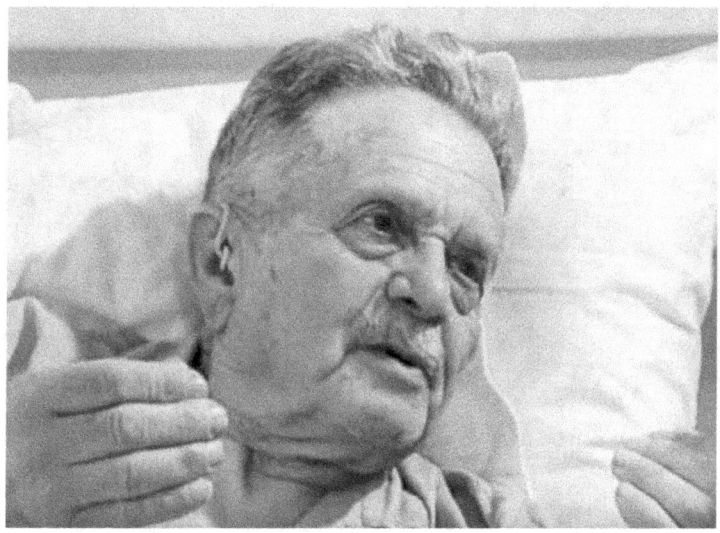

Last photo of Vilmos Nagybaczoni Nagy c. 1976 • Images taken by permission from András Kisfaludy's documentary film: *The Fateful Years* (Munkart Budapest 1994)

Béla Nagybaczoni Nagy and his son Dr. Béla Nagybaczoni
• Nagybaczoni Nagy Family Archives

Commemorative Wreath Laying Ceremony, Piliscsaba Cemetery May 30, 2009. Left seated: Vilma Nagybaczoni Nagy (daughter), center standing: Dr. Béla Nagybaczoni, speaker: Dr. József Ferenc Holló, Lt. General, Director of the Hungarian Military Institute and Museum.
• Museum of Military History Budapest

Commemorative Wreath Laying Ceremony, Piliscsaba Cemetery, May 30, 2009. Dr. Imre Lebovits retired professor and chief librarian at the Budapest University of Technology and Economics, author of "The Jewish Laws – Saviors of Jews". Dr. Lebovits honors the memory of Vilmos Nagybaczoni Nagy by leaving a small stone on his grave as it is customary in the Jewish faith. • Museum of Military History Budapest

Courtyard of the Museum of Military History: Budapest

"We commemorate a patriotic soldier who in a time of great inhumanity remained humane". Plaque dedicated to vitéz lofő Nagybaczoni Nagy Vilmos, 18 June, 2003 with the active promotion of the Jewish Communities of Hungary, along with the Hungarian Federation of Forced Laborers, and the National Memorial and Reconciliation Commission of Hungary.

Portrait of Nagybaczoni Nagy Vilmos circa 1942 painted after he was promoted to Lt. General painted by General Béla Szenteneményi, the director of the Military Museum and Archives Budapest. • Museum of Military History: donated by the Nagybaczoni Nagy Family

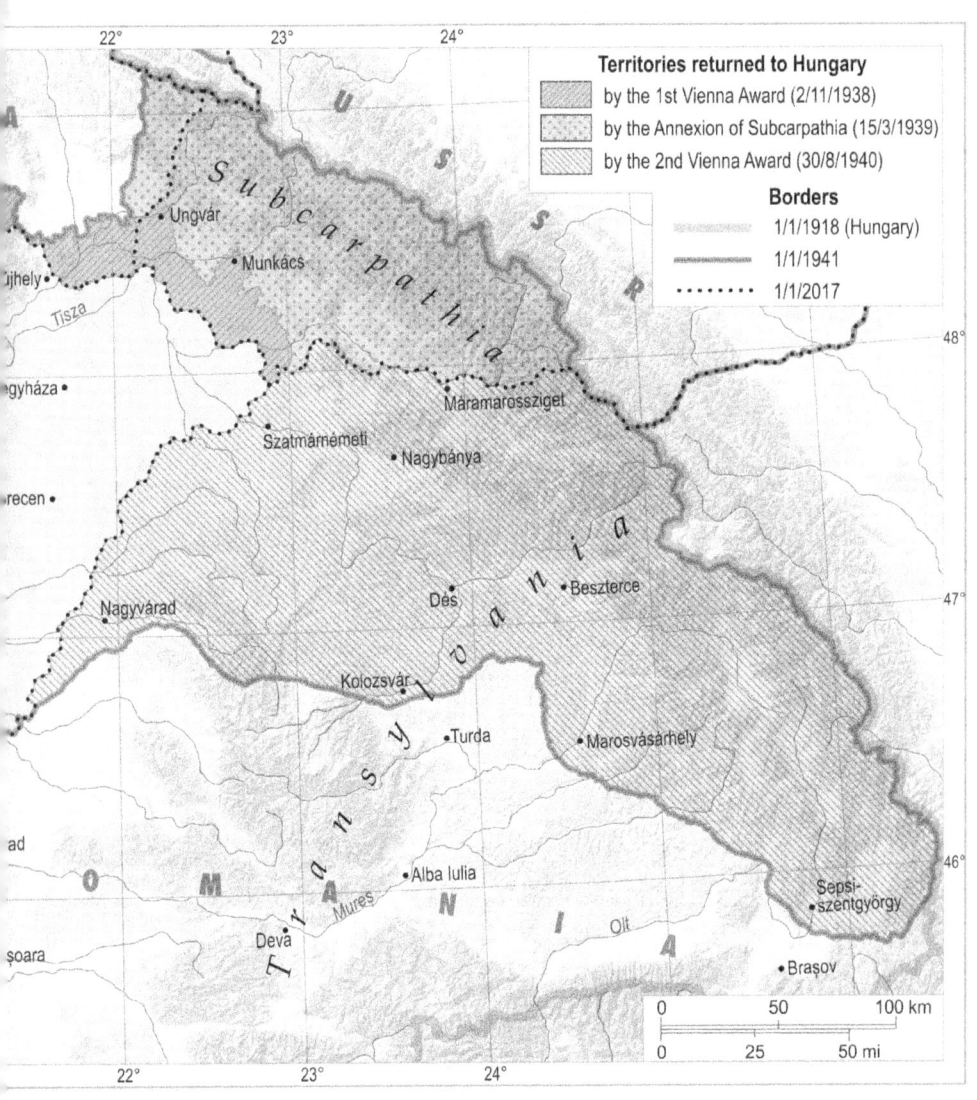

www.ingramcontent.com/pod-product-compliance
Lightning Source LLC
Chambersburg PA
CBHW070040230426
43661CB00034B/1452/J